Race Relations in the United States, 1960–1980

Race Relations in the United States, 1960–1980

THOMAS UPCHURCH

Race Relations in the United States
Ronald H. Bayor, General Editor

GREENWOOD PRESS
Westport, Connecticut • London

Library of Congress Cataloging-in-Publication Data

Upchurch, Thomas.
  Race relations in the United States, 1960–1980 / Thomas Upchurch.
    p. cm. — (Race relations in the United States)
  Includes bibliographical references and index.
  ISBN 978–0–313–34171–7 (alk. paper)
1. United States—Race relations—History—20th century.   2. Racism—United States—
History—20th century.   3. Civil rights movements—United States—History—20th
century.   4. Civil rights—United States—History—20th century.   5. Minorities—Civil
rights—United States—History—20th century.   6. Minorities—United States—
Social conditions—20th century.   7. African Americans—Civil rights—History—20th
century.   8. African Americans—Social conditions—20th century.   9. United States—
Social conditions—1960–1980.   I. Title.
  E184.A1U64 2008
  305.800973—dc22   2007038738

British Library Cataloguing in Publication Data is available.

Library of Congress Catalog Card Number: 2007038738
ISBN-13: 978–0–313–34171–7 (vol.)
        978–0–313–33717–8 (set)

First published in 2008
Greenwood Press, 88 Post Road West, Westport, CT 06881
An imprint of Greenwood Publishing Group, Inc.
www.greenwood.com

Printed in the United States of America

The paper used in this book complies with the
Permanent Paper Standard issued by the National
Information Standards Organization (Z39.48–1984).

10   9   8   7   6   5   4   3   2   1

To my son Caleb Upchurch, whose youthful generation lives today on the cultural frontier settled by the civil rights pioneers of the 1960s and 1970s.

Contents

Series Foreword

W.E.B. Du Bois, an influential African American civil rights activist, educator, and scholar, wrote in 1903 that "the problem of the twentieth century is the problem of the color line." Although Du Bois spoke only of the situation affecting African Americans, we now know that the twentieth century brought issues to the fore that affected all of America's racial and ethnic groups. It was a century that started with vicious attacks on Blacks and other minority Americans as evident in the 1906 Atlanta race riot and included within its years substantial civil rights gains in legislation and public attitudes as revealed by the Civil Rights Act of 1964 and the Voting Rights Act of 1965. Everything that occurred took place during the time of two world wars, the Great Depression, the Cold War, the turbulent 1960s, the Civil Rights and Women's movements, the rise of the Conservative movement, and the Persian Gulf and Iraqi wars.

The first volumes in the *Race Relations in the United States* series include coverage of significant events, influential voices, race relations history, legislation, media influences, culture, and theories of inter-group interactions that have been evident in the twentieth century and related to race. Each volume covers two decades and encapsulates the state of race relations by decade. A standard format is followed per decade, allowing comparison of topics through the century. Historians have written the topical essays in an encyclopedic style, to give students and general readers a concise, yet authoritative overview of race relations for the decade studied.

Coverage per decade includes: a Timeline, Overview, Key Events, Voices of the Decade, Race Relations by Group, Law and Government, Media and Mass Communications, Cultural Scene, Influential Theories and Views on Race, and a Resource Guide. Furthermore, each volume contains an introduction to the two decades and a selected bibliography and index. Historical photos complement the set.

The volumes not only deal with African Americans, Native Americans, Latinos, and Asian Americans but also with religious entities such as Jewish Americans. The history is a fascinating story that deals with such personalities as

Henry Ford, Marcus Garvey, Martin Luther King, Jr., Cesar Chavez and Dolores Huerta, Russell Means, and George Wallace; defining events such as the imprisonment of Japanese Americans during World War II, the 1943 Zoot suit riots in California against Mexican Americans, the Selma to Montgomery Civil Rights march in 1965, and the American Indian Movement's occupation of Wounded Knee, South Dakota in 1973; and legislation and court cases deciding who could enter the country and who could become a citizen. The 1960s as a decade of new civil rights acts, immigration laws and cultural changes are covered along with the increase in new immigration that marked the 1980s and 1990s. The volumes will familiarize readers with the role of the Ku Klux Klan, the fear of a "Yellow Peril," and the stereotypes that impeded the attainment of equality for many minorities.

The books' focus will enable readers to understand the progress that has been made in the face of relentless persecution and oppression. As the year 2000 approached and passed, the United States was a different country than it had been in 1900. Many problems remained in relation to immigration and civil rights, but the days of lynching, racially discriminatory laws, and culturally negative stereotypes have largely faded. The story is a positive one of growth and change, but one that provides lessons on the present and future role of race relations.

One of the enduring changes that can be seen is on TV where the human landscape has evolved from ugly images of racial and ethnic groups to more multicultural and accepting views. When television first appeared, African Americans, Native Americans, Asian Americans and Hispanic Americans were portrayed in negative ways. Blacks were often portrayed as ignorant servants and Native Americans as savages. "Stepin Fetchit," Charlie Chan, wild Indians, and the "Frito Bandito" are gone. These negative images evident in the 1950s would not find a place in today's media. By itself, that represents a significant change in attitudes and indicates the progress that has been made in intergroup relations. How this happened is what students and general readers will find in these volumes.

Ronald H. Bayor
General Editor

Acknowledgments

I wish to thank editors Ron Bayor of Georgia Tech and Wendi Schnaufer of Greenwood Press, for their helpfulness in improving this book and my friend and mentor Stanly Godbold for supplying heretofore unpublished sources on Jimmy Carter, Clennon King, and the 1976 presidential election. I also appreciate the support of John Black, Tim Goodman, David Bartram and all of East Georgia College as I put other important business on hold to complete this project. Finally, my wife Linda deserves recognition for her unwavering commitment to me during this time when family matters were occasionally put on hold. Thank you all!

Introduction

For students today, few decades in American history are as full of excitement and drama as the 1960s and 1970s. These twenty years saw great changes take place, some for the better, some for the worse, but all historically significant. Two issues dominated the times: the Cold War in foreign affairs and the civil rights movement in the domestic arena. Only fifteen years removed from World War II, the United States continued in the '60s and '70s to try to define its role as superpower and defender of the free world. The task was made more difficult by the constant threat of nuclear war that hung over the heads of all Americans like Damocles' sword. In 1962, the Cuban missile crisis made the world collectively hold its breath for 13 days as the Americans and Soviets brokered a stand-down. Beginning in 1965, the Cold War spawned another problem, as a small country on the other side of the earth, Vietnam, played host to the longest war and the worst foreign quagmire in American history. Then there was the race to the moon, which saw the Soviets take an early lead only to be eclipsed by superior American know-how in 1969. In the 1970s, the United States tried to reduce Cold War tensions through *detente* and two SALT treaties with the Soviets while opening trade with communist China. By the end of the decade a new, non–Cold War foreign issue had emerged—the threat of Muslim fundamentalist extremism in Iran—which served essentially as the opening salvo in the current "war on terror."

Against the backdrop of these foreign affairs issues, which held the fate of the United States and its people in the balance, came a revolution in American race relations, as African Americans stood up en masse and demanded the equality they had been granted on paper in the Reconstruction Amendments nearly a century earlier. As they and their white liberal allies pushed the envelope of change in the early 1960s, they inspired other, smaller minority groups to emulate their actions. By the end of one decade and the beginning of the next, Hispanics and American Indians had stood up for their rights, as well. Despite the notable precursors of the 1950s—*Brown v. Board of Education*, the Montgomery bus boycott, and the Little Rock school integration crisis—white America was still not really prepared for the deluge of civil rights activity that came in the 1960s. The movement took too many different forms, was spearheaded by too many different groups and leaders, who attacked on too many different fronts, and came too swiftly for most of the presidents, congressmen, governors, mayors, and law enforcement officials to handle, much less for most comfortable, middle-class, white Americans to appreciate. Indeed, the civil rights movement was not merely one, single movement, but a collection of several submovements all working toward the common goal of racial equality, although sometimes working against one another to achieve it.

Consider this: before whites had a chance to digest the school and city bus integration issues of the 1950s, the sit-ins of 1960 started. Before they could get used to the idea of desegregated lunch counters, the freedom rides of 1961 started. Before they could grasp integrated interstate busing, integration of southern universities began. In 1963 came mass marches in the deep South and in the nation's capital. Next, voter registration drives and striving for the ballot took precedence. As whites struggled to keep up with these rapid changes, they could at least count on three things that all these reform movements had in common—they were nonviolent, they were taking place in the South, and they all required cooperation from whites and government officials to be successful. In 1965, however, things changed. The black protest for equal rights turned violent, it moved out of the South to both the West and the North, and it came *after* the U.S. government had passed the most sweeping legislation for racial equality in American history. From 1966 to 1968, the question became not whether there would be race riots in the cities but how many and how severe. By the end of the decade, the nonviolent civil rights movement had largely been displaced by the Black Power movement, which in turn spawned the Brown and Red Power movements of Hispanics and Native Americans. These various "Power" initiatives turned the civil rights *movement* into a racial *revolution* that proved largely self-destructive. All that remained in the 1970s was to clear the debris left from them and see what, if anything, had actually been accomplished by this whirlwind of racial change.

No one had a tougher job through all this turmoil than the presidents of the United States. The moderate Republican Dwight Eisenhower had been no crusader for racial justice in the 1950s, and he offered no support to the college students staging sit-ins in 1960. He left office glad that he did not have to preside over the coming civil rights era. The campaign of 1960 pitted John F. Kennedy, of Massachusetts, a Democrat and a social liberal, against the Republican Richard M. Nixon, of California, a moderate conservative. Kennedy won the election narrowly, thanks to key black votes in Illinois and South Carolina, and made civil rights reform one of the major foci of his domestic agenda. Sidetracked by foreign issues in Cuba, Kennedy had little time to devote to race relations and even less support on Capitol Hill for doing so. The main civil rights issues that he actually had a chance to deal with were not of his choosing but had been thrust upon him by eager African Americans. Ultimately, his tragic assassination, in

1963, cut short his presidency and his chance to go down in history as *the* great civil rights president.

Lyndon Johnson, well known as an economic liberal from Texas, took over and surprised everyone with his concomitant social liberalism. He immediately seized the opportunity to pass Kennedy's civil rights bill and to solidify the Democratic party as the party of racial justice. Elected in his own right in a landslide in 1964, he passed a major voting rights bill a year later, but his attempts to make good on his campaign promise to create the "Great Society" went awry. Despite his best efforts, the Great Society fell into ignominy, the result of race riots at home and an unpopular war abroad. With Johnson's withdrawal from the campaign of 1968, Robert F. Kennedy, a younger brother of the former president, became the Democratic frontrunner. More inclined to support civil rights reform than even his brother or Johnson, Bobby would have likely carried the banner of racial justice forward into the 1970s, but it was not to be. He was assassinated before the election, and the Democratic party spun into chaos, divided over Vietnam, urban race riots, and related issues.

In 1968, the presidential torch thus passed to Richard Nixon, who won a close election against the Democrat, social liberal, and then vice president Hubert Humphrey. Nixon had learned hard lessons about the fickleness of American voters during the lean years of the '60s. The losing Republican candidate in 1964, Barry Goldwater, had taught him that a strong foreign policy coupled with moderate social agenda would not produce victory at the polls. The strong showing of Governor George Wallace of Alabama in both the '64 and the '68 contests had, by contrast, taught him that a hard line on racial issues coupled with a strong foreign policy might be a winning formula. With that formula in hand, plus some political smoke and mirrors, Nixon easily won re-election in 1972, catering to the "silent [white] majority," while effectively putting a damper on civil rights reform. By then, however, he could do little to reverse the changes that had already been made at the hands of Democrats in the previous decade. Nor did the silent majority call for rolling back civil rights, anyway; it just advocated letting well enough alone. Nixon's subsequent Watergate scandal, impending impeachment, and ultimate resignation brought cheers from most racial minorities.

Gerald Ford, a moderate Republican from Michigan, took over the presidency in 1974, but his shortened term, his pardon of Nixon, his inability to solve the energy crisis and related economic problems, and the disgraceful end to the Vietnam war all mitigated against his administration going down in history as successful on any front, much less on civil rights. Defeating him in 1976 was Jimmy Carter, a Democrat from Georgia, who inherited all the problems accumulated from Johnson to Ford. His impotence in solving the Iran-hostage crisis and in bringing down high interest rates and fixing related economic problems, as well as the general feeling of "malaise" that hung palpably in the air in the late '70s, doomed him to the one-term dustbin of history. Although he likely would have been a civil rights reformer under other circumstances, he lacked the number and type of opportunities to distinguish himself as such that had been presented to Kennedy and Johnson in the '60s.

The Democratic presidents of the 1960s had their job of reforming American race relations made somewhat easier through the help of a liberal Supreme Court run by Chief Justice Earl Warren, who was ironically an Eisenhower appointee. The Burger Court, which followed it in the 1970s, while still mostly liberal, was tempered with a greater degree of conservatism, and it worked to the advantage of the Republican presidents, who wished at least to slow the pace of reform if not altogether reverse it. Civil rights cases in the 1960s typically produced verdicts that, although not always favorable, showed a pattern of ever-increasing racial integration, equality, or justice. Similar cases in the 1970s tended to meet with mixed results, ending in failure as often as success.

Meanwhile, the job of the Democratic presidents of the 1960s was made more difficult by the adamant opposition of southern governors such as fellow Democrats Ross Barnett of Mississippi and George Wallace of Alabama, who were determined to do all in their power to preserve segregation and white supremacy for as long as possible. Southern Democrats in Congress, such as Strom Thurmond of South Carolina and James O. Eastland of Mississippi, likewise did all they could to stop civil rights legislation in the '60s. Their efforts came to naught, and by the '70s virtually all white southern politicians had made their peace with the fact that their black neighbors would now be voting and that political success would from now on depend on securing black votes. Settling that issue once and for all made the job of the 1970s presidents slightly easier than that of their predecessors.

Not all was about political issues in the '60s and '70s, however, and not all was bad. These decades also saw great triumphs of the human spirit and American technology, as NASA made several successful moon landings, as music festivals such as Woodstock brought hundreds of thousands of people together peacefully to enjoy new cultural experiences, as women made great strides toward equality with men, and as the United States celebrated its Bicentennial. It seems there were just enough of such positive developments to buoy the American people in a sea of uncertainty and against the waves of confusion that the Vietnam War and the racial revolution had brought.

African Americans were perhaps the biggest winners of all in the sweepstakes of life in these decades, as they made impressive showings in newly integrated sports and entertainment venues. They dominated professional boxing, with Muhammad Ali, Joe Frazier, George Foreman, and Sugar Ray Leonard becoming icons of their sport. They dominated collegiate and professional basketball, too, as Wilt Chamberlain, Bill Russell, Kareem Abdul-Jabbar, and Julius "Dr. J." Erving became household names. They came to dominate football a littler slower but had done it by the mid-1970s with such legendary players as Jim Brown, Walter Payton, "Mean" Joe Green, and dozens of others. Dominance in baseball was elusive, but they certainly proved equal to whites, as well as Hispanics and Asians, in the sport, with Hank Aaron becoming the all-time home run champion in major league history (until his record was broken, in 2007, by the slugger Barry Bonds). In Olympic competition, they excelled in track and field, setting multiple world records in various sports.

In entertainment, African Americans broke the color barrier in pop music in the '60s, with Motown artists such as the Supremes and Stevie Wonder and with traditional record labels that sported Ray Charles and James Brown, among others. They conquered television, as well, with stars such as Bill Cosby and Flip Wilson, sitcoms such as *The Jeffersons* and *Sanford and Son*, and the miniseries *Roots*. Hollywood, Broadway, and all points in between likewise became fair game for blacks with skill and talent by the end of the '70s, as did Madison Avenue, the corporate world, the ivory tower, and the arena of books and letters. Every success they had opened doors for other minorities sooner or later and ushered in a new era in which American Indians and Asians would be portrayed sympathetically as noble, courageous, and worthy of white respect. In the 1950s, white resistance had made such respect almost unthinkable; by the 1980s, it had become commonplace and even quite fashionable.

For every member of a racial minority who achieved success in one of these highly visible fields, a hundred were left behind in the ghettos of the big cities, on the wrong side of the tracks in a small southern town, or on a squalid reservation. Negative demographics plagued the black, brown, and red communities throughout the 1960s and 1970s, as the minority unemployment rate typically hovered around twice the white rate and as rates of school dropouts, teen pregnancies, drug addiction, crime, and incarceration were equally disproportionate. The civil rights movement clearly did not solve all the social ills of minorities; in fact, it seems to have made them worse in some ways, as the ever-increasing welfare state came to replace fathers, husbands, and the nuclear family as the main financial providers for the poverty-stricken. Yet, when the presidential adviser Daniel Patrick Moynihan pointed out, in his "Moynihan Report" (1965), the tragic irony that the "Great Society" was rapidly going bad, he was met with jeers and howls from most civil rights activists, who seemed blinded to any possible negative consequences of massive federal economic aid to their people. Moynihan, like a prophet of doom, might arguably have been right, but, if so, he was saying something that many people did not want to hear. He was not the only one, though. The social scientists Robert Fogel and Stanley Engerman likewise caused a stir when, in the mid-1970s, they published their controversial book *Time on the Cross*, on American slavery, which critics said amounted to giving a scholarly thumbs-up to the peculiar institution. Criticism went both ways, however. Those who advocated paying reparations to African Americans for slavery, American Indians for broken treaties, or Hispanics for conquered Mexican territory were met with either outrage or laughter from most whites. Likewise, those who argued that "ebonics," a form of English that incorporated grammatical variations often used by black youth, should be accepted into the mainstream of American culture were simply too far ahead of their time.

This volume explores these and many related topics. It presents the story of changing American race relations in terms of politics, law and government, media, racial theories, and culture through the eyes of individuals and groups, from the vantage point of blacks, whites, American Indians, Hispanics, and Asian Americans, with both the powerful and the powerless represented. It documents the triumphs and defeats of the civil rights movement, and it memorializes those who gave their lives to make America a better place for all races. It is in many places an ugly story, full of human weakness and mortal stains, but overall it is a story of past progress, present challenges, and future hope.

1960s

TIMELINE

1960

February 1	Greensboro Four in North Carolina start the sit-in movement, which quickly spreads all through the South.
April 16	Student Nonviolent Coordinating Committee (SNCC) is founded in Raleigh, North Carolina, and Marion Barry, the future mayor of Washington, D.C., is elected first SNCC national director.
May 6	President Dwight D. Eisenhower signs the Civil Rights Act of 1960 into law.

1961

January 21	A black Air Force veteran, James Meredith, completes his first application for admission to the all–white University of Mississippi (Ole Miss), at Oxford.
February 1	James Farmer is elected national director of the Congress of Racial Equality (CORE).
February 2	President John F. Kennedy (JFK) begins the federal Food Stamp program.
March 6	JFK issues Executive Order 10925, creating the Equal Employment Opportunity Commission (EEOC) and beginning affirmative action.
May 4	The first Freedom Ride begins in Washington, D.C., sparking violent white resistance in South Carolina, Georgia, and Alabama.

1962

September 30	Meredith's admission to Ole Miss causes a riot, in which two people are killed.
	The labor leader Cesar Chavez, in California, creates the National Farm Workers Association.
November 20	JFK issues Executive Order 11063, beginning federal oversight of racial discrimination in housing.

1963

April 3	The Reverend Dr. Martin Luther King, Jr. (MLK), leads his first march in Birmingham, Alabama.
April 12	MLK's "Letter from Birmingham Jail" is published in the *Birmingham* (Alabama) *News*.
April 23	A Baltimore postal worker, William Moore, is assassinated in Alabama as he makes his solo Chattanooga Freedom March.
May 2	MLK and Birmingham civil rights leaders begin using children in marches.
May 12	The first serious riots begin in Birmingham over civil rights marches and Ku Klux Klan (KKK) bombings.
May 13–18	Black protests against racial discrimination begin in Cambridge, Maryland.
June 10	The first Cambridge riot breaks out over civil rights demonstrations.
June 11	JFK announces his plans to send a major new civil rights bill to Congress.
June 12	Medgar Evers, field secretary for the Mississippi NAACP, is assassinated at his home, in Jackson.
June 22	President Kennedy meets with African American leaders in the White House to discuss his civil rights bill and their proposed March on Washington.
	Kennedy issues Executive Order 11114, extending affirmative action requirements to federally funded construction projects.
July 2	MLK and other black leaders meet in New York City to finalize plans for the March on Washington.
August 18	Meredith graduates from Ole Miss.
August 28	The March on Washington, at which MLK makes his "I Have a Dream" speech, takes place.
September 9	Birmingham schools begin desegregation.

September 15	KKK bombs the Sixteenth Street Baptist church in Birmingham, killing four children.
November 22	JFK is assassinated in Dallas; Lyndon B. Johnson (LBJ) is sworn in as president.

1964

January 8	LBJ makes his first State of the Union Address, promising to support civil rights reforms.
March 8	Sioux Indians in San Francisco stage the first occupation of Alcatraz Island.
June 21	Three civil rights workers are murdered near Philadelphia, Mississippi.
July 2	LBJ signs the Civil Rights Act of 1964.
August 4	The Federal Bureau of Investigation (FBI) begins probing the murders near Philadelphia, Mississippi.
August 20	LBJ signs the Equal Opportunity Act, creating the Job Corps and Vista (Volunteers in Service to America).
August 24–27	The Democratic National Convention (DNC) is held at Atlantic City, New Jersey; the Mississippi Freedom Democratic Party stirs controversy there.
November 3	LBJ is elected president.

1965

January 18	MLK begins the Selma campaign in Alabama.
February 18	The black civil rights worker Jimmie Lee Jackson is killed during the Selma campaign.
February 21	The Black Muslim leader Malcolm X is assassinated in New York City by fellow Black Muslims.
March 7	Hosea Williams leads a failed march from Selma to Montgomery, resulting in the beating of marchers by Alabama authorities at the Edmund Pettus Bridge.
March 9	MLK leads a march to the Edmund Pettus Bridge, kneels in prayer, and returns to Selma.
	A white northern preacher, James Reeb, is killed during the Selma campaign.
March 13	LBJ meets with Governor George Wallace of Alabama in the White House and warns him to end the violence against demonstrators.
March 17	LBJ sends his black voting rights bill to Congress.

March 21–25	MLK leads the Selma-to-Montgomery march.
March 25	Viola Liuzzo, a white woman from Detroit, is killed during the Selma campaign.
August 6	LBJ signs the Voting Rights Act into law, guaranteeing blacks the right to vote by providing strict federal enforcement and harsh penalties for racial discrimination in voting and in registering voters.
August 11–17	The Watts riot in Los Angeles erupts, becoming the most deadly race riot since 1943.
August 20	The white northern preacher Jonathan Daniel is killed while participating in ongoing Alabama civil rights activity.
September 24	LBJ issues Executive Order 11246, increasing affirmative action requirements in federally funded construction projects.

1966

January 7	MLK announces his plan for a Northern Freedom Movement.
January 26	MLK takes up temporary residence in a Chicago slum to kick off his Chicago campaign.
February 23	MLK leads his first march in Chicago.
June 6	Meredith is shot in north Mississippi while attempting his solo March against Fear from Memphis to Jackson.
June 17	Stokely Carmichael, national director of SNCC, begins using the "Black Power" slogan in defiance of MLK's nonviolent strategy.
July 10	MLK starts his better-housing campaign in Chicago.
July 10–15	Major rioting erupts in Chicago, but it is not directly related to MLK's activity.
July 30–31	More civil rights marches lead to white backlash riot in Chicago.
August 21	Another march in Chicago leads to a counterdemonstration by the American Nazi Party.

1967

April 15	MLK leads a march and delivers an antiwar speech at Central Park in New York City.
June 13	LBJ appoints Thurgood Marshall to become the first African American on the U.S. Supreme Court.
July 12–17	A riot breaks out in Newark, New Jersey, resulting in more than twenty deaths.

July 22–27	Detroit riot breaks out, topping the 1965 Watts riot as the most devastating of the 1960s.
July 23	A Black Power conference is held in Newark, stoking the fires of black anger already burning in America.
July 24	H. Rap Brown, national director of SNCC, encourages blacks to burn down the town of Cambridge, Maryland, sparking yet another riot there.
August 25	George Lincoln Rockwell, head of the American Nazi Party, is assassinated by a former party member.
August 30	Thurgood Marshall is confirmed by the U.S. Senate as a Justice of the Supreme Court.
November 30	LBJ begins his Model Cities program.

1968

February 8	A massacre at Orangeburg, South Carolina, results in many black college students being killed or wounded by authorities.
February 15	Cesar Chavez suffers through his 25-day hunger strike to draw attention to the plight of migrant farm workers in California.
February 29	The National Advisory Commission on Civil Disorders issues its "Kerner Report" on the causes of the riots of 1967.
March 11	Chavez ends his hunger strike, meets with Robert F. Kennedy (RFK).
March 28	MLK leads a poor people's march in Memphis, resulting in riots by black youth.
April 3	MLK delivers his last public address, "I've Been to the Mountaintop" at a church in Memphis.
April 4	MLK is assassinated in Memphis by a white supremacist.
April 4–8	MLK's murder sparks riots throughout the nation, one of the worst being in Washington, D.C.
April 9	MLK's funeral in Atlanta becomes the largest ever held for a private American citizen.
April 11	LBJ signs the Civil Rights Act of 1968 into law.
May 12	Coretta Scott King and Ralph Abernathy open Resurrection City in Washington, D.C., as part of MLK's posthumous Poor People's Campaign.
June 5	RFK is assassinated in Los Angeles while campaigning for president.
June 19–20	King and Abernathy lead Solidarity Day demonstration in Washington to close Resurrection City.

July 23–27	Rioting erupts in Cleveland.
August 5–8	The Republican National Convention meets in Miami, resulting in rioting and two deaths.
August 26–30	The Democratic National Convention meets in Chicago, resulting in rioting and the media-circus trial of the "Chicago Eight" over the next two years.
November 19–20	Indians in San Francisco begin another occupation of Alcatraz Island, this one to last more than a year and a half.

1969

March 5	President Richard M. Nixon creates the Office of Minority Business Enterprise.
April 26	The National Black Economic Development Conference meets in New York; James Forman formulates the "Black Manifesto" there.
May 4	Forman disrupts a church service in New York City to present his Black Manifesto demands.
August 8	Nixon signs Executive Order 11478, extending affirmative action to all federal government agencies and jobs.
August 15–18	The Woodstock music festival is held in upstate New York.
October 29	The Black Panther Bobby Seale is first bound and gagged in court in the Chicago Eight trial.
November 5	Seale's case is separated from that of the remaining "Chicago Seven."

OVERVIEW

The dominant issue in American race relations in the 1960s was the series of events commonly known as "the civil rights movement." More than a single movement, the struggle for civil rights for African Americans and other minorities was really a collection of movements. There was a movement to end segregation in education and public facilities, a movement to get and secure voting rights, a movement to improve job opportunities, housing, and living conditions in general, a movement simply to gain both self-respect and respect from the white majority, and ultimately a movement to assert independence from white society through Black Power.

In addition to these many different strands running through the fabric of the civil rights movement, there were also two sides to its story. The well-known side, which garnered national news media coverage at the time, which has appeared in most high school and college survey textbooks ever since, and which is the main subject of most civil rights film documentaries, largely follows the trail of Martin Luther King, Jr. From his ascension to leadership, in 1955, through his death, in 1968, wherever King went, reporters and television crews followed. Likewise, virtually all decisions coming from the American president or Congress regarding civil rights during the 1960s were made in consultation with King. Although other civil rights leaders occasionally stole the spotlight from King temporarily, they could not keep it long, for King was a star, a media darling, a charismatic and likeable fellow, and an African American whom all but the most hardened segregationists could embrace.

The not-so-well-known side took place concomitantly with King's story, but it did so without the benefit of national news coverage and without garnering the attention of the president or Congress. In dozens of small towns and isolated farms in the rural South, hundreds of local black denizens and their few white allies fought for their civil rights with scarcely a notice outside their own communities. Likewise, in dozens of big cities, from Boston to Los Angeles and from Seattle to Miami, demonstrations occurred that made the local news but barely made a ripple in the vast sea that is the history of the civil rights movement. Thousands of people of all races and colors participated in this great reformation of American race relations, many of whom will never be properly recognized in history for their courage or sacrifice.

KEY EVENTS

1960: THE GREENSBORO SIT-INS

On a cold Monday afternoon, the first day in February 1960, the civil rights movement, which had been trickling along, burst into a torrent. The metaphorical dam of white supremacy, black fear, and government complicity that had been holding it back suddenly sprang a leak in the unlikely, out-of-the-way place of Greensboro, North Carolina. There, in a department store and restaurant owned by F. W. Woolworth's, a national chain headquartered in New York, regional law and the custom of racial segregation met in an awkward confrontation. What started that day as a poorly planned but flawlessly executed act of defiance mushroomed by chance into a submovement that overspread the South and quickened the pace of the larger civil rights movement, as it quickened the pulse of young African Americans. It was the "sit-in" movement, and it would soon draw the eyes of the nation and the world to the American South and keep them there throughout the 1960s, as they watched a revolution in race relations take place.

It began at Scott Hall, a boy's dormitory on the campus of the local black North Carolina Agricultural and Technical College. There, on Sunday night, January 31, four black male teens, freshmen students on academic scholarships, formed an impromptu pact and plan. The students were Franklin McCain, Ezell Blair, Jr., Joseph McNeil, and David Richmond. Their plan was simply to go down to the local Woolworth's, which was in that generation roughly what Wal-Mart is today, walk up to the whites-only lunch counter, sit down on the bar stools, and ask for coffee. It would not be the first time blacks had tried to desegregate public facilities by walking in and asking to be served, but it would be the first time it would be done successfully and the first time it would spark a fire of public attention. None of the "Greensboro Four," as they would later be dubbed in history books and civil rights lore, expected to become celebrities or heroes of the civil rights movement.[1] What they expected, in fact, was to be arrested or beaten up at best or lynched at worst. What happened instead when they arrived at the Woolworth's on South Elm Street at approximately 4 P.M. that Monday was that everyone else at the lunch counter ignored them. The pregnant black waitress behind the counter, Geneva Tisdale, refused to serve them, fearing for her job and her health. On order from the store manager, Curly Harris, the white employees likewise ignored them. Amazingly, white patrons already seated and eating also generally ignored them. One elderly white lady, however, walked past them on her way out, patted them on the back, and told them she was proud of them; somebody should have done this years ago, she said. That sentiment was echoed by a local white merchant, Ralph Johns, who had long been encouraging blacks to step up and challenge the Jim Crow system. It was he who tipped off the local newspaper that a major story was developing downtown. At 5 P.M. the store closed for the day as usual. The Greensboro Four hurried back to campus, hearts racing, pride swelling, feet not touching the ground from the surreal feeling of excitement over what they had just done. It would not be the end of their "sit-down protest," however, as the local newspaper called it, but just the beginning.[2]

That evening, the four recruited at least 19 other students to go back to Woolworth's with them the next day and repeat the "sit-in," as it would later come to be known. This second day's sit-in lasted longer and drew more attention from local media and other civil rights leaders. The national media also picked up the story before day's end. The news spread like wildfire, partly by media reports and partly by word of mouth. By the third day, the students were not coming only from North Carolina A & T but from other area colleges, as well, including the black female school Bennett College. In addition to going co-ed, the sit-ins also became integrated at that time, as several white students joined the protest. Altogether some 85 people participated. The Greensboro Four did not limit themselves to recruiting students, however. They also contacted Floyd McKissick, a young, energetic, ambitious, talented attorney working for the National

Association for the Advancement of Colored People (NAACP), and a local preacher named Douglas Moore. They, in turn, spread word of the sit-ins to other groups of student activists outside the state. Thus, a local incident quickly turned into a regional phenomenon. Neither did the protestors limit themselves to sitting in the Woolworth's but soon added other local establishments to their sit-in movement.

By the fourth day in Greensboro, local whites had decided to retaliate, to taunt and threaten the integrationists, and to save seats for regular white patrons at the Woolworth's and other cafes. By the end of the week, the situation had grown chaotic, as hundreds of blacks and whites, students and townspeople, citizens and public officials, onlookers and reporters all converged on downtown Greensboro to be part of the action. The Ku Klux Klan also made its presence known, and Curly Harris had no choice but to close Woolworth's altogether. City officials pleaded with the student activists to agree to a two-week truce so they could have time to reach some sort of solution or, at the very least, a compromise before the situation escalated into a bloody conflagration. They agreed. Greensboro thereafter returned to the sleepy little city it had always been for the next month and a half.

Meanwhile, the sit-in fever spread like a contagion into neighboring cities in North Carolina: Raleigh, Durham, Winston-Salem, High Point, Charlotte, Fayetteville, Elizabeth City, Concord. By the end of the second week, sit-ins had been staged in Hampton, Virginia, and Nashville, Tennessee. By the end of February, there were sit-ins going on in 31 cities in eight southern and border states. They ranged from as far north as Baltimore to as far south as Tallahassee. In Portsmouth, Virginia, and Chattanooga, Tennessee, what started as nonviolent sit-ins erupted into riots in the streets—a harbinger of things to come in other venues of the civil rights movement in the 1960s. All told, over the next two years, it is estimated that some 70,000 people participated in sit-ins in the South. By 1963, although some sit-ins were still going on, other explosive events in the civil rights movement had occurred that relegated the comparatively peaceful sit-ins to back-page news coverage.

The Greensboro Four had originally formed no plan beyond their first week of activity in their own city. Once the movement had gone nationwide, someone needed to step in and bring order and planning to the sit-ins. In April 1960, Martin Luther King, Jr.'s Southern Christian Leadership Conference (SCLC) joined the sit-in movement, taking it to the next level in terms of organization and legitimacy. With SCLC backing and resources, the student protesters met at Shaw University, in Raleigh, and formed the Student Nonviolent Coordinating Committee (SNCC). Of the Greensboro Four, only Ezell Blair, Jr., attended the formative meeting of SNCC. The locus of power in the new organization came from Nashville students, including Marion Barry, John Lewis, James Bevel, and Dianne Nash, and their mentor, James Lawson, himself a theology student and teacher of Gandhian nonviolent resistance in the vein of King. The nonviolent strategy of SNCC has been described as passive-aggressive behavior in which black youth expressed their pent-up resentment against segregation and second-class citizenship not by open hostility but by quiet irreverence. SNCC members crossed the invisible color line and then stood there, or sat there, and waited—to be arrested, harassed, or possibly killed—with never an option to strike back. By making themselves potential victims, they also became the ultimate victors in the struggle to reform southern race relations, claiming the moral high ground while leaving their segregationist foes in the muck below.

Back in Greensboro, the city officially desegregated all its public facilities over the summer of 1960, less than six months after the first sit-in. Ironically, none of the Greensboro Four were among the first African Americans to be served at the previously whites-only lunch counter at Woolworth's. Instead, that honor went to the black waitress there, Geneva Tisdale, who ordered an egg salad sandwich that she had prepared herself in the kitchen that morning.

1961: THE FREEDOM RIDES

On May 4, 1961, 13 volunteers from the Congress of Racial Equality (CORE) bought bus tickets in Washington, D.C., bound for New Orleans. Seven of the 13 were black, six were white, seven were northerners, six were southerners, eleven were men, and two were women. The oldest was 61, the youngest 19. They were as diverse as a group could be, but they had one thing in common: a burning desire to see the walls of racial segregation and inequality torn down in America. They divided into two groups, one group riding on a Greyhound bus, the other a Trailways bus, so if one was attached they would still have a chance of achieving their mission. In case one met violent opposition and did not make its destination, perhaps the other would. The riders would sit in racially mixed black and white pairs, or the blacks would sit in the front of the buses and the whites in the back. Their main objective was to test the recent U.S. Supreme Court ruling in *Boynton v. Virginia*, which outlawed segregated facilities in interstate transportation, to see whether the southern states would abide by it and whether the U.S. Justice Department would enforce it. Their lesser aims included getting to New Orleans by May 17, the seventh anniversary of the *Brown v. Board of Education* ruling, to participate in a civil rights rally scheduled for that day. Lastly, they wanted to draw attention to the ongoing struggle for racial justice in America.

These death-defying "Freedom Rides" were the brainchild of CORE's new national director, James Farmer.[3] Having assumed his position on February 1, he had been on the job only three months when he staged the Freedom Rides. Determined to begin his tenure with a bang, he simultaneously ensured that the new president, John F. Kennedy, would begin his likewise—with a civil rights bang that Kennedy did not want and for which he was not prepared. Farmer sent letters from CORE to the various agencies of the federal government that dealt with civil rights issues, including the White House, the Justice Department, the Interstate Commerce Commission, and the FBI, notifying them of the plan for the Freedom Rides. He also notified both the Greyhound and Trailways bus companies. All ignored his correspondence. Responding to Farmer, however, were a few Washington area news reporters, who naively assumed they would be taking notes on a back-page, small-print story.

Farmer had prepared the participants for the worst-case scenario of being beaten, taunted, and tormented by Ku Klux Klansmen and their ilk in the Deep South. He used Gandhi's proven method of nonviolent resistance, which CORE had advocated since its inception in the 1940s and had also been used effectively already by Martin Luther King and the SCLC in recent boycotts and sit-ins. Little did any of the volunteers know just how valuable their training would be. Indeed, they would experience the worst-case scenario in real life by the second day of their journey. Having made it safely across the Potomac River, through Virginia and North Carolina, they encountered their first physical opposition at the bus terminal in Rock Hill, South Carolina. There, local whites bloodied a black rider, John Lewis, who would go on to fame for his exploits in the civil rights movement and beyond, and others for attempting to integrate the men's room.

Meanwhile, as the Freedom Riders rolled on across the Savannah River, the new U.S. attorney general, Robert F. Kennedy, made his first important speech on civil rights just up the road at the University of Georgia. He promised to enforce the law of the land to the fullest, regardless of white southern opposition. Little did he know he would have to make good on that promise over the next two weeks by sending U.S. marshals to protect the Freedom Riders. Neither he nor his brother the president wanted to deal with such a crisis, especially at that crucial time when the Bay of Pigs disaster already had them in a Cold War foreign affairs quandary. Likewise, little did he know that some agents in the FBI were working with southern law enforcement officials to allow the Ku Klux Klan to stage an attack on the Freedom Riders in Alabama, but, indeed, that was the case.

The buses rolled into and out of Atlanta without incident, except for a small cadre of student civil rights supporters who cheered them on. Next stop: Anniston, Alabama, where, unbeknownst to the Freedom Riders, the Klan eagerly awaited their arrival. The Greyhound bus arrived at the terminal at 1 P.M. on Sunday, May 14—Mother's Day—right after most local churches had let out. Many of the Klansmen and their families and friends had left church headed for the terminal, still dressed in their Sunday best. The violence began immediately, with broken windows, slashed tires, and verbal threats. Anniston policemen stood guard but did nothing to stop the act of terrorism in progress. After a brief stop, the bus pulled out of the terminal, escorted to the city limits by the police, with a convoy of cars and trucks loaded with Klansmen and fellow racists following close behind. Six miles south of town, flat tires forced the bus driver to pull over on the side of the highway. Angry white Alabamians immediately swarmed the bus, beating it with clubs and demanding that the passengers step outside. Alabama highway patrolmen arrived on the scene to witness the mobbing but did nothing. Emboldened by the patrolmen's passivity, the mob threw a firebomb into the bus, setting it on fire, and sent thick black smoke billowing out the windows and choking the Freedom Riders, who then had no choice but to escape the burning bus. They were met at the doorway with baseball bats to the head.

Within a few minutes, an ambulance arrived, but the driver initially refused to take integrated patients on board. He finally relented, and the ambulance whisked the Freedom Riders to the local hospital in Anniston, where they were welcomed coolly by a single white nurse but no doctors. The Klan followed them there and threatened to burn down the hospital if the integrationists and "agitators" did not leave town immediately. With their bus a charred heap on the side of the highway, they had no way to leave. Frantic phone calls to various people, including the Justice Department in Washington, yielded no results, until the local civil rights leader Fred Shuttlesworth in Birmingham arranged impromptu transportation out of town. Having received minimal treatment for their burns and wounds, they were off to Birmingham.

At the same time this tragedy was taking place, across town at the Anniston Trailways station, the second bus arrived to a similar fate. Beatings left several riders unconscious or semiconscious, battered, and bludgeoned. Yet, they escaped the city with their bus intact, heading for Birmingham. As they arrived in the largest city in Alabama and the one which would soon earn a reputation as the most racist city in America, the streets teamed with whites spewing hatred and carrying chains, pipes, sticks, and clubs. The attack began before the bus stopped rolling. The police department's contribution to the affair was to keep the way clear for the Klansmen to do their dirty work. The white terrorists were careful not to kill anyone; beating them up would be enough to scare them off and keep other outside agitators away and to prevent the aggressors' being prosecuted for murder. By sheer providence, it just so happened that the CBS News national correspondent, Howard K. Smith, was in town and on the scene. CBS broadcast his eyewitness account via radio, which incited a strong national public reaction and forced the Kennedys to change their view of the civil rights struggle from merely a political to a vitally important moral issue.

After the initial ordeal in Birmingham, the Freedom Riders intended to merge into one bus, but they were stranded for hours waiting for arrangements to be made with one of the two bus companies. The next day they ended up being flown out of town instead, in a desperation move arranged hastily by Robert Kennedy, to New Orleans. This ended the saga of the first Freedom Rides for the original 13, but it merely began the full-scale Freedom Ride movement. SNCC and fellow civil rights activists in Nashville took up the cause at that point. Integrating a bus in Tennessee, the small group headed for Birmingham, where they hoped to continue the itinerary scheduled for the original riders, stopping in Montgomery, Jackson, and finally New Orleans, still in time for the *Brown v. Board of Education* commemoration on May 17. When they arrived in Birmingham, the police, headed by Bull Connor, who would soon go on to infamy in the civil rights movement as the symbol of white racist intransigence, simply arrested them, drove them back to the Tennessee state line, deposited them unceremoni-

Freedom Rider bus went up in flames in May 1961 when a fire bomb was tossed through a window near Anniston, Alabama. The bus, which was challenging bus station segregation in the south, had stopped because of a flat tire. Passengers escaped without serious injury. AP Photo/str.

ously on the side of the road in the dark, and warned them not to come back to Alabama. They rejected that advice and caught a ride back to Birmingham, piling into cars rather than buses. This time, Connor planned to escort them to the Mississippi state line, by way of Montgomery.

Arriving in Montgomery, this second group of Freedom Riders found itself in dire straits, as the bloodiest attacks yet awaited. Robert Kennedy had sent his special assistant for civil rights issues, John Seigenthaler, to meet them in Montgomery and to offer them assurance of protection. Instead, Seigenthaler walked straight into the mob attack in progress to save a victim and became a victim himself. The mob paid no respect to his federal office and beat him unconscious. To Attorney General Kennedy, this was the final straw. He had a falling out with John Patterson, the Alabama governor, and sent U.S. marshals to Montgomery. Meanwhile, Martin Luther King, Jr., the SCLC, and other civil rights activists converged on Montgomery to rally at the black First Baptist Church. The Klan laid siege to the church, however, forcing the occupants to hole up inside for days. Finally, Kennedy arranged to have them escorted out of Alabama aboard a Trailways bus by the National Guard. As they departed, one Freedom Rider, James Bevel of Nashville, commented that it seemed more like a military operation than a civil rights protest. A second busload followed aboard Greyhound.

Once the activists were across the state line in Mississippi, Kennedy made sure they were met again by the National Guard, having prearranged it with Ross Barnett, the governor of Mississippi. They rode safely into the terminal in Jackson, where they were simply arrested and hauled off to jail. Mississippi was careful not to replicate the public relations disaster that Alabama had just caused. Following the strict CORE policy of staying in jail rather than posting bail, the Freedom Riders were just beginning their torturous journey. It was still May 1961, and the last of the convicts would not be released for another year.

The publicity generated by these first spectacular episodes resulted in hundreds of idealistic students, ministers, and concerned citizens around the nation joining the Freedom Ride movement. In all, over the next eight months, there would be 60 separate Freedom Rides carried out by 436 individual Freedom Riders. Most ended up in a Mississippi jail thereafter, rather than suffering beatings at the hands of the Klan. There were, however, isolated incidents of violence in Monroe, North Carolina; McComb, Mississippi; and Washington, D.C. Other repercussions faced by the Freedom Rides included the predictable white backlash. Lincoln Rockwell's notorious American Nazi Party drove a so-called Hate Bus to New Orleans in mockery.[4] White Citizens Councils in Louisiana and other Deep South states likewise arranged *Reverse* Freedom Rides in which they paid the fare of poor blacks who wanted to move to the North. One group of Reverse Freedom Riders was dumped with much media attention in Hyannis, Massachusetts, the home town of the Kennedys.

In the end, the Freedom Rides faded strangely into semiobscurity in the history books, partly because more compelling and explosive events occurred in the civil rights movement immediately thereafter and did not abate for a decade. After all, for all the violence, bloodshed, and misery inflicted on the riders, none of them actually paid the ultimate price with their lives, whereas several people would later become martyrs for the movement in other episodes. Partly, too, the symbolic messiah of the movement, Martin Luther King, Jr., merely offered moral support to the Freedom Ride cause rather than joining it himself.

1962: THE INTEGRATION OF OLE MISS

Nestled in the rolling hills of north Mississippi, the quaint little university town of Oxford had a population of barely 5,000 people in 1962. It was home to the University of Mississippi, called Ole Miss, a small school with a student body of fewer than 3,000. Its great claim to fame was that it had produced the brilliant southern novelist William Faulkner a generation earlier. Otherwise, it produced most of the lawyers who had become the political leaders of the Magnolia State since antebellum times. In the 116 years of its history, never had either the town or the college seen so much commotion as the day a black man, James Meredith, arrived on campus to register. It would be a bloody affair, leaving two people dead and several wounded, and it would capture the attention of the nation like no other civil rights event had ever done. It would leave the state of Mississippi with a reputation as the most recalcitrant of all southern states on civil rights issues.

James Meredith grew up in the red clay hills of central Mississippi, in rural Attala County. In the 1950s, he spent nine years in the Air Force, where he was stationed in Japan, among other places, and where he took night classes and correspondence courses offered by various colleges, including the Universities of Maryland and Kansas. Having earned respectable grades from those institutions, the 27-year-old Meredith dreamed of continuing his education at his home state's flagship university, Ole Miss. Upon leaving the Air Force, he moved back to Mississippi and enrolled temporarily in the premier school for blacks in the state, Jackson State College. He sent his first letter of application to Ole Miss on January 21, 1961, ironically and coincidentally the day after John F. Kennedy was inaugurated as president of the United States. Kennedy had spoken of taming the "new frontier" of civil rights, and Meredith intended to be one of the pioneers on that new frontier.[5]

Meredith knew that Ole Miss would reject his application once the registrar realized he was black, so he immediately began seeking legal counsel. He first went to Medgar Evers, the NAACP field secretary in Mississippi, whom he had previously never met. Evers put him in touch with Thurgood Marshall, the national director of the NAACP Legal Defense Fund. Marshall, who was already famous for his litigation of the *Brown v. Board of Education* case and who would soon be named the first black Justice of the U.S. Supreme Court, showed great interest in Meredith's cause. He assigned Constance Baker Motley to manage his case. The judicial process would prove arduous, lasting nearly two years and moving from state court to federal district court to federal appeals court, and would ultimately require the services of a U.S. Supreme Court Justice. It would move from the town of Meridian to Biloxi to Jackson and finally to New Orleans. It would involve about a dozen different judges, some of whom vehemently disagreed with the others about the constitutionality of racial integration, leading to a back-and-forth of stays, set-asides, and injunctions. And it would pull the U.S. Justice Department and the president himself into the fray.

The initial ruling, which was unfavorable for Meredith, came in June 1961, while the Freedom Riders were doing their best to fill up the jails in Mississippi. The state already seethed with racial tension exacerbated by outside agitation, and this case would soon make it explode. Meredith received a different verdict from the U.S. Fifth Circuit Court of Appeals, which had a rotating panel of judges who might hear any particular case. On June 25, 1962, the presiding judges ruled that Ole Miss must accept his application. On July 18, another judge, who had not been on that panel, issued a stay on that order. On July 27, another panel of judges from the Fifth Circuit set aside the stay. The two sides tried to outmaneuver and outlast each other four times. In September, U.S. Supreme Court Justice Hugo Black was called in to mediate. He sided with Meredith and the NAACP against Ole Miss and the state of Mississippi, issuing an injunction, the most authoritative action a court could take.

At that point, Mississippi's governor, Ross Barnett, stepped into the picture on behalf of his race, state, and alma mater. He appointed himself temporary registrar of the University of Mississippi, and he made a public proclamation that he intended to defy the injunction. In the same week, a state court judge ordered

James Meredith, center with briefcase, is escorted to the University of Mississippi campus in Oxford on October 2, 1962, by Chief U.S. Marshal James McShane, left, and an unidentified marshal at right. To the far right is one of the U.S. Army troopers stationed on the university grounds. Meredith, a civil rights activist, was the first black student to attend the University of Mississippi after integration. His presence sparked riots on the Oxford campus. AP Photo.

the nullification of the decisions of the federal courts, ruling that they had no authority to interfere in local matters such as this one involving a Mississippi citizen (Meredith) and a Mississippi institution (Ole Miss). The next day, the state legislature weighed in, giving its full support to the governor and the state court. These actions amounted to a declaration of political war, with states' rights pitted against the authority of the U.S. government, and the situation even threatened to escalate to another full-blown civil war.

At the same time, the U.S. Justice Department, headed by the president's younger brother, Attorney General Robert F. Kennedy, took control of enforcing the injunction, lining up a single U.S. marshal and a lawyer for the task initially. Both he and the president also had telephone conversations with the governor, in which they tried to negotiate a peaceful settlement of the issue. They ultimately agreed on a staged presentation, in which the governor would save face with his constituents by putting up a stiff fight but would back down in the end under threat of overwhelming national military power. On September 20, the team from the Justice Department escorted Meredith along the sixty-mile drive from Memphis to Oxford. There, several thousand local whites, several dozen state troopers, reporters, the governor, and miscellaneous state officials met them on campus. Meeting Meredith face-to-face, the governor read a statement and summarily denied Meredith admission to the university. The next day, the court proceedings resumed. The U.S. Fifth Circuit Court of Appeals in New Orleans held Barnett in contempt.

Because of the quickness of the events from day to day, on September 25, the next scene in the staged drama shifted to the state capital Jackson, which made travel more convenient for all parties coming from New Orleans. There Barnett again denied Meredith admission to Ole Miss. Again the court in New Orleans held Barnett in contempt, slapping him with a $10,000-per-day fine. The following day, Meredith and the Justice Department team flew from New Orleans to Oxford, landing at the small-town airport, where again they were mobbed by local whites, reporters, and law enforcement personnel. On this third attempt to register, Meredith faced Lieutenant Governor Paul B. Johnson, who would soon go on to succeed Barnett as governor. Johnson had much to gain politically with his white constituents by taking a hard line approach in this situation. In a media spectacle rarely seen in American history, the thin, little Johnson, backed by a team of state troopers, stood toe-to-toe with U.S. Marshal James McShane, clenched a fist in his face, gritted his teeth, and dared the bigger man and his group to try to pass. They did try to pass, which led to pushing, shoving, and a scene reminiscent of boys scuffling on a playground. In the end, the federals backed down once again, this time heading back to Memphis to await their next move.

Robert Kennedy had planned to make a fourth attempt at having Meredith escorted into Oxford by a larger force of U.S. marshals. In the middle of the journey, however, the mission was aborted, as word came that the president himself had issued an executive order federalizing the Mississippi National Guard. Now Meredith would be flown into Oxford and protected by the National Guard as he registered and matriculated. It was Sunday night, September 30, when Meredith finally stepped onto campus without opposition. He and his team were housed in a dormitory for the night, and the next day, October 1, 1962, he registered and attended his first classes at Ole Miss. While the media frenzy died down after Meredith's enrollment, the saga had just begun for the now-29-year-old black veteran.

At the time all this happened, in September 1962, the general public did not know about the staging of the whole affair between the Kennedys and Meredith and the NAACP. The scuffle between Johnson and McShane yielded one of the most famous photographs of the entire civil rights movement, making its way into newspapers around the world. It seemed to show the weak but determined little state government fighting the all-powerful federal government. White Mississippians reveled in the idea that their chosen representatives, Barnett and Johnson, had the courage to fight the big bully, the U.S. government. Black Mississippians, meanwhile, silently gloried in the triumph of one of their own over what they perceived to be the big bully—the state of Mississippi.

1963: THE MARCH ON WASHINGTON

In many ways, Wednesday, August 28, 1963, was just like any other day in the hustle and bustle of the workweek in the nation's capital, Washington, D.C. Parents went to work, stores opened for business, traffic buzzed around the city, and everyone fought the summer heat and humidity of coastal mid-America. There was one notable exception, however, to this everyday routine: the six most prominent African American civil rights organizations in the country had teamed up to produce the first-ever "March on Washington for Jobs and Freedom."[6] Its aims included sending a message to Congress to pass President Kennedy's civil rights bill, showing solidarity of purpose among the often competing civil rights groups, and building a bridge between grass-roots blacks and whites. Critics said it could not be done, that it would not draw more than a few thousand radicals, that it would result in riots in the streets, and that it would damage the civil rights movement, rather than strengthen it. Against all odds, however, the organizers' efforts resulted in a peaceful, nonviolent protest attended by an estimated crowd of 170,000 blacks and perhaps 30,000 whites, representing all regions of the country. They came to make their presence felt, to have their voices heard, and to push the civil rights movement forward at an accelerated pace.

As early as the World War II years, the black union chieftain A. Philip Randolph, of the Brotherhood of Sleeping Car Porters, had threatened to lead a march on Washington. At the time, he hoped to convince President Franklin Roosevelt to guarantee fair job opportunities in the federally funded defense industry. Roosevelt's quick and smart response to the threat, however—the issuance of Executive Order 8802, creating the Fair Employment Practices Committee—made the march unnecessary. Over the next two decades, the idea lay dormant as civil rights leaders made major advances by other means, such as litigation, boycotts, sit-ins, and localized demonstrations. For reasons that seem partly unclear today but which included the need to take advantage of the Kennedy administration's sympathetic overtures to oppressed blacks, the idea of staging a march on Washington seemed ripe once again in 1963. The now-aged Randolph took the lead in resurrecting the idea. He began by communicating his plan to the other members of the "Big Six": Roy Wilkins of the NAACP, Martin Luther King, Jr., of the SCLC, James Farmer of CORE, Whitney Young of the National Urban League (NUL), and John Lewis of SNCC.[7] He also lined up influential white leaders such as Walter Reuther of the United Auto Workers Union, Eugene Carson Blake of the National Council of Churches, Joachim Prinz of the American Jewish Congress, and Patrick O'Boyle, the Catholic archbishop of Washington. Most important, he began the process of convincing a skeptical President Kennedy of the seriousness and feasibility of the plan.

Beginning in June, the planning was done swiftly amid the backdrop of the recent assassination of Medgar Evers in Mississippi; violent civil rights demonstrations in Alabama, Maryland, and Virginia, among other places; a problematic sort of reverse-discrimination court case that involved a protest in southwest Georgia; FBI surveillance of civil rights leaders; and Kennedy's introduction of his heralded civil rights bill. On June 22, Kennedy met with the Big Six at the White House to discuss the civil rights bill he had sent to Congress 11 days earlier. He questioned the wisdom of their staging a march on Washington with such an important piece of legislation pending. He feared it would cause a backlash among the roughly one-third in Congress who could be swayed to vote either way and who might decide to vote against the bill if they saw anarchy in the streets surrounding them on Capitol Hill. Failure of the march would ensure failure of the bill, he believed. Each of the Big Six in turn tried to assure the president that they would maintain strict control over the crowd and that the march would proceed in the nonviolent, Gandhian tradition already established in earlier demonstrations. King, as was so often the case, made the most astute observation and memorable statement in response to Kennedy, saying of the march, "It may seem ill timed. Frankly, I have never engaged in any direct action movement which did not seem ill timed."[8] In other words, to wait for a more convenient time to stage a march would be folly. The president acquiesced.

On July 2, the Big Six met in New York City to finalize their plans. Randolph held the esteemed position of elder statesman, while Roy Wilkins held the title of leader of the most influential of the civil rights groups, the NAACP. Randolph handed the job of organizing the actual march to his controversial but talented lieutenant, Bayard Rustin. This move stirred hard feelings because Rustin was a known homosexual, a socialist, and a former communist, and his reputation preceded him. Ultimately, they reached a compromise in which Rustin would serve as a behind-the-scenes choreographer of the march, while Wilkins and King would serve as the public relations team for fielding questions from the news media. Rustin's job was not merely to figure out a way to get people to sacrifice their time and money to come to Washington in the middle of the workweek but also to stage a dramatic, all-day event for them once they got there. He ultimately planned the actual march to take place from the Washington Monument to the Lincoln Memorial, with opening ceremonies on one end and closing ceremonies on the other. The alliance between Wilkins and King was critical to the success of the march because, according to a *Newsweek* magazine article published at the time, King had the support of 88 percent of blacks, and the NAACP still had the longest track record of any civil rights groups of successfully working with whites. Their alliance thus gave more legitimacy to each man than either would have had working alone on such an enormous project.

Throughout July, J. Edgar Hoover and the FBI monitored King, tapping into his personal life, as part of its ongoing efforts to flush communists and "pinkos" into the open or otherwise to obtain dirt on him and other civil rights activists that might discredit them publicly. Upon finding evidence that a King staffer in New

Rev. Martin Luther King, Jr., gives his famous "I Have a Dream" speech to the crowds gathered in front of the Lincoln Memorial during the March on Washington, August 28, 1964. Courtesy of Photofest.

York was a former communist organizer, the FBI gleefully leaked it to the media, which trumpeted the news to the world. Moreover, evidence obtained from wiretaps revealed that King was, in Hoover's words, a "tomcat" with the ladies.[9] Hoover chose to give that information to Kennedy rather than the media, with the intention of convincing the president that he should have no dealings with civil rights leaders because they were hypocrites and could not be trusted. The FBI also leaked information to Congress on Rustin's tawdry personal life, which the southern segregationist Senator Strom Thurmond of South Carolina eagerly made public in a Senate speech. With all these distractions testing the resolve of march organizers, it seems a wonder they managed to keep their composure and go through with their plan at all, much less do it with such grandiose results.

As the day approached in August, the things that did the most to jeopardize the success of the march came from unexpected sources. One of the Big Six, James Farmer, sat in jail in Louisiana for leading a demonstration there. It was his and CORE's official position not to post bail but to suffer incarceration and fill up the jails out of righteous indignation. Whether to follow that policy at such a critical time, when his presence would be sorely missed at the march, became a dilemma for Farmer, and a bone of contention for the other march leaders. Farmer ultimately chose jail over appearing on stage in front of the eyes of the world on August 28. Another problem arose when John Lewis of SNCC, the youngest of the Big Six, prepared a controversial speech for his moment behind the microphone. Helped by James Forman in the drafting of the speech, Lewis planned to threaten a "scorched-earth" policy in the Deep South if the federal government did not take swift and serious action to destroy racial discrimination.[10] On the day before the march, Archbishop Patrick O'Boyle previewed the speech, found it inflammatory, and said he would not participate in the march if such language was used. This led to a chain reaction throughout the ranks of the organizers to get Lewis to reword his speech for the sake of keeping unity. The organizers could not afford to lose the support of key white participants by appearing to advocate violence or retribution. At the time of this flare-up, the Black Muslim Malcolm X happened to be in the lobby of the Washington Statler-Hilton Hotel, where Rustin had gathered his forces to work out a compromise. Upon hearing of the dispute, Malcolm took the opportunity to mock the nonviolent, integrationist approach of the Big Six, calling their planned march the "Farce on Washington," a label that reporters sent straight to the front page.[11] The dispute over Lewis's speech would not be solved that day. Meanwhile, as Rustin fought that battle behind the scenes, he also had to prepare for violence breaking out at the hands of onlookers, counterdemonstrators, or others not affiliated with march organizers, by coordinating with local police and special security personnel.

By the day of the march, FBI agents, at the behest of Hoover, began calling celebrities slated to appear at the event and warned them to stay inside, ostensibly out of fear that there would be rioting in the streets but more likely because Hoover hoped to discredit the march's leaders with a poor showing of support from celebrities. Undeterred, however, the celebrities poured in, along with the hundreds of buses and trains carrying the common people. White movie stars such as Charlton Heston and James Garner marched beside black stars such as Harry Belafonte and Diahann Carroll. At 10 A.M. the festivities began with performances by the white folk singers Joan Baez, Bob Dylan, and the trio of Peter, Paul, and Mary, among others. The CBS television network covered the event live, from beginning to end, with ABC and NBC joining later in the day. In the midst of what would have been an otherwise purely joyous day, word came from Africa that the man most responsible for founding the NAACP back in 1910, W.E.B. Du Bois, had died. It was ironic but somehow appropriate that the old icon of the integrationist movement had passed away on this particular day, and the current NAACP director, Roy Wilkins, had the unenviable honor of announcing his passing to the world.

In the early afternoon, the focus shifted to the Lincoln Memorial stage, where Archbishop O'Boyle still threatened not to give the opening invocation unless Lewis's speech was toned down. The Big Six and their lieutenants and allies argued vehemently among themselves back stage over the wording, and Rustin persuaded O'Boyle to proceed, promising him a more conciliatory speech from Lewis. When time came for Lewis to speak a few minutes later, the "scorched-earth" language had been removed, and the public audience never missed it.

Lewis's speech was second only to King's climactic "I Have a Dream" speech in its impact on the crowd. In between those two dramatic orations, there were more celebrities, and there was more music. To conclude the program, A. Philip Randolph introduced King as "the moral leader of our nation," and the crowd welcomed him as such.[12] King's brief speech became an instant classic and has since been named among the three or four greatest speeches in American history. President Kennedy, watching the march on television from the safety of the White House, applauded King's ability to hypnotize an audience, saying, "He's damn good."[13]

After the benediction to conclude the march, the crowd dispersed, happy with the event they had watched and helped create and equally glad to get out of the blistering heat. At 6 P.M., Kennedy welcomed the Big Six and their lieutenants into the White House for another brief summit about where to go from here in getting the civil rights bill passed. It would be the last time most of them would ever talk face-to-face again, as the dapper young President had only three more months to live.

1964: FREEDOM SUMMER, DEADLY SUMMER

Philadelphia means "city of brotherly love." The town of Philadelphia, Mississippi, however, was anything but a city of brotherly love in 1964. It became instead a city of civil rights activity, Ku Klux Klan reaction, racial strife, murder, FBI probes, and international media attention. The two-month hunt for three missing civil rights workers turned the eyes of the world on the little backwater town and its corrupt law enforcement officers. The discovery of the bodies of Mickey Schwerner, James Chaney, and Andrew Goodman ultimately led to a murder trial conducted by the U.S. Justice Department in a federal court in Mississippi that marked a turning point in southern race relations. Whereas all-white local juries in the Deep South had a history of acquitting their white peers of racial hate-crime charges, this time it was different. This time, an all-white local jury returned a guilty verdict against seven fellow whites, including a sheriff, a deputy sheriff, a former sheriff, a city policeman, and the Imperial Wizard of the White Knights of the Ku Klux Klan. These convictions gave hope to the hopeless, showing the black population of Mississippi that a new day had dawned, a day when justice, rather than whiteness, would prevail. This happy ending, however, obscures the tragedy that occurred on June 21, 1964, as three innocent young men were murdered, so it is the story of that tragedy that now must be told.

A town of 5,000 in a county of only 20,000, Philadelphia sits in the middle of Neshoba County, in the east-central red clay hills. About 40 miles from the Alabama line and 70 miles from the state capital, Jackson, Philadelphia is also a mere 30 miles from where James Meredith, the protagonist of the 1962 Ole Miss integration crisis, grew up. The town's great claim to fame prior to 1964 was its annual Neshoba County Fair, held every summer dating back to the 1800s (except during World War II). The week-long fair has traditionally been the state of Mississippi's great showcase for political stumping during election years, and the likes of governors James K. Vardaman, Theodore G. Bilbo, and Ross Barnett made some of their fieriest orations there. Even presidential candidates such as Ronald Reagan have spoken there. The only other distinguishing feature separating Neshoba County from most of the other 82 Mississippi counties was its Choctaw Indian reservations. The presence of more than half of all the Choctaws in the state gave Neshoba County a racial milieu that no other county could match. While one might suppose this triad of races should have prevented whites and blacks from polarizing, it did not. Whites were just as determined to maintain their position of superiority there as they were in Birmingham or any other hotbed of civil rights activism. Maybe more so, considering that, upon visiting the town in 1966, Martin Luther King, Jr., remarked that it was the worst, most racist place he had ever been.

On the night of June 21, 1964, indeed it was the worst town that Schwerner, Chaney, and Goodman, three out-of-towners, could have been in. At 24, Michael Henry "Mickey" Schwerner was the oldest of the three, and the leader. Raised in a Jewish family in New York City, he graduated from Cornell University in 1961 and continued his education at Columbia University. He was married, and both he and his wife joined CORE in 1963. In January 1964, they moved to Meridian, Mississippi, and set up a "COFO" (Council of Federated Organizations) office to coordinate the efforts of CORE, SCLC, SNCC, and NAACP in preparing for "Freedom Summer"—a statewide black-voter-registration drive. There they met Chaney, a 21-year-old local black construction worker and college student. Together they canvassed the rural countryside that spring and summer, talking to the largely uneducated and fearful black residents and holding meetings in black churches to promote voter registration. In June, they spent a few days in Ohio training white college students to come south for the summer and help. There they met Goodman, a 20-year-old Jewish student from New York City, who was new to the Freedom Summer project and who accompanied them back to Mississippi.

The presence of COFO workers in rural black areas in Mississippi stirred white resentment not only around Philadelphia but throughout the state in 1964. The state government created auxiliary or supplementary police units to serve as facades to allow Klansmen and other radical segregationists to meet under cover and protection of the law. As civil rights activity increased, random acts of Klan violence, such as beatings, church burnings, and even murder, increased from Holmes County to Hattiesburg, from Neshoba County to Natchez. Philadelphia had no history of being any worse than any other town in terms of racial terrorism, although, rather inexplicably, it was singled out for a Klan campaign in the spring of 1964, playing host to 12 separate cross burnings in April, one of which took place on the courthouse lawn. Meanwhile, the auxiliary police unit in the region met at the National Guard Armory in Philadelphia. Part of the tragedy of these murders is that, of the 1,000 COFO volunteers in Mississippi during

Freedom Summer, these three had the misfortune of being in the wrong place at the wrong time. The same could have happened to any of the other volunteers, had they been caught in a similar situation—alone and defenseless at night on a rural stretch of highway, at the mercy of corrupt law enforcement officers.

The prelude to the murders began on Tuesday evening, June 16, when the Mount Zion Methodist Church, a black congregation's modest old edifice, held a combination church meeting and political forum. The Klan had been keeping an eye on the church for weeks, knowing it served as the organizing point for local civil rights activism. As the attendants left the building that night, three of them were assaulted by Klansmen, and one was beaten within an inch of his life. Later that night, the church building went up in flames and burned to the ground. On Sunday, June 21, Schwerner, Chaney, and Goodman drove in a station wagon northwest from the local hub city of Meridian to Neshoba County, a 40-mile trek up state highway 19, to investigate the beatings and the arson. Cecil Price, the local sheriff's deputy, identified the car as the one that had been seen around the area lately and that belonged to one of those so-called invaders from up North. He pulled the car over, citing the driver, Chaney, for allegedly speeding. Under normal circumstances, any other driver would have been issued the citation and sent on his way. This, however, was by no means a normal circumstance. The deputy seized the opportunity to teach these integrationists a lesson and hauled them off to the Neshoba County jail. This happened around 4 P.M. The deputy detained the three men for approximately six and a half hours. At around 10:30 P.M., he allowed Chaney to pay a $20 fine and released him. Price and a city policeman, Richard Willis, then tailed their station wagon to the edge of the city limits, moving southwest toward Meridian. That was the last anyone saw of them, at least according to the officers, who then went back to their daily vocation of helping run bootleg whisky around the dry state.

When the missing-persons report came out the next day, the vast majority of local whites dismissed it as a hoax. They convinced themselves that the three COFO workers had staged their own disappearance in order to draw more attention to their Freedom Summer campaign and thus to enlist more volunteers and collect more donations. Meanwhile, FBI agents arrived within two days to begin an investigation, as did reporters for *Newsweek* and the *New York Times*. All received a chilly welcome from most townspeople. By the end of the week, the FBI had set up a special new office in Jackson for handling the investigation, and J. Edgar Hoover himself, the long-time director of the FBI, soon came to dedicate the office. At the same time, 400 naval cadets from the nearby military base in Meridian were on the scene, combing through the swamps looking for bodies. The station wagon had already been found by then, nowhere near the place Price and Willis had claimed but rather 12 miles away on the opposite side of town, burned and gutted. About six weeks later, on August 4, the FBI located the bodies, buried beneath 15 feet of dirt in a nearby pond levee. Now, at least the families could get some closure.

The timing of these murders in the big scheme of American history was monumentally important. The Civil Rights Act of 1964, the most important civil rights law ever enacted, was passed on July 2, right in the midst of the missing-persons hunt. It gave the Justice Department enforcement clear powers to prosecute civil rights violations to a greater extent than any law before it. The timing of the discovery of the bodies could not have been worse for local whites, who tried to maintain a business-as-usual approach to opening the Neshoba County Fair on August 10, a mere six days later. Although the fair did go on as scheduled, and turnout was not much less than the normal 50,000, racial strife, the FBI presence, and outside interference in local matters generally cast a dark shadow over the festivities.

It took the FBI another four months of questioning witnesses to gather enough evidence to press charges against anyone. Altogether they charged 21 men initially, although some of the charges were later dropped and others dismissed in court. Through legal maneuvering, the defense managed to ensure that the first court proceedings did no harm, and what followed was a lengthy process of retrials and appeals. While the slow and sometimes frustrating American system of justice took its course, national attention shifted away from Philadelphia and on to other civil rights battlegrounds. During this respite, the black members of Mount Zion rebuilt their church and dedicated it to the memory of the three slain COFO workers, in February 1966.

Four months later, in June 1966, national attention returned to Mississippi, as James Meredith attempted to stage a solo march from Memphis to Jackson but was shot shortly after crossing the state line south of Memphis. This Meredith March, although nowhere near the town of Philadelphia, had important ramifications for it, nonetheless. Upon the shooting of Meredith, many other now-famous civil rights leaders, including the SCLC's Martin Luther King, Jr., and Stokely Carmichael of SNCC took up the march where their fallen comrade had left off. Although mainly remembered in civil rights history as the march that created the "Black Power" slogan and thus helped change the direction of the movement away from nonviolence to black retaliation, it also afforded King the opportunity to visit Philadelphia for the first time, since he was in the state anyway.[14] While there, he led a small march downtown that was scheduled to end at the Neshoba County Courthouse. Again, however, local law enforcement officers stood against the marchers, preventing King from stepping foot on the courthouse lawn. King thus improvised and delivered the brief speech from the curb of the street, then proceeded to lead the marchers back in the direction from whence they had come, all the while being taunted and heckled and ultimately attacked by a white mob. King later recalled that this attack was one of only two times in his life that he felt truly afraid for his life (the other being in a similar march in a suburb of Chicago a month later).

By February 1967, the FBI's case had wound through the federal court system, all the way to the Supreme Court and back, and was ready for final prosecution.

This time, the Justice Department charged 19 men with either violating the civil rights of Schwerner, Chaney, and Goodman, conspiring to violate their civil rights, or committing outright murder. The jury that deliberated at the trial was composed of five white men and seven white women, all citizens of the state of Mississippi. The basic story they heard through testimony picked up where the original Price and Willis version ended: the two had indeed let the three go free and then followed them out of town, but they had by then also organized a whole posse to help them carry out a lynching. The officers had immediately stopped the three young men again, forced them into a car, driven them to a dirt road far out in the county, taken them out one by one, and executed them by shooting. They then loaded the bodies into the back of their own station wagon, dumped them in the bottom of the levee, which was then under construction by one of the conspirators, who in turn bulldozed them under right then in the middle of the night. One of the conspirators then took the car to a different location and set it afire. Upon hearing this gruesome story pieced together by various witnesses, the all-white jury quickly returned guilty verdicts against the seven ringleaders, while acquitting the rest. This verdict showed that federal civil rights laws could be effective, that the U.S. government fully intended to enforce them, that even the most recalcitrant of southern states could not stop their enforcement, and that the future might thus be brighter than the past for blacks in Mississippi.

1965: THE WATTS RIOT

A sprawling metropolis of 2.5 million and growing, Los Angeles sat comfortably in the 1960s as the third largest city in the United States. Just like today, it was then the home of Hollywood, the preferred residence and hangout of many of the rich and famous, a favorite vacation spot of people from all over the world, the host city of two national collegiate sports powerhouses, the University of Southern California (USC) and the University of California–Los Angeles (UCLA), and in many ways the ultimate American dream city. It attracted people of all races, cultures, and backgrounds, some for its glamour and excitement, but most for basic economic opportunity. Although a majority-white city, it housed hundreds of thousands of poor blacks and Hispanics in communities such as Watts, as well as in its multiple suburbs. Known for its tolerance and progressiveness in race relations, Los Angeles would have appeared to the casual observer a model city, a prototype for how the American melting pot assimilated diverse racial and ethnic groups. So it seemed until Wednesday, August 11, 1965, a date that has lived in infamy ever since, a day that shattered the illusion of the idyllic TinselTown city, and a day that would mark a turning point in the civil rights movement and in American race relations generally.

It began on a typically hot, dry day in southern California. The temperature still hovered in the mid-90s at 7 P.M., as afternoon began to give way to evening. People went about their business as usual. There were no warning signs that something bad was about to happen, much less that the black residents of the Watts community were sitting on a powder keg and needed only a single case of police brutality to set it off. Lee Minikus, a white, 31-year-old California highway patrolman, saw nothing out of the ordinary that day about pulling over a car that seemed to be moving erratically down Avalon Boulevard. A black motorist had flagged him down to tell him there was a drunk driver behind the wheel. He gave chase, caught the vehicle in question, and stopped it. In the driver's seat sat a 21-year-old African American, Marquette Frye, while his 22-year-old brother Ronald sat in the passenger seat. Ronald had just returned from military service, and the two young men had gone out to celebrate his homecoming with drinks. Minikus followed standard procedure when dealing with drivers suspected of being under the influence. He instructed Marquette to perform a series of sobriety tests. Rather than resisting arrest, Marquette cooperated fully, albeit with too much enthusiasm, in Minikus's opinion. He seemed to treat the tests as a joke, which appeared to the patrolman's trained eye as a drunk man's response. Minikus cited him with driving while intoxicated, informed him that he was under arrest, called for a police car to take him to the station, and requisitioned a tow truck to take his car to be impounded. Ronald asked to be allowed to drive the car home, which was only two blocks away. Minikus refused and told Ronald to walk home.

Meanwhile, Frye's outlandish behavior while standing on the side of the road, dancing, hopping, and making a spectacle of himself, drew a small crowd of local resident observers. Within minutes, the squad car and tow truck arrived, but so did the young man's mother, Rena Frye, whom Ronald had informed of the problem. She scolded her son for drinking, and the two argued. She then tried to convince the white officers that they should let her drive the car home. By then, however, Minikus had already made his decision to tow the car and proceeded accordingly, oblivious to the mother's pleading. The frustrated mother made a scene with a loud, verbal outburst, drawing the officers' ire. Sensing a hostile situation developing, the officers then called for backup, as they had been trained to do. As they prepared to cuff Marquette and usher him into the car, the young man resisted arrest and began yelling that the police would have to kill him. As the officers manhandled Marquette, he tried to defend himself, and they wrestled over control of the policeman's nightstick.

Within a few minutes, two more squad cars arrived on the scene, and two white officers jumped out to help control the swelling crowd of black spectators. One of the policemen wielded a shotgun, which he did not fire but used merely for intimidation to hold the crowd at bay. The other wielded a nightstick, which he immediately jabbed hard into Marquette's abdomen, ostensibly to shut him up, teach him a lesson, and put him in his place. The blow doubled him over, and another to the head sent him to the ground. Even if such force was necessary under the circumstances, the black crowd clearly did not think it was. It provoked Rena and Ronald Frye into a defensive rage, causing them to try to intervene physically. The mother actually jumped on Minikus's back and ripped his shirt. The officers peeled her off, then arrested all three members of the Frye family.

By this time, about 25 minutes had elapsed since the beginning of the episode, several more law enforcement backups had arrived, and the crowd had grown to number approximately 100 in the immediate vicinity and 1,000 in the general area. Just when it seemed the incident had been brought under control, some-one in the crowd spat on an officer named Vaughn. He and his fellows reacted violently, bursting into the mob to identify and catch the perpetrator. They grabbed a young hairdresser, yanked her forcefully into the clearing, and pushed her unceremoniously into the back of the police car. Many in the crowd realized they had picked the wrong person, and, to make matters worse, this particular woman looked pregnant, which made the white officers' actions reek of unjustifi-able police brutality. The crowd consequently exploded in anger, throwing bottles, bricks, rocks, and chunks of concrete at the police car. The officers followed their standard procedure for dealing with such situations, however, and, at 7:40 P.M., withdrew from the scene, hoping the crowd would disperse and the incident would pass. It did not work, however. The black residents of Watts continued to mill around the street corners from 116th and Avalon to 122nd and Avalon, fuming over what they had just witnessed and feeling helpless, frustrated, and angry. They took out their frustration on passing white motorists, assaulting and beating some, vandalizing the cars and property of others. The riot had begun, and it lasted sporadically until the next morning.

The events of that first night were serious, to be sure, but they had not risen to the level of a full-scale riot. Consequently, the highest-ranking officials in the government and law enforcement were not immediately called in. The next day, Thursday, August 12, John Buggs, the Los Angeles human relations com-missioner, talked to the city gang leaders and asked them to try to help calm the black youth of Watts. He believed developing such a rapport with those who could best relate to the rioters would be the surest way not only to bring imme-diate peace but also to help the restoration and healing process begin. Deputy Police Chief Roger Murdock, however, thought it ridiculous to get street toughs to do what his police were paid to do—restore law and order. He decided to countermand Buggs's initiative and send the police back to Watts in a strong show of force. Technically, he was acting according to the protocol of the police manual in so doing, but it would soon become evident that the manual needed serious revisions in light of changing times. The presence of the police in Watts backfired, because the black youth saw them increasingly as the oppressors. At 5 P.M. that day, in the midst of heavy police occupation, the vandals descended to the next level and began looting stores owned by nonblacks. Soon after, the first arson was reported. That evening and throughout the night, without plan-ning, the rioting youth set fire to 46 square miles of the Los Angeles metropolitan area.

Realizing that a bad situation had grown much worse, the police then sprang into emergency mode, taking control of the city as if it was a war zone. Now Chief of Police William Parker got involved, but his leadership skills seemed lacking in the face of such a serious problem. He refused to ask for help from law enforcement outside the area or from the National Guard. He did talk to the mayor, Sam Yorty, and to Lieutenant Governor Glenn Anderson about the problem, but he assured them he had the problem under control. They believed him. Thus, on the third day of the riot, Friday, August 13, both the mayor and the lieutenant governor went about their business as usual. Each, ironically, had a separate meeting scheduled in the San Francisco Bay area. Likewise, by sheer coincidence, Governor Pat Brown was not only out of state but out of the country, vacationing in Greece at the time. Elected officials were of almost no help, therefore, as the violence and burning escalated even further that day. It was Friday the 13th, and a nightmare was unfolding in Watts.

Finally, Chief Parker admitted he could not bring the situation under control without outside help. At about 11 A.M., he phoned Anderson and asked him to deploy the National Guard. Anderson denied that request. Instead, he said he would fly back to Los Angeles, meet with city leaders, and take command. The lieutenant governor refused to fly on a regular commercial plane, however, like a lowly citizen. He required the services of the governor's official plane. Unfortunately, the plane was not available immediately. The delay cost Anderson nearly three hours—precious time on a day when Watts was going up in flames and people would soon be dying by the minute. Upon arriving, he discovered that most of the city leaders were, like Mayor Yorty and Governor Brown, away on business or vacation. He took charge, ordering the affected area to be cordoned off and placed under curfew. No one entered or exited the area that day or night without permission. This action contained the riot within a specified area, but it did nothing to end the arson, vandalism, and homicides within it. That evening and night, 16 people were killed.

At 5 A.M. on Saturday morning, the first National Guardsmen arrived, and over the next four days some 14,000 troops would occupy Watts. Some of the black residents of Watts welcomed them as saviors, while others spurned them as just another group of oppressors. The Guard did not totally quell the riot, but it limited the individual acts of vandalism, looting, arson, and murder. Even so, 18 more people were killed after the arrival of the troops. The Guard was not alone in patrolling Watts but received help from almost 1,000 policemen and 700 deputies. This incredibly large law enforcement and military occupation resulted in the arrest of nearly 4,000 people for engaging in riotous activities, yet it could not prevent 34 people being killed, more than 1,000 being wounded seriously enough to require medical treatment, at least 1,000 buildings being destroyed or damaged, and at least $40 million (in 1965 dollars) in property damage being done. The Watts riot lasted for six days. By Tuesday, August 17, all of the rioters were either spent or locked up. The authorities lifted the curfew, the National Guard withdrew, and the difficult task of cleaning up the mess began.

As city officials and residents began reconstruction and restoration, Governor Brown took the lead in finding out why this tragic riot had occurred. He appointed CIA Director John McCone to investigate and report on the causes. McCone's preliminary report turned out to be too superficial to satisfy many observers, so social scientists took up where the McCone report left off. What they determined was that of the roughly 100,000 black residents of Watts and the surrounding area, approximately one-third participated actively in the rioting, while the other two-thirds watched. The active participants have been labeled "New Urban Blacks."[15] They were born in the city, having never lived in the rural South as their parents had. They were mostly in their teens and twenties, and they were better educated than any previous generation of African Americans. They seem to have been disappointed in the slow pace of civil rights reform rather than excited like their parents about the prospect that reform was happening at all. They had tasted of the good life in the city of Angels, and they wanted more. In essence, the Civil Rights Act of 1964 and the Voting Rights Act of 1965 had merely whetted their appetites for absolute equality under the law in all walks of life. Sociologists have called this phenomenon the "rising expectations" syndrome.[16] The New Urban Blacks' specific grievances were aimed primarily at Jewish storeowners who they believed artificially inflated the price of their goods, absentee landlords who had no stake in the community except their own financial interests, and grocery stores—regardless of who owned them—that sold spoiled meat and rotten produce. Finally, they may have been reacting to a general sense of second-class citizenship they felt because they lived in a racially segregated area of the city.

Los Angeles did not allow de jure segregation, but de facto segregation was just as noticeable there as anywhere else in America. It was not that whites could not live in Watts, they just chose not to and did not have to. Likewise, blacks were free to live where they chose, if they could afford the rent or mortgages. All employment opportunities were legally open to blacks, but in practice many whites would not hire African Americans for the more desirable jobs. The white people of the city, including the political leaders and new media personnel, held a typically Anglo-centric worldview that, though unpremeditated and subconscious, was wrapped inside a smug liberalism that prevented them from seeing how insulting the New Urban Blacks perceived them to be. An example can be seen in the Los Angeles Times's coverage of the deaths of the 34 riot victims. Thirty-two of them were black or Mexican American, while only two were white. The paper covered the funerals of the two white victims—a fireman and a deputy—individually and with compassion. It did not cover the other 32 funerals at all. Another example can be seen in Chief Parker's callous description of the rioters as animals and himself as the zookeeper. He wanted to keep the police in the power position and the animals under control. When white city leaders looked for a scapegoat for the riot, they looked to the Deep South, rather than in their own backyard. They blamed the riot on recent civil rights turmoil in Louisiana and Georgia, saying that it had had a bad influence on their model black youth.

Perhaps the greatest tragedy of the Watts riot lay in the fact that it set a new, negative tone for black-white race relations in America just at the time when it seemed that the greatest civil rights progress was being made. Other, smaller riots had happened in 1964, but none had remotely approached the catastrophic nature of this one. Indeed, this one set a precedent for the more frequent and more deadly riots that were to come in the long, hot summers of 1966, 1967, and 1968.

1966: MARTIN LUTHER KING AND THE CHICAGO FREEDOM MOVEMENT

America's second largest city, Chicago, had a population in the 1960s of 3.5 million, not counting the suburbs. Beginning with the first "great migration" of black southerners to the North during the World War I years, by the 1960s the "Windy City" had become the home of more African Americans than lived in the whole state of Mississippi. Attracted there by jobs and opportunity, most found the welcome of white Chicagoans just as chilly as the winter wind blowing across Lake Michigan. Many of these whites were first- or second-generation immigrants themselves, and they tended to huddle together in neighborhoods and communities that did not easily accept outsiders, no matter their race. Not surprisingly, blacks likewise huddled together in vast, sprawling, working-class areas on the south side, although more by necessity than choice. Only two real estate firms in the Chicago area would sell homes in white neighborhoods to black buyers, and only 1 percent of all home listings were open to an integrated market. Many banks and mortgage companies also discriminated, refusing to lend to blacks. White city leaders had long imposed a pseudolegal form of racial segregation on the black population, restricting their access to the better neighborhoods and schools. Indeed, Jim Crow was just as alive and well in Chicago as any place in the Deep South.

In 1955, while Martin Luther King, Jr., was leading the now-famous Montgomery Bus Boycott in Alabama, in Chicago Richard J. Daley was winning election as mayor, partly because of his successful strategy to win black votes. Daley, a Democrat, would go on to serve as mayor throughout the rest of the 1950s and 1960s, becoming the most powerful mayor in America. In the early 1960s, he secured federal funding to build bigger and better public housing for African Americans on the south side, but these projects ended up serving more as traps to keep blacks stuck in their own communities than as homes that would raise their residents' standard of living. Meanwhile, neither the Daley administration nor the Chicago public school system made any effort to implement the *Brown v. Board of Education* ruling, and in 1961 the U.S. Supreme Court got involved through *Webb v. Board of Education of Chicago*. Still, the city followed the example of the Deep South states, and, rather than integrate with all deliberate speed, it took its sweet time improving the school situation for black students, who, incidentally, made up nearly 47 percent of all Chicago public school students.

In 1965, in the midst of his ongoing struggle to integrate the South, King, against the advice of some of his supporters, began looking for an opportunity to take the civil rights movement north. Local Chicagoans such as Al Raby and SCLC leaders in the Chicago office, including James Bevel, had been asking King for months to come and lead a demonstration there. After considering several possible locations for his northern campaign, and after visiting the Windy City, he finally decided that Chicago was the right place. It had a large black underclass, it suffered from many of the same ills that he had been dealing with for years in the South, it had an obstinate white power structure, headed by Daley, and it had already seen a demonstration recently when James Farmer and CORE had held a "pray-in" there earlier in the year. Once King made public his decision to start the Chicago Freedom Movement, Daley condemned it in no uncertain terms. He did precisely what southern governors such as George Wallace of Alabama and Ross Barnett of Mississippi had done in the face of civil rights agitation—he condemned King as an outside agitator and told him to mind his own business. Daley wanted to protect his turf, and he had powerful allies in the black community, such as the Reverend J. H. Jackson, who benefited from a quid pro quo with the mayor; they delivered black votes to him, and he delivered patronage to them. King, however, was not deterred by such alignments against him, having withstood similar ones in the South for a decade.

On January 7, 1966, King issued his plan for what he called the northern "freedom movement."[17] It included himself, his wife, Coretta, and several of his staff living in a dilapidated building on the southwest side in order to get a feel for real life in a Chicago slum. On Wednesday, January 26, he took up a two-day residence in a building in the North Lawndale community, which locals called "slumdale."[18] The building had a dirt floor, an open entrance with no door, and inadequate heat, and it reeked of urine because of the homeless people who used it as a public bathroom. After surviving the first night there, King walked the neighborhood the next day, meeting the residents and drumming up support for the campaign. Business in Alabama later in the week gave him an excuse for pulling out of the ramshackle tenement. Upon returning to Chicago a few days later, he slipped into a clean hotel, saying he just could not let his wife stay in such a deplorable place, although he had no problem letting his staff stay there.

After making weekly trips back and forth from Alabama to Chicago, with day trips on the side to New York and other places, on February 23 King led his first march through the streets of Chicago. He took 200 supporters and commandeered some of the worst buildings in the ghetto, cleaning and repairing them for the benefit of their poor tenants. Legally, he had no authority to do it, but he wanted to thrust the issue squarely in the face of both the slumlords who owned the buildings and the city leaders who let them get away with renting them. He then called a public meeting in which he confronted the slumlords to their face, and they mostly agreed to the reforms he demanded. These actions embarrassed the proud Mayor Daley, and he determined to grab the headlines away from King. He immediately publicized his own plan for the renovation of the black section of town over the next two years. With haste he sent a team from city hall to visit some 100,000 poor Chicagoans and offer them whatever assistance they needed, and he funded a project to eradicate the rats in the ghetto. Within days, he announced that more than 1.5 million rats had been destroyed. On March 17, he led a march of 70,000 supporters down the main thoroughfare, State Street, in a well-planned show of his power, designed to let King know who ran the town.

Undaunted by Daley's power plays, on May 27 King announced that 163 local organizations had joined with him and the SCLC to clean up the slums of Chicago. He also said he intended to lead a march down State Street on June 26. That march never took place, however, because events down in Mississippi diverted everyone's attention from Chicago in the month of June. At that time, James Meredith, who had integrated Ole Miss in 1962, was shot while attempting a solo march from Memphis to Jackson. King and a whole array of other civil rights leaders descended upon Mississippi to take up the Meredith March on their fallen comrade's behalf. The march ended at the destination of Jackson on June 26. During this march, the most infamous rift in civil rights movement history occurred, as the new leader of SNCC, Stokely Carmichael, began opposing King's nonviolent philosophy by trumpeting the "Black Power" slogan. This episode created dissension in the ranks that would never be repaired, headed the civil rights movement in a new direction, contributed to the outbreak of violence and rioting that would soon characterize American race relations for the rest of the 1960s, and arguably killed the movement in the long run.

All of the consequences of the advent of Black Power can be seen in retrospect, but at the time, in July and August 1966, they were not yet evident. King had no idea how much the credibility of his nonviolent demonstrations had been challenged by Black Power. He soon found out. Back in Chicago, he kicked off his better-housing campaign on July 10. Coincidentally, the same day, just down the road from where he had set up headquarters to coordinate his activities and meet with the media, a minor race riot erupted. It started with an ice cream truck getting stranded in the road and black children taking advantage of the opportunity to loot it. It was 98 degrees outside, and these and many other children just like them routinely played in the water gushing from fire hydrants in their neighborhoods. The white police, responding to the looting of the ice cream truck, had no way of finding the guilty parties, so they decided to punish all the local black children by turning the water off at the hydrants. A black man came behind them, however, and turned the water back on. The police responded by arresting the man and locking the hydrants. An angry mob formed and began rioting. King and fellow civil rights leaders, upon hearing the news, rushed out to calm the crowd, and temporarily it seemed that a full-scale riot might be averted. Then, on Wednesday, July 13, the rioting broke out anew for no apparent reason. On Friday, Mayor Daley called for the National Guard to intervene. The riot, although nothing to laugh about, ended with far less damage done than had occurred in Watts the year before. It would likewise pale in comparison to the series of race riots about to erupt later in 1966 and 1967. It has consequently been consigned to a footnote in history among the many cataclysmic events of the 1960s.

King continued his Chicago campaign as if nothing had happened. The next week, he called for a picket line to be formed outside a local real estate company known for its discriminatory practices. The picketers, led by James Bevel, were heckled so badly that they ended their demonstration before the day was over. The next day, Saturday, July 30, a civil rights march of 250 people took place through a white community near Marquette Park, which brought a violent response from the residents, who threw bottles, rocks, curses, and epithets at the integrationists. The following day, the march continued, this time moving back in the opposite direction with 550 marchers under supposed police protection. The white mob, however, weaved in and out of the police line as if it was not there, assaulting the marchers and vandalizing their parked cars. Mayor Daley called on the white citizens of Chicago to end the violence, saying if they would just leave the integrationists alone to march in peace, the marchers would soon exhaust themselves and go home, and nothing would have to change. He believed that if whites ignored the marchers, they would not want to continue their demonstrations, because getting attention was what really fueled them. Whites certainly heard the mayor, but they did not listen to him. Instead, they ignored him, rather than ignoring the integrationists.

Despite so many obstacles, still King persevered. On August 5, he led another march near Marquette Park. Nearly 1,000 police showed up in full riot gear, but they were outnumbered five to one by the white mob. King, the star attraction, arrived late. Upon entering the street to lead the march, he was struck in the head with a rock by someone in the white crowd behind the police line. The blow sent the Reverend to his knees. Chaos ensued. Even with a bloody lump behind his ear, King still led the march. At the end of the day, he returned to his home base in the city, New Friendship Baptist Church, where he vowed to supporters and reporters alike not to end his Chicago campaign, even though he claimed never to have known such hate in his life as he had encountered in Chicago, not even in Alabama or Mississippi. All the attention that King drew to the city caused a backlash, however, among the American Nazi Party of Lincoln Rockwell. On Sunday, August 21, as King led yet another march in south Chicago, Rockwell and his neo-Nazis, along with some Klansmen and other assorted racists, staged a counterdemonstration at Marquette Park, which amounted to little more than preaching to the bigots' choir.

King's next and final move in Chicago came with the announcement of his intention to lead a march through the most violently racist suburb of Chicago, Cicero. His new protégé, Jesse Jackson, who happened to be living in Chicago and attending seminary there at the time, had already declared his intention to march in Cicero. King reiterated the pledge, setting the date for September 4, which caused Governor Otto Kerner to deploy the National Guard a day in advance to keep the peace. As it turned out, King never led that march, although it went on as scheduled, led by local civil rights leaders. There was another minor riot that day, but, all in all, it was an anticlimactic affair.

The final result of the Chicago Freedom Movement in 1966 was that King and his civil rights cohorts had to accept a modified version of their list of demands. The campaign was not a complete failure, but it certainly did not represent the finest moment of either King or the civil rights movement. Some people at the time, and some historians since, have viewed it as a failure because it did not bring about an overnight, dramatic turnaround of racial discrimination in Chicago. It did sow the seeds of change, however, and that makes it a valuable piece of the mosaic of civil rights history. It showed an ugly reality about the United States that white northerners had for the most part managed to keep under cover before then—that racism was a national, not merely a southern, problem.

1967: THE LONGEST, HOTTEST SUMMER

The civil rights movement had begun with nonviolent demonstrations by blacks against a white establishment that often reacted violently in return. By 1963, the first of a long series of summertime race riots erupted in which black youth changed that dynamic, turning violent in the face of white oppression. The number of riots increased the following summer, and in 1965 the Watts riot pushed the boundaries of race rioting to a new level. The long, hot summer of 1966 topped all previous years for rioting, with 43 recorded in various cities around the nation. It was just a primer for the longest, hottest summer of all—the summer of 1967. No fewer than 150 race riots were recorded that year, including one, in Newark, that rivaled Watts for carnage and another, in Detroit, that surpassed it. The Newark and Detroit riots were so severe that President Lyndon Johnson, the architect of the "Great Society" initiatives to improve the living conditions of minorities, created the National Advisory Commission on Civil Disorders, in July, to find out what went wrong in those cities. In a sense, these riots became the beginning of the end of both his presidential administration and his hope for a Great Society. Indeed, such racial unrest in America's largest cities proved that not only was the idea of a Great Society not being realized, but, for urban black youth, the very concept reeked of hypocrisy and doubletalk. For them, their inner-city ghetto neighborhoods did not even qualify as *good* societies, much less *great* ones.

The Newark riot, on June 20, 1967, unlike the Watts riot, did not just explode without warning. Prior to that time, several lesser riots, some of which were fairly serious, had broken out in other cities, such as Tampa, Cincinnati, and Atlanta just days before. These earlier riots had created a tense mood in urban black neighborhoods around the nation, and the thought of rioting as a way to lash out at the white power structure of each city spread like a contagion. Inner-city black youth in Newark and the surrounding communities in New Jersey seemed to be primed for a bout of "civil disorder" that summer.[19] All the conditions were right: the city had a large, poverty-stricken black underclass with an extremely high public school drop-out rate, a high rate of teen pregnancy, many broken homes and single-parent homes, a severe unemployment problem, and was plagued by crime. Its crime rate was, in fact, among the highest in the nation. Its black youth, out of school for the summer, had nowhere to go and nothing to do but hang out on the streets. Its unemployed adults likewise whiled away the hours in idleness, boredom, and frustration. It was all a classic stereotype of life in an inner-city ghetto in postwar America.

Besides these depressing demographics, Newark also suffered from both a housing shortage and substandard housing. In many cases, absentee landlords would refuse to renovate their deteriorating rentals, claiming that high taxes sucked all the profit out of their enterprise. Whether this was true or not, the properties were mostly out-of-sight, out-of-mind for them. This housing problem merely inflamed tensions that had been bubbling under the surface for several years between the poor black majority, which was largely powerless, and the wealthier white minority, which still controlled the political and economic machinery of Newark. As the white-flight phenomenon ripped through the northern industrial cities like a cyclone after World War II, Newark followed suit. As whites exited by the thousands for the more hospitable suburbs, Newark was left with a sizable black majority. Out of a population of about 400,000, about 275,000 were black. Until the 1950s, the city had traditionally held a white majority and had been dominated by Irish American political bosses. In the 1960s, however, Italian Americans made an alliance with the black majority and took control. This new group of white power brokers spread just enough graft to black leaders to keep them loyal, but the alliance was always tenuous. Meanwhile, the Newark police department continued to be overwhelmingly made up of whites, while most of the citizens they arrested were black. Complaints of police brutality had been voiced repeatedly in the early 1960s, but the answer from City Hall was always the same: each case is turned over to the FBI, a neutral federal agency, for review. Although this answer seemed to quiet the rumblings in the black community, it was political smoke and mirrors, pure and simple. The FBI actually had no jurisdiction in these local police brutality cases.

Further complicating matters, the nonviolent resistance portion of the civil rights movement had largely bypassed Newark, yet the Black Power mentality had made serious inroads. Black Muslims thrived there, running a "Spirit House" that became an impromptu civic meeting place for disaffected and disenfranchised blacks.[20] They actively recruited the youth in street-corner rallies during the summer. From among the Muslims, Colonel Hassan Jeru-Ahmed (a.k.a. Albert Ray Osborne) emerged as a spokesman. He claimed to lead the Blackman's Volunteer Army of Liberation, which existed in name only. Yet, he attracted attention and followers, as did LeRoi Jones (a.k.a. Amiri Baraka), a nationally known writer and poet. The civil rights group with the most prominent presence in Newark was the Congress of Racial Equality (CORE), an organization devoted to nonviolence and integration, but even it was tainted by the poisonous racial climate of northern New Jersey. The Newark chapter of CORE was more militant than any other in the nation. It, like SNCC in the South, had fallen victim to the Black Power heresy.

Thus, to recap, the racial tension in Newark grew to the breaking point in June 1967 because of rioting in other cities, an impending housing shortage in an already underhoused ghetto, fear and distrust of the police, and an increasingly militant Black Power mentality. All that was needed was an incident to light the fuse under the powder keg. The first incident occurred on Tuesday, June 20. It began with a city Planning Board meeting in which the board decided to use its power of eminent domain to confiscate a 150-acre tract of land right in the middle of the black community and sell it to the state so that a new medical and dental college could be built there. The African American population of Newark could not afford to lose this housing, however. Black leaders complained vehemently, going through the official channels, following protocol, but to no avail. The city planners would not change their position. The black community was already upset, therefore, when, a week later, the second spark flared. On June 27, Mayor Hugh Addonizio named a white friend the new Secretary of the Newark Board of Education. African Americans complained again, because this particular white man had merely a high school education, while several well-respected, college-educated blacks in the city would have been better qualified. Still, no rioting occurred. On July 8, yet another spark flared when the white (and Catholic) police broke up a street-corner rally of Black Muslims. Some of the Muslims fought back against the police, resulting in a brawl between the most polar-opposite groups imaginable, as race, religion, and social status all came into sharp contrast. Now the fuse was lit, and the spark was running quickly toward the powder.

The final straw came on Wednesday evening, July 12, at approximately 9:30, when the police stopped a cab driver for tailgating. Police found that the driver, John Smith, a 40-year-old black veteran from Georgia, had a revoked license, having been involved in several motor vehicle accidents in recent years. According to the police, Smith became belligerent and resisted arrest. They used force to subdue him, then drove him to the Fourth Precinct Police Station. Some black observers witnessed the alleged beating and screamed, "Police brutality!"[21] Word of the incident spread throughout the black community quickly, and local civil rights leaders showed up at the police station within the hour, demanding to speak to the victim. After talking to him, they demanded that the police take him to the hospital. The police acquiesced to their demands and drove him to the hospital. Meanwhile, a black mob thronged around the police station, each member feeding off the resentment and anger of the others. Within a few minutes, someone began throwing Molotov cocktails at the station. As the flames licked the building, civil rights leaders from CORE, the United Community Corporation, and the Newark Legal Services Project tried to calm the crowd and channel their energy into a nonviolent march on City Hall. The march began all right, but it soon degenerated into chaos as more policemen arrived on the scene and tried to disperse the marchers. As the crowd scattered in all directions, looters began to smash store windows. The looting lasted only a little while, however, and, by the next morning, it seemed the riot was over.

Actually, the riot had just begun. Thursday morning, a false rumor circulated that Smith had died from the beating. The militant-minded blacks congregated at the Spirit House again that day and fomented more hatred for the white police. That night, they gathered outside the police station once again and began throwing rocks and assorted objects while chanting, "Black Power!"[22] In a near-repeat of the night before, the police dispersed the crowd once again, which just sent individuals and small groups out to start fires and loot stores. By the wee hours of the morning, now Friday, the city leaders had contacted Governor Richard Hughes, seeking help. Hughes sent in the state police and the National Guard. The coordination between local police and the state troopers and soldiers was poor. Many of the law enforcement personnel were not properly trained to deal with this kind of situation, and they shot at unarmed looters, occasionally hitting innocent spectators and even children inside their own homes. They even shot at each other, thinking a rioter was sniping at them. These sporadic shooting incidents continued even after daylight and all through the day Friday.

To protect against looting, some store owners painted "Soul Brother" across their windows and storefronts, even if they were not black.[23] What they saved from being attacked by black rioters, however, was often lost when the white police targeted their stores for shooting raids, thinking they were black-owned and harboring rioters. On Saturday and Sunday, the rioting waned but did not completely end. By Monday, it had petered out completely. The final toll: 23 dead, of whom 21 were black and two white. Included in that number were some women and children. Seemingly, just as many innocent bystanders had been killed as actual rioters. As the situation in Newark came to a merciful conclusion, the racial tension merely shifted to the surrounding New Jersey communities. Over the next few days, the cities of Elizabeth, Englewood, Jersey City, Plainfield, and New Brunswick would experience smaller riots of their own. The worst was in Plainfield. There, a white policeman shot a black man in the back as he ran away into an all-black neighborhood. A crowd of black residents immediately swarmed around the policeman as he tried in vain to run back the way he had come. As he tripped and fell, the mob beat him to death.

As the nation watched New Jersey go up in flames, about 600 miles to the west, in Michigan, an even worse riot was about to explode. It began on Saturday night, July 22, when police raided several illegal black gambling houses and nightspots called "blind pigs."[24] Such raids were not uncommon, but, considering the tinderbox situation in Detroit resulting from riots in other cities and recent white hate crimes against blacks in the Motor City, these raids seemed unusually ill timed. Besides, African Americans in Detroit had a long history of clashing with the white police. In the midst of World War II, in 1943, one of the worst race riots in American history had broken out in Detroit. Going into the 1960s, experts had predicted that this industrial city was the most likely candidate for another major riot. The only surprising thing about the 1967 riot, therefore, was that it did not happen sooner. Like Newark, Detroit had all the same kinds of negative demographics within its black ghetto. The only difference was that Detroit's were worse. This car-manufacturing capital of the world far exceeded Newark in overall population, black population, and density of population in its ghetto. Twelfth Street was the heart of the ghetto, and a place where crime and vice of all kinds could be found. The housing was dilapidated and overcrowded, and even those with decent apartments stayed outside on the street much of the time.

On this particular Saturday night, the mostly white police force had already raided four blind pigs without incident. By the wee hours of Sunday morning, the police went after a fifth one, this time on Twelfth Street. They normally arrested a handful of people in such raids, but this night they arrested 82 from this one joint. The reason for the large number was that two Vietnam veterans who had just returned home were being toasted. Even though the black population at large opposed the Vietnam War more stridently than did whites, these Detroit blacks rallied around their veterans as they would members of an extended family. Thus, the police showed extreme impropriety in arresting them and their fellows in this situation. Multiple police cars had to go back and forth to take the large number of people arrested down to the station. This gave plenty of time for a crowd of black observers to form into a mob, as they watched car after car take away their buddies. The last car drove away at 5 A.M. As it left, someone in the crowd threw a bottle at it and shattered a window. Then someone smashed a store window and tried deliberately to incite a riot, but there were few takers at that time of the morning. At 8 A.M., the police came back to Twelfth Street and made a sweep of the area to round up any remaining criminal suspects. The police presence only aggravated an already tense situation, however, and the crowd on the street grew larger.

Although the makings of a riot already existed, the police department and the news media had formed a pact long before this incident to keep such events quiet. Publicity, they believed, only encouraged more people to join the rioters. It was a good theory, but it had absolutely no effect on the black multitudes in inner-city Detroit. The mob never dissipated, and discontent traveled by word of mouth, rather than by media broadcasts. Looting, arson, and miscellaneous acts of vandalism and violence began, strangely, on a beautiful Sunday morning. Thinking it would prevent their stores from being looted, many owners followed the Newark example and painted "Soul Brothers" on their windows. Looters totally ignored such signs, however, and ransacked stores indiscriminately. Witnesses described the rioters in Detroit with different terminology than had been used in Watts, Newark, or any other city where some sense of reason and rationale guided their actions. In Detroit, rioters seemed to be engaged in anarchy—destructive behavior without purpose, hateful action without conscience, the epitome of nihilism. One man, for instance, set fire to a row of apartments starting on one end of the block; his own apartment lay at the other end. The wind swept down the street, and he ended up burning down his own dwelling.

A young black Democratic congressman named John Conyers, who represented a mostly African American ghetto constituency, went out into the street early that Sunday morning to try to persuade the swelling mass to disperse, but his effort failed. Instead, someone in the crowd yelled that if he was defending the police, he was no better than their white oppressors. The crowd basically booed and hissed him off the street and continued beating the drum of black resentment and frustration. By 2 P.M. that day, Mayor Jerome Cavanaugh had assembled the city leaders, and they agreed they needed outside help; their own police force could not contain the growing riot, and their fire department could not keep pace with the flames. At Cavanaugh's request, Governor George Romney sent in the state police immediately, although the first National Guard troops could not be mobilized and on the scene until 7 P.M. Meanwhile, 56 neighboring towns sent in fire truck crews to help douse the flames. The mayor set a curfew from 9 P.M. to 5 A.M., but even with the curfew and the extra law-enforcement help, nothing stopped the riot from turning deadly that night. The killings followed the typical pattern: store owners and policemen shot looters, looters beat to death store owners who got in their way, rioters shot or beat to death white motorists passing along the wrong street at the wrong time, and police and National Guardsmen accidentally shot innocent bystanders and sometimes each other. In addition to these routine casualties, two people were electrocuted by touching a downed power line.

National Guardsmen, called in to restore order by Governor George Romney, stop their tank near a Detroit firetruck in the neighborhood that was ravaged by rioting on July 24, 1967. At least three people were killed. AP Photo.

After midnight, going into Monday morning, Cavanaugh and Romney appealed to Vice President Hubert Humphrey for federal troops. Humphrey passed the request on to President Johnson, who, after daylight, authorized paratroopers and special forces to go in. The general in charge of the operation was John Throckmorton. He and representatives of the Johnson administration personally toured the affected areas throughout the day Monday. The rioting had quelled enough during the daytime to deceive Throckmorton into thinking it was over. He decided no federal troops were necessary. His assessment was premature. With nightfall came a reintensification of rioting, and Throckmorton was forced to reverse his order. As if in a war zone rather than a riot zone, tanks rolled down the streets of the Detroit ghetto. Even then, the riot continued in spasms until Thursday, July 27, by which time it had finally played itself out. Thereafter, the troops and the curfew remained in place for several more days. When it was over, 43 people lay dead. Of them, 33 were black, 10 were white. Seventeen of them were looters, one was a National Guardsman, one a fireman, and one a policeman. Two civilians had been burned up or asphyxiated by smoke, two had been electrocuted, one had been beaten to death, and the rest died from gunshot wounds.

While Detroit still smoldered, President Johnson created the National Advisory Commission on Civil Disorders, better known as the Kerner Commission, to study the riots—to find what caused them and to seek ways to prevent possible future riots. Headed by Governor Otto Kerner of Illinois, the commission felt pressured to work quickly, because another riot could erupt in any city at any time. Yet, as the commission did its work, summer gave way to fall and winter, and 1967 went out on a quiet note. The commission's report, long and detailed, came out on February 29, 1968. It can be summarized as saying that de facto segregation in the North was just as harmful to the black psyche as de jure segregation in the South and that until African Americans got a genuinely fair shake in this country—in jobs, housing, law enforcement, schools, and the rest—these kinds of racial revolts would not go away. Sadly and ironically, less than a month after the report hit the shelves, a new wave of race riots erupted in towns and cities across America. This time it was not discrimination against blacks that caused them but the assassination of Martin Luther King. Once again, despite the best efforts of Lyndon Johnson to figure out a way to make the Great Society a reality, he had missed the mark. Soon, with the combination of race riots, assassinations, and the quagmire in Vietnam, he would be a humbled man, his presidency broken beyond repair.

1968: CESAR CHAVEZ'S *LA CAUSA: HUELGA!*

The civil rights movement grew in complexity every year in the 1960s as it moved from the rural South to the urban North and West. Over time, it morphed from a nonviolent resistance struggle to an assertion of Black Power, from peaceful protests to bloody riots. While it started as a black-white issue, it evolved into an all-minorities-versus-the-white-majority issue. By 1968, Mexican Americans had joined ranks prominently with African Americans in the movement for equality. The epicenter of this brown liberation movement was California, where a boycott against grape farmers by the little-known union leader Cesar Chavez culminated in a 25-day hunger strike that drew the attention, sympathy, and praise of Senator Robert Kennedy, Vice President Hubert Humphrey, Coretta Scott King, and the American people at large. This event put the plight of migrant workers on the nation's intellectual radar screen for the first time since the Great Depression.

The story begins on the West Coast in the early 1960s. California at the time had all the attractions of the American dream—the third largest city, Los Angeles, home of Hollywood and Disneyland; historic San Francisco, with the Golden Gate Bridge and Alcatraz Island; Yosemite National Park and other parks with giant redwood and sequoia trees; a thousand miles of beautiful Pacific coastline; the second tallest mountain in the contiguous United States, Mount Whittier; some of the most respected universities in America and the world, such as Stanford and the University of California; and, last but not least, the nation's most productive agricultural region, the 200-by-60-mile San Joaquin valley, with its fruit and vegetable farms and plantations. The attractiveness of life in California drew thousands of Americans every year, making the Golden State the fastest-growing state in the nation. California likewise attracted foreign immigrants, mostly from neighboring Mexico. Like all immigrants throughout American history, they came seeking a higher standard of living, a better quality of life. Prior to 1964, many came from Mexico as official guests of the U.S. government through the Bracero program, which granted temporary visas to migrant farm workers. These Braceros gave the landowners a stable, low-paid labor force that allowed them to keep their prices down as they sold their goods on the market. Despite the success of the Bracero program, Congress ended it on December 31, 1963, and the labor situation in California became tumultuous for the next decade.

The Braceros had never accounted for the total number of migrant farm workers in California—far from it. Many thousands of American citizens also made their livelihoods as migrants. Going back to the infamous Dust Bowl of the 1930s, multitudes of desperate victims of Mother Nature and the Great Depression left their homes in the Great Plains and journeyed to California to take some of the lowest-paying jobs in America. Immortalized in John Steinbeck's 1939 novel (and the movie made from it) The Grapes of Wrath, migrant workers faced conditions that had not really changed over the 30 years from the 1930s to the 1960s, except that no longer were most of the migrants white. They were now mostly Mexican or Filipino Americans, but they still endured a dismal existence. The Bracero program had proven a mixed blessing for them. On the one hand it gave them competition from foreigners, but on the other hand it stabilized their wages at the same rate the Braceros were required by law to receive—$1.40 per hour in the early 1960s. The end of the Bracero program spelled the end of guaranteed wages for the American citizen migrant workers, as they were left to negotiate their wages with individual landowners. More often than not, however, little negotiation actually took place. The landowners just set their wages on a take-it-or-leave-it basis, and, of course, the migrants were in no position to reject the offer.

Long before the Bracero program ended, various people and labor unions had tried to unionize the migrant farm workers in the hope that solidarity would produce higher wages. None had been successful. By 1960, experts had decided it could not be done. Organizing migrants, they said, was like trying to herd cats or hit a moving target. Not only was there the problem of constant movement among the workers, but the landowners held all the cards—political connections, corporate funding, and near-limitless legal counsel. Altogether, California farmers and planters generated some $8 billion of taxable revenue per year. Some small or family farming operations consisted of 10,000 acres and 2,000 employees during peak seasons. The largest plantations were corporate-owned, and some were in excess of 100,000 acres. How could the lowly and despised fruit pickers take down such an enormously wealthy and powerful foe? Only by finding a leader with incredible skill, unstoppable drive, indefatigable ambition, and superhuman charisma. Or by such a man finding them.

In 1962, that leader appeared. His name was Cesar Chavez. He not only proved the experts wrong about the possibility of organizing the migrants but actually galvanized the migrants into one of the most prominent labor unions in America by the end of the decade. Chavez was an American citizen of Mexican heritage. Born in Yuma, Arizona, he lived the typical life of a poor minority in the Southwest. After receiving only an eighth-grade education, he served honorably in the U.S. Navy and then moved to Los Angeles in the 1950s. There he got involved in the Community Service Organization, ultimately becoming its vice president, and helped organize urban Chicanos into a labor union. Despite his success in that venue, he remained a small-town guy at heart. Specifically, his heart lay in the fields with the migrant workers, and he soon left the city to help his compadres in the country.

On September 30, 1962—ironically, the same day that James Meredith precipitated the showdown between the Kennedy administration and the state of Mississippi at Ole Miss—Chavez created the National Farm Workers Association (NFWA). Although he intended it to be a union, he deliberately omitted that word from the title of the organization, realizing the incendiary effect of the word on employers. Headquartered on the outskirts of the farming town in the valley, Delano, in a community called the Forty Acres, the NFWA flew a flag of Chavez's design, featuring a black eagle on a white circle surrounded by bright red. The flag would later become the union symbol that would appear on the boxes of grapes picked with union labor. It took Chavez nearly three years to show any notable success in getting migrants to join, but soon after the Bracero program ended, wages for migrants plummeted. The Filipinos commanded a higher price than Chicanos, but both groups still fell far below the $1.40 per hour they had earned prior to 1964. By 1965, the Filipinos, who represented a small minority of the Chicano-dominated migrants, decided to go on strike. This created a golden opportunity for Chavez and the NFWA. If the higher-paid Filipinos would strike, surely the lower-paid Chicanos could not continue working. Chavez convinced Chicanos to unite behind the NFWA and to strike in unison with the Filipinos. The success of this preliminary unionization garnered the attention of one of the most powerful unions in America, the Teamsters. The Teamsters tried to muscle in on the NFWA and organize migrants in other parts of the Valley. Chavez would be forced to battle the Teamsters for the next three years until he finally joined with that union's great rival at the national level, the AFL-CIO.

Meanwhile, the protest against the grape planters began in 1965 with the NFWA's rallying cry, "*Huelga!*" ("strike" in Spanish).[25] It became such a powerful slogan that the sheriff of Kern County, California, outlawed its use in the midst of the strike. Although "*Huelga*" made an effective and easy-to-remember slogan, it really just represented one strategy employed in "*la causa*" (the cause), which was to raise the wages and living standards of the migrant workers.[26] From the beginning, Chavez decided he would carry on *la causa* by nonviolent protest. Heavily influenced by Martin Luther King and other civil rights leaders' successful use of Gandhian tactics in the South, Chavez invited SNCC and CORE representatives to come to Delano and train his NFWA staff in nonviolent resistance. They arrived, and Chavez became a true believer who would never waver from his commitment to nonviolence, even during the most trying times. The times became trying almost immediately. The Watts riot in Los Angeles focused attention on more pressing racial issues in 1965, and within a year the Black Power movement had emerged in the South, resulting in a rejection of the nonviolent philosophy by many civil rights leaders and a rift in the previously unified façade among them. By 1967 and early 1968, the nonviolent contingent of the civil rights movement had been almost totally eclipsed by the more titillating Black Power and race-riot contingent. Some Chicanos urged Chavez and the NFWA to follow suit, arguing that the NFWA should become a Brown Power organization. Chavez adamantly refused and clung tenaciously to nonviolence.

Even so, by January 1968, *la causa* was suffering from burnout and lethargy. The migrants had grown weary of the three-year standoff, which dragged on day after day with little change. If anything, the change was for the worse, as the problem of Mexican scab workers crossing the border and breaking the strike had grown to epidemic proportions. The NFWA's major initiative in early 1968 was to help the U.S. Border Patrol catch the scabs. Even after the NFWA got Attorney General Ramsey Clark to crack down on border security, the scabs still poured in and took the migrants' jobs. Chavez, sensing that his grip on the situation was loosening and needing desperately to figure out a way to get a new grip, decided to go on a hunger strike. The idea was to show the people that he was willing to pay any price, to perform an almost unthinkable personal sacrifice, to keep *la causa* alive. He began on February 15, 1968, by sequestering himself in a small back room behind a service station at Forty Acres, where he slept on a cot. Initially, he wanted seclusion in order to get himself mentally prepared for the ordeal to come. The first four days passed without notice, as neither he nor his closest staffers disclosed what he was doing. Before the end of the first week, word had leaked out, and immediately the migrants rallied around their leader. They came from miles around to visit him, as if he were a saint on a holy fast—something these Catholics could understand and relate to. By the second week, the hunger strike had become a national news story, and Latinos from all over the Southwest made pilgrimages to Delano to stand in a line of hundreds to visit their venerable hero. Some joined with him in the hunger strike in a show of solidarity, although none lasted the whole 25 days.

During the fast, Chavez complained of having nightmares about food for the first few nights. He also developed muscle pains and a severe backache. He persevered, drinking plain water but eating nothing, until by the end of the first week he no longer craved food. By the second week, physical weakness set in, although his mental dexterity actually improved. He was able to get by on as little as two hours of sleep per night. By the third week, however, he grew more and more exhausted. By the fourth and final week, he could not stay awake more than two hours before collapsing. He became too feeble to walk without assistance and too weak to make a public speech. On the eleventh day of the fast, Chavez was summoned to court to answer charges by one of the large grape planter families that the NFWA had violated a court order against picketing their company 12 times. When he arrived outside the courthouse, his people staged a silent but extremely powerful show of support. Approximately 1,000 of them lined the walkway on their knees in quiet, reverential prayer for their champion. This

United Farm Workers labor leader, Cesar Chavez, speaks during a news conference on May 24, 1968. The location is not known. AP Photo.

spectacle angered the prosecution at the moment but soon caused them to realize the nature of the fight they were engaged in; they realized it made them look like the bad guys, so they dropped the charges and asked that the case be dismissed.

For Chavez, this victory was no cause for celebration, because his work was not finished. He continued to fast until March 11. By that time, the notoriety of Chavez's *causa* had reached the top echelon of American politics and society. Senator Robert F. Kennedy of New York, the former attorney general, a strong supporter of civil rights reform and soon to be the frontrunner in the race for the Democratic nomination for president, dropped in to take communion with Chavez and the migrants at the county park near Delano. Four thousand farm workers showed up for Mass and to listen to Kennedy speak. The holy bread that Chavez ate at that time was the first morsel of food he had eaten in 25 days. Kennedy asked the priest to give the leader a double portion. After Kennedy made his speech to the adoring crowd, a friend read Chavez's brief, prepared statement. In it, Chavez explained why he had fasted and called upon his fellows to sacrifice similarly in whatever ways were necessary to make *la causa* successful.

The exuberant reception that Kennedy received that day in Delano, some people believe, was the final thing that convinced him to run for president. Whether true or not, the tragic irony is that within three months he would be dead, shot while campaigning just 150 miles south in Los Angeles. Equally ironic, the death of Kennedy made possible the election of the Republican candidate, Richard Nixon, whose family had been in the Orange County, California, citrus fruit agribusiness for several years and who consequently took the side of the planters rather than that of the migrant workers. Equally tragic, less than three weeks after March 11, Chavez's role model, Martin Luther King, Jr., was assassinated. Although both murders took their toll on Chavez emotionally, neither prevented him from continuing *la causa*. Likewise, despite a severe backache that kept him bedridden for most of 1968, he plugged away with the boycott of the grape growers. The following year, the grape growers began to soften, and in 1970 all 26 of them in the Delano area caved in to the union's demands. Thereafter, Chavez began working for other migrant causes, such as boycotting lettuce growers. He did not confine his work to California, however, but traversed the country to stand with poor workers. In so doing, he became an icon for Mexican Americans, much the same as King became for African Americans.

1969: THE INDIAN OCCUPATION OF ALCATRAZ

On November 19, 1969, at 2 o'clock on a cold, foggy San Francisco Bay morning, a group of about 80 American Indians assailed the heights of Alcatraz Island, taking it from the United States as a prize for their people. Composed primarily of college students from San Francisco State College and several campuses of the University of California, the group called itself "Indians of All Tribes."[27] Acting on treaties made between the U.S. government and various tribes from 1868 to 1934, the Indians claimed that they had a right to seize any unused federal property, provided they made substantial improvements to it within a reasonable period of time. They intended to use the 19-acre island to start an American Indian university, museum, and cultural center, or so they claimed. In reality, they understood they were making only a political statement, but it was a strong and dramatic one. It captivated the attention of the media and the American people like nothing Indians had done since killing Custer in 1876. It served as the long-overdue turning point in U.S. government–American Indian relations and began the reformation of white people's collective attitude toward their Native neighbors.

Alcatraz is a Spanish word dating to the 1700s meaning "pelican."[28] The quarter-mile-by-eighth-mile island was once home to many of the large, white, big-billed birds. Situated one mile from San Francisco in the bay, the island rises to 110 feet at its tallest point. The United States acquired Alcatraz during the Mexican War of 1846–1848 when it took possession of all California. In the 1850s, the government used it as a military fort to help protect the West Coast. Once the Civil War broke out, in the 1860s, the Federals turned it into a military prison. After the war, in the 1870s and beyond, the military authorities converted it into a prison for troublesome Indian warriors taken off the battlefields of the Great Plains, the Rocky Mountains, and the West Coast. In the early twentieth century, the government made it a general-inmate federal prison. Not until 1934 did it become the keystone institution in the federal prison system, garnering the nickname "the Rock," for which it has been immortalized in legend and in movies.[29] Although the island was thought to be inescapable, in 1962, an inmate, Frank Morris, and some accomplices successfully escaped the prison; whether they survived the frigid, shark-infested waters that surround it is not known. The dank, salty air had made the escape possible by corroding and weakening the prison's physical buildings and components. A year later, the combination of that escape and the continual deterioration of the buildings convinced the Kennedy administration to close down the prison. Thereafter, it became *unused* federal property, although not *abandoned* land, because a federal caretaker remained on the premises to look after it.

In 1952, while Alcatraz was still in operation, the U.S. Bureau of Indian Affairs began trying to improve the conditions of the Native American population by relocating Indians from reservations to urban dwellings and jobs. California had the largest Indian population of any state in the nation, and one of the cities with the largest influx of Indians was, not surprisingly, San Francisco. By 1964, there were approximately 20,000 relocated Indians there. On March 8, 1964, five of these Indians, all Sioux, went to Alcatraz and staked their claim to the property. One of them, Allen Cottier, was president of the Bay Area American Indian Council. Citing 1868, 1887, and 1934 laws, he declared that the Sioux had a right to the property and offered the government the same price for it that the government had recently given California Indians for reservation land—47 cents per acre. On advice from their attorney, after making their intentions publicly known, they left the island to proceed with the bureaucratic paperwork. After the Indians waded through a mountain of red tape and filed a federal law suit, nothing came of this initial attempt to take Alcatraz. It caused a brief and minor sensation in the Bay area, but it did not attract much national attention. Meanwhile, Alcatraz remained under the control of the Government Services Administration (GSA), and for the next five years various federal and state agencies tried to figure out what to do with it.

Throughout the mid-1960s, the African American civil rights movement picked up momentum and won major changes and notable legislation to help the largest minority group in the country. Hispanic Americans soon joined in, seeking their own civil rights reforms. It was only natural that the oldest minority group, the Indians, should likewise jump on the civil rights bandwagon, and it is

Group of American Indians, part of the Indians of All Tribes Inc., occupying the former prison at Alcatraz Island, stand under graffiti welcoming Indian occupiers to United Indian Property on the dock of Alcatraz Island, San Francisco Bay, November 25, 1969. The occupiers are demanding a visit by Secretary of the Interior to discuss possession of the surplus mid-bay property. AP Photo.

not surprising that it was primarily the young Indians—college students—who led the charge. Having been raised in urban environments such as San Francisco and Los Angeles, this new generation of Indians was both educated and streetwise. Among these student leaders were Richard Oakes (Mohawk), Joe Bill (Eskimo), and Ross Harden (Winnebago), of San Francisco State College, and LaNada Boyer (Shoshone), of the University of California at Berkeley. They worked in teaching and administrative positions, in conjunction with older Indians such as Steve Talbot, at the University of California-Berkeley, Jack Forbes, at the University of California-Davis, Louis Kemnitzer, of San Francisco State College, and Adam Nordwall, of the United Bay Area Council of American Indian Affairs, who helped them plan their 1969 takeover of Alcatraz. Although none of these older supporters were Sioux, and all realized that the Sioux were the only Indians specifically granted the right to seize abandoned property, they believed they could stage the takeover as a civil rights demonstration, if nothing else.

To prepare for their takeover, Oakes and about 50 others took a tour boat around the island on November 9, to scope it out. Five of the Indians decided to jump overboard and swim to Alcatraz, but only four made it. The four walked around on the island for about 10 minutes, were confronted by the government caretaker, Glen Dodson, who asked them to leave, and went to the dock to await a boat to pick them up. Later that day, 14 of them returned on another boat and stayed overnight. The next day, the regional director of the GSA, Tom Hannon, received word that the Indians were there, and he immediately headed out to Alcatraz to tell them they were trespassing and would be arrested by U.S. marshals if they did not leave. They left after a 19-hour occupation. This eviction did not deter them, however. Instead, it energized them to come back a third time, with a larger, more determined force that intended to stay.

On the evening of November 19, about 80 of the Indians massed at the San Francisco Indian Center, chartered a boat to Alcatraz, and embarked on what would turn out to be a 19-month occupation. They feared that the Coast Guard had been tipped off to their plans and would stop them, but it did not happen. They spent the night on the island, and the next morning, the authorities were notified of their presence. Curiously, television news crews arrived in helicopters to cover the event before any representative of the government showed up to confront the Indians. The occupiers, led by Richard Oakes, immediately began posting signs saying, "You Are on Indian Land" and "This Land Is My Land," as well as scratching out portions of U.S. government signs to make them read "Warning: Keep Off Indian Property," and similar statements. They issued a statement to the press called "Proclamation to the Great White Father and His People," in which they sarcastically explained why Alcatraz would make a perfect habitation for Indians: like a reservation it was cut off and dilapidated and had no transportation or sanitation services, no hospital, no school, and no jobs. Their sarcasm extended to creating a "Bureau of White Affairs" and to painting over two of the old cell blocks the names of President Nixon and Vice President Agnew.[30]

Although the FBI monitored the situation, the Coast Guard blockaded the island, and the GSA stayed in touch with U.S. marshals and the federal district attorney from the beginning, no government agency took any precipitous action against the occupiers. Despite having the ability to remove the Indians forcibly, none did, on orders from the president of the United States. President Nixon had been apprised of the situation by his special advisor for minority affairs, Leonard Garment, on the first day, and he issued strict orders for all agencies to stand down and not provoke a bloodbath. He instructed his people to talk diplomatically to, and negotiate with, the Indians. The thought was that, once the Indians had their day in the media spotlight and got their demands heard, they would quickly tire of being on that desolate rock and go home. Nixon underestimated the resolve of this particular group, of course, and as the first week came to a close, not only had no Indians left the island, but many more had come and joined the original demonstrators, some of them women and children.

On November 25, after five days of the standoff, Richard Oakes made front-page news once again by proclaiming that Alcatraz represented not the end of the Indian campaign to retake their land from the white man but only the beginning. Next, they would take Alaska! The timing of all the media attention could not have been better for the Indians, because November 27 was Thanksgiving Day. Although they did not originally plan their occupation to coincide with Thanksgiving, the fact that it did allowed them to stage the most dramatic episode of the long occupation. Their supporters on the mainland shipped in large amounts of food and supplies, even a band for entertainment, and the Indians invited the white news reporters to come and be the Pilgrims as they celebrated a re-creation of the first Thanksgiving at Plymouth Rock in 1621. After that media spectacle, the Indians could have very well considered their mission accomplished and gone home. Instead, the occupation gradually turned into a war of attrition with the federal government.

During the last month of 1969, the GSA and the U.S. Department of the Interior began trying to coax the Indians to leave, telling them (truthfully) that the buildings on Alcatraz had been condemned and were not safe for human habitation. The Indians were housing about 200 men, women, and children in the ramshackle apartments that had formerly served as the prison guards' family homes up to 1963. Although the Indians naturally thought the warning was just a ploy, on January 3, 1970, Richard Oakes's 13-year-old stepdaughter fell through the stairwell of one of the buildings to her death. Rather than convince Oakes and his cohorts to leave the island, however, this tragedy seemed to make them more determined than ever to stay. And stay they did. Over the next few months, the government authorities turned off the water supply and electricity to the island and announced that Alcatraz was now part of the new Golden Gate National Recreation Area in an attempt to pressure the Indians to leave. Still they stayed.

The American public's attention waned quickly in 1970, however, as events in Vietnam and demonstrations against the war intensified. The lack of attention doomed the Indians' cause. By 1971, the number remaining on Alcatraz had dwindled to about 20. On June 11, Nixon ordered U.S. marshals in to remove them. The Indians gave up without a fight. As had always happened in every instance in American history when the government and the Indians conflicted, the government eventually won. The Indians could claim a symbolic victory, however, as they had brought their civil rights issues to the forefront of American society and had, like blacks and Hispanics, forced the white man to begin a multicultural reformation of the United States.

VOICES OF THE DECADE

JAMES MEREDITH

The African American student James Meredith's courageous integration of the University of Mississippi, in 1962, set up one of the most spectacular showdowns between the federal government and a state government since the Civil War. It took multiple court cases and ultimately nothing less than President Kennedy's decision to send in a small army of National Guardsmen and U.S. marshals to get Meredith registered. Amid the violence, vandalism, and death, the black Air Force veteran from rural Attala County, Mississippi, managed to remain fairly calm and confident in what he was doing. He required only one year of additional classes to get his degree from "Ole Miss," but it took two years for him to get registered. Here he reflects on his three-year saga in the little town of Oxford.

On September 30, 1962, I had flown into the university airport with the U.S. marshals from Tennessee. That day two men were killed and several hundred were wounded in the fighting between the United States and Mississippi. The next day I was enrolled as a student. This was the first time in the history of the state that a Negro had ever been enrolled in a school which Mississippi had reserved for its privileged whites.

On August 18, 1963, I drove out of Mississippi with the U.S. marshals to Tennessee, after receiving a degree from the University of Mississippi. . . . After a while my father got me away from the crowd for a private talk. He wanted to express his satisfaction at having lived to see this day. As he evaluated the University of Mississippi ordeal and the graduation exercises, he told me his surprising conclusion about the Mississippi whites: "The people can be decent." . . .

My exit from Mississippi on August 18, 1963, marked the end of my three years in that state; it marked the end of this particular stage of my struggle to break the system of "White Supremacy" and to carry out my "Divine Responsibility."

From James Meredith, *Three Years in Mississippi* (Bloomington: Indiana University Press, 1966), pp. 327–28.

MARTIN LUTHER KING, JR.

In 1963, Birmingham was a hotbed of civil rights activity. King arrived in April on behalf of the SCLC to lead the protests against segregation that were already under way. On April 12, he was arrested for violating an Alabama state court injunction against such demonstrations. While in jail, he read a letter written by an assortment of Alabama "moderate" ministers, published in the *Birmingham News*, which disapproved of the civil rights demonstrations and King's determination to push the movement forward. King's response, which became an instant classic statement of why immediate, persistent, and unified protest by black Americans for civil right was a necessity, is excerpted here.

My dear Fellow Clergymen,
    While confined here in the Birmingham city jail . . . I pause to answer criticism of my work and ideas. . . . I am in Birmingham because injustice is here. . . . I cannot sit idly by in Atlanta and not be concerned about what happens in Birmingham. Injustice anywhere is a threat to justice everywhere. . . . Birmingham is probably the most thoroughly segregated city in the United States. Its ugly record of police brutality is known in every section of this country. Its injust treatment of Negroes in the courts is a notorious reality. There have been more unsolved bombings of Negro homes and churches in Birmingham than any city in this nation.
    . . . We know through painful experience that freedom is never voluntarily given by the oppressor; it must be demanded by the oppressed. Frankly, I have never yet engaged in a direct action movement that was "well-timed," according to the timetable of those who have not suffered unduly from the disease of segregation. For years now I have heard the word "Wait!" It rings in the ears of every Negro with a piercing familiarity. This "Wait!" has almost always meant "Never." . . . We have waited for more than 340 years for our constitutional and God-given rights . . . and we still creep at horse and buggy pace toward the gaining of a cup of coffee at a lunch counter. I guess it is easy for those who have never felt the stinging darts of segregation to say "Wait."
    . . . I have almost reached the regrettable conclusion that the Negro's great stumbling block in the stride toward freedom is not the White Citizen's Counciler or the Ku Klux Klanner, but the white moderate who is more devoted to "order" than to justice. . . .
    Yours for the cause of Peace and Brotherhood,
    Martin Luther King, Jr.
    From Paul D. Escott et al., eds., *Major Problems in the History of the American South*, Vol. II: *The New South* (Boston: Houghton Mifflin, sec. ed., 1999), pp. 360–66.

The apex of the civil rights movement came on August 28, 1963, with the March on Washington. Nearly a quarter-million people, blacks and whites, southerners and northerners, and members of various civil rights organizations, participated. The all-day event centered around the Lincoln Memorial, where King delivered his most famous oration, commonly called the "I Have a Dream" speech. The most memorable part is excerpted here.

So I say to you my friends, that even though we must face the difficulties of today and tomorrow, I still have a dream. It is a dream deeply rooted in the American dream that one day this nation will rise up and live out the true meaning of its creed—we hold these truths to be self-evident, that all men are created equal.

I have a dream that one day on the red hills of Georgia, sons of former slaves and sons of former slave-owners will be able to sit down together at the table of brotherhood.

I have a dream that one day, even the state of Mississippi, a state sweltering with the heat of injustice, sweltering with the heat of oppression, will be transformed into an oasis of freedom and justice.

I have a dream my four little children will one day live in a nation where they will not be judged by the color of their skin but by the content of their character. I have a dream today!

I have a dream that one day, down in Alabama, with its vicious racists, with its governor having his lips dripping with the words of interposition and nullification, that one day, right there in Alabama, little black boys and black girls will be able to join hands with little white boys and white girls as brothers and sisters. I have a dream today!

I have a dream that every valley shall be exalted, every hill and mountain shall be made low, the rough places shall be made plain, and the crooked places shall be made straight and the glory of the Lord will be revealed and all flesh shall see it together.

This is our hope. This is the faith that I go back to the South with.

From Thomas Gentile, *March on Washington: August 28, 1963* (Washington, D.C.: Self-published, 1983), pp. 242–49.

Barely more than a month after the Kerner Commission issued its report, the nation was again convulsed in race riots. This time the cause was the assassination of Martin Luther King, Jr. In Memphis to lead a strike of garbage collectors against the city, King made his last speech on April 3, 1968, at a church, the night before he was assassinated. This famous oration, which alludes to the Bible story of Moses being taken by God to the top of a mountain overlooking Canaan, the "promised land," came to be known as the "mountaintop" speech. It seemed prophetic, as if King knew his end was near. Here is an excerpt.

We've got some difficult days ahead. But it really doesn't matter with me now. Because I've been to the mountaintop. I won't mind. Like anybody, I would like to live a long life. Longevity has its place. But I'm not concerned about that now. I just want to do God's will. And he's allowed me to go up to the mountain. And I've looked over, and I've seen the Promised Land. I may not get there with you, but I want you to know tonight that we as a people will get to the Promised Land. So I'm happy tonight. . . . I'm not fearing any man. Mine eyes have seen the glory of the coming of the Lord.

From "Martin Luther King, Jr., 1929–1968," *Collier's 1969 Year Book* (New York: Crowell-Collier Educational Corporation, 1969), p. 182.

CESAR CHAVEZ

Beginning in 1965, Cesar Chavez led his Hispanic National Farm Workers Association, soon to become the United Farm Workers Union, on a strike against the grape growers of California. In 1966, he led a march on Sacramento to draw attention to the strike. In 1968, for three weeks, he went on a hunger strike, which drew the attention of Attorney General Robert Kennedy, among other influential leaders. Here, in a speech he was too weak from hunger to deliver, he gives the rationale for his actions to a crowd of 8,000, including Kennedy. On March 11, 1968, the Reverend James Drake read the speech on his behalf.

I undertook this fast because my heart was filled with grief and pain for the sufferings of farm workers. The fast was first for me and then for all of us in this union. It was a fast for nonviolence and a call to sacrifice.

Our struggle is not easy. Those who oppose our cause are rich and powerful and they have many allies in high places. We are poor. Our allies are few. But we have something the rich do not own. We have our own bodies and spirits and the justice of our cause as our weapons.

When we are really honest with ourselves we must admit that our lives are all that really belong to us. So it is how we use our lives that determines what kind of men we are. It is my deepest belief that only by giving our lives do we find life. I am convinced that the truest act of courage, the strongest act of manliness, is to sacrifice ourselves for others in a totally nonviolent struggle for justice. To be a man is to suffer for others. God help us to be men.

From Stephen M. Gillon, *The American Paradox: A History of the United States since 1945* (Boston: Houghton Mifflin, 2003), p. 88.

BOBBY SEALE

One of the founders of the Black Panthers, in Oakland, California, in 1966, Bobby Seale helped formulate the organization's charter. Although the official Ten Points of the Black Panthers's Platform and Program have been published and are widely available, the following version is Seale's summary, as given in a speech in 1968.

Now, when we first organized the Black Panther Party for Self-Defense, Huey said, "Bobby, we're going to draw up a basic platform. . . .

Huey said, "First we want freedom, we want power to determine the destiny of our black communities.

"Number two: We want full employment for our people.

"Number three: We want housing fit for shelter of human beings.

"Number four: We want all black men to be exempt from military service.

"Number five: We want decent education for our black people in our communities that teaches us the true nature of this decadent, racist society that teaches black people and our young black brothers and sisters their place in the society, for if they don't know their place in society and in the world, they can't relate to anything else.

"Number six: We want an end to the robbery by the white racist businessmen of black people in their community.

"Number seven: We want an immediate end to police brutality and murder of black people.

"Number eight: We want all black men held in city, county, state, and Federal jails to be released because they have not had a fair trial because they've been tried by all-white juries, and that's just like being tried in Nazi Germany, being a Jew.

"Number nine: We want black people when brought to trial to be tried by members of their peer group, and a peer being one who comes from the same economic, social, religious, historical and racial background . . . they would have to choose black people from the black community to sit up on the jury. . . .

And number ten: Huey said, let's summarize it: "We want land, we want bread, we want housing, we want clothing, we want education, we want justice, and we want peace."

From Gene Marine, *The Black Panthers* (New York: New American Library, 1969), pp. 35–36.

RACE RELATIONS BY GROUP

AFRICAN AMERICANS

In 1960, African Americans made up about 12 percent of the nation's population. They were not spread evenly throughout the United States, however, but were concentrated in the South and in the big industrial cities of the North and West. In states such as Mississippi, South Carolina, and Louisiana, they accounted for about one-third of the population, as they did in cities such as Chicago and Detroit. These numbers had unfortunately not translated into any significant political, economic, or social improvements, as most blacks in the

Deep South were cut off from the ballot, locked into inferior schools and low-paying jobs, and shut out of decent housing. Except for northern urban blacks having the right to vote, their economic and housing conditions were equally deplorable.

In most cases, these problems resulted from deliberate actions by white citizens and the various governments they controlled—local, state, and federal—to keep the better jobs, housing, and schools, and certainly the political power, for themselves. In the South, many forms of racial discrimination were of the de jure variety, meaning made official by state law. In the North and West, more often than not, racism tended to be of the de facto variety, meaning unofficial and illegal, yet widely practiced and tacitly approved by government authorities.

Although various civil rights groups and individual black leaders had attempted to reform these problems over the decades, by the 1960s there had been few successes. The National Association for the Advancement of Colored People (NAACP) had been the most productive civil rights organization and had been responsible for the most important development, the U.S. Supreme Court's 1954 *Brown v. Board of Education* ruling. White opposition to integrated public schools had effectively stifled the implementation of the ruling, however, and by 1960 still only about 2 percent of blacks in the Deep South attended integrated schools. Yet the NAACP persevered, under the direction of Roy Wilkins, bringing case after case to the federal courts, involving not only school integration but all types of racial discrimination. It labored largely in anonymity, though, until certain of its cases made it to the Supreme Court and were decided in what were invariably controversial rulings.

The other widely known civil rights group in 1960 was Martin Luther King, Jr.'s Southern Christian Leadership Conference (SCLC). This organization was founded in 1957 as a result of the successful 1955 campaign to desegregate the city bus line in Montgomery, Alabama. Only three years old, it had not yet accomplished anything memorable as the new decade dawned. As its name suggests, it was primarily a Christian organization devoted to nonviolent forms of protest against discrimination. Less well-known but arguably more important at the time was the Congress of Racial Equality (CORE). Formed in the 1942 in Chicago, it had spent most of its time trying to end northern discrimination, although it had made forays into the South at times. Led by James Farmer, CORE was a pacifist group committed to nonviolent but direct and confrontational actions.

Other smaller, less-famous, or less important groups extant in 1960 included the Fellowship of Reconciliation, which was an international, interreligious body that promoted understanding across national, religious, and racial boundaries and which gave several black civil rights leaders their start; the Brotherhood of Sleeping Car Porters, a socialist labor union devoted to black workers' rights, led by Asa Philip Randolph; the National Urban League, which fought to improve conditions for blacks in the inner cities, and which from 1961 to 1971 was led by Whitney Young. Also existing at the time but not working in con-

Malcolm X, 1964. Courtesy of Photofest.

junction with these other groups for integration was the Nation of Islam (NOI), headed by Elijah Muhammad in Chicago but made famous by the ubiquitous Malcolm X. Classified loosely as a civil rights group, the NOI worked for black separatism and independent nationhood through a peculiar, racist version of Islam.

Standing cautiously alongside these mostly African American civil rights groups were individual white moderates scattered throughout the South and social liberals throughout the nation. In the South, calling someone a "moderate" was an insult; basically, it was a euphemism for "nigger lover," another term that hardened segregationists frequently used. Each southern state had its core of influential moderates. In Mississippi, for instance, newspaper editors such as Hodding Carter and Hazel Brannen Smith made life hard for themselves merely by being open-minded on civil rights issues; Smith's own white neighbors targeted her paper for annihilation and eventually succeeded. Ministers such as Will Campbell likewise jeopardized their own careers for racial justice, as did professors such as James Silver. In the North and West, there were throngs of liberal politicians, celebrities, ministers, professors, and ordinary citizens—far too many to name—ready to stand up for African American civil rights, but as of 1960 few had actually done so.

Standing in opposition to all these civil rights groups and white moderates were primarily the White Citizens' Council, formed in Mississippi, in 1955, to oppose school integration; the American Nazi Party, founded, in 1959, by Lincoln Rockwell, to oppose all forms of racial integration; and the Ku Klux Klan, which at the time was a disunited collection of local klaverns. Despite stinging defeats in Montgomery and Little Rock in the late 1950s, most white segregationists had not yet experienced being on the losing side in the civil rights struggle, and they would not easily accept it once it happened in the 1960s. They had mostly managed to forestall court orders and circumvent federal civil rights legislation, and they had no reason to believe this would change going into the new decade. Indeed, at the beginning of 1960, there seemed to be a stalemate between the opposing forces, as if both sides were waiting for someone or something to alter the status quo. They did not have to wait long.

In the midst of the stalemate, four young black college students, none of whom were affiliated with any civil rights organization, emerged to break the status quo. On February 1, 1960, in Greensboro, North Carolina, four students from North Carolina Agricultural and Technical College started the Greensboro sit-in at the local Woolworth's lunch counter, thus unwittingly launching one of the first, most dramatic, and most successful submovements in the civil rights crusade, the sit-in movement. The tactic was simply to enter an all-white public establishment and quietly sit and wait to be served. Despite retaliation from white segregationists, the success of the Greensboro sit-in prompted students in other North Carolina towns to pick up the tactic almost immediately. Within a couple of weeks, sit-ins were going on in several other states, and soon they had spread throughout the South. Just as important, within a few months, the SCLC had launched a new youth group, christened the Student Nonviolent Coordinating Committee (SNCC), to organize the thousands of black *and* white students into a unified force.

Just days before the presidential election of 1960, Martin Luther King, Jr., was arrested and jailed for leading a sit-in in his hometown of Atlanta. John F. Kennedy, the Democratic nominee, seized a golden opportunity to win points with black voters, soothe his own conscience, and basically do the right thing, by calling King's wife, Coretta, and offering sympathy. His younger brother Robert, however, took the initiative to call the judge who had sentenced King to four months of hard labor in a Georgia prison and to plead the mercy of the court. The judge agreed, King walked free on bail, and candidate Kennedy won the respect of black voters while winning the election by the narrowest of margins. The president-elect then appointed his brother Robert attorney general. Although John Kennedy became the president, Robert became the foremost ally of African Americans and of the civil rights movement for the next few years. Meanwhile, King's stock as the leader of the civil rights movement increased as a result of his brief incarceration. Sit-ins continued thereafter for the next three years, although by 1961 they had for the most part lost their headline-grabbing status.

In 1961, the sit-ins were displaced in the headlines by the Freedom Rides. Sponsored by CORE, the Freedom Rides involved integrated passengers boarding previously segregated Trailways and Greyhound buses in Washington, D.C., and riding them across state lines through the Deep South. The ultimate destination was New Orleans, but the first buses never made it that far. Violent white resistance in Alabama, and later in Mississippi, doomed them. The courage of those first Freedom Riders in the face of death, however, captured the imagination of many of those engaged in sit-ins and other civil rights activities, and they joined the cause. By the end of the year, more than 400 separate Freedom Riders had participated in one or more of 60 freedom rides. Likewise, the Kennedy administration, reeling from the Bay of Pigs issue and reluctant to tackle Deep South segregationists head-on, ultimately had no choice but to take a stand on the Freedom Rides. Offering them the protection of federal marshals and National Guard troops as necessary, Kennedy indirectly helped the Freedom Riders integrate many of America's national transportation carriers.

Although the Freedom Rides had ended by 1962, the sit-ins continued, as did other forms of protest for racial justice in the South. In December 1961, SNCC stirred the waters by launching a campaign to desegregate the town of Albany, Georgia, by using the Freedom Rider strategy of packing the jails. After the students took the arrows as pioneers, Martin Luther King, Jr., moved in and stole the spotlight by getting arrested twice and garnering the media coverage afforded celebrities. When he left town thereafter without having actually accomplished anything in the way of desegregating the town, many SNCC members began to grow bitter toward him. This would be just the beginning of what would become an increasingly harmful rift between SNCC and King as the years went by.

For most of 1962, the Kennedy administration still had little clout with Congress, southern governors, or at least half of the white public of the country in advancing the civil rights battle. That soon changed when, in September, a black Air Force veteran provoked a showdown between the U.S. government and the state of Mississippi. James Meredith applied for admission to the state's flagship university, Ole Miss, and, upon being denied admission because of his race, he sued. His case was appealed through the courts until it reached the Fifth Circuit Court of Appeals, in New Orleans, where a liberal majority of judges found in his favor. Governor Ross Barnett, acting as temporary registrar of the university, had no intention of complying with the court order, however, and stalled for time, hoping Meredith would back down. Instead, he relentlessly pursued his dream, which forced the Kennedy administration to get involved in enforcing the court order. Again, as he had done a year earlier for the Freedom Riders, Kennedy sent in federal marshals and National Guard troops. In the ensuing riot between the federal personnel and local whites on September 30, two people were killed. In the end, Meredith won, matriculated, and graduated the following year. Although he owed his success largely to help from the NAACP, he repudiated the organization afterward, preferring to make a stand for racial justice independent of any civil rights group.

Kennedy gained enemies in the South as a result of his heavy-handed use of federal law enforcement officers in the Meredith case. He had no time to take stock of his civil rights agenda, because a more serious problem arrived on his desk within the next week. It was the 13-day Cuban missile crisis of October 1962. His brilliant leadership through that most difficult situation largely rescued him from whatever negative effects might have resulted from the Meredith case, because there was only one thing white segregationists cared about as strongly as racial issues, and that was national defense. Even though his popularity increased significantly in the polls going into 1963, Kennedy still did not have a mandate for pushing civil rights legislation through Congress. That did not stop him from considering the possibility, however. He felt pressure from Martin Luther King, Jr., and other black leaders to ride the wave of momentum. He was cautious not to move too far, too fast, though, and he did not respond immediately to the prodding.

Meanwhile, many other developments began taking place in early 1963, as sit-ins continued, mass marches began, and relatively minor white backlashes of violence occurred around the nation. As the journalist Milton Greenberg put it at the time, "The American Negro took to the streets in 1963 in a nationwide protest against a century of second-class citizenship. Utilizing the techniques of civil disobedience and mass demonstrations, including a march on Washington in August, Negroes forced white Americans to take note of the discontent."[31] During this year of protest, national attention focused primarily on four cities: Birmingham, Alabama; Jackson, Mississippi; Cambridge, Maryland; and Washington, D.C. Partly because Birmingham was widely considered the most racist city in America, and partly because local blacks such as the Reverend Fred Shuttlesworth were begging for help there, Martin Luther King, Jr., and the SCLC made it their first major target since Albany in 1961. The peaceful marches began on April 3, but by April 12, King was in jail in the iron and steel capital of the South. While there, he penned the first of his masterful treatises on nonviolent but immediate and confrontational protest. Published in the local Birmingham newspaper, it has since become known as the "Letter from Birmingham Jail." In it, he chided white moderates who supported the overall objective of the civil rights movement but did not want it to move so fast that fellow whites would not have a chance to get used to it, thus causing a backlash. Nine days later, he was again bailed out with help from the Kennedy administration.

As King planned his next assault on Birmingham, just up the road from there, the first of the highly publicized assassinations of the civil rights era occurred. The victim was William L. Moore, a postal worker from Baltimore, who had come to Chattanooga to stage a one-man "freedom walk" to Jackson, Mississippi.[32] Making it about 50 miles into Alabama on Highway 11, he was shot near Gadsden on April 23. Immediately, SNCC and others took up marches all over the South in his honor. By the end of May, "sympathy demonstrations" had been held in faraway Los Angeles and San Francisco that drew racially mixed crowds of 20,000 in commemoration of Moore and southern integrationists in general.[33] National attention, however, remained mostly with King in Birmingham.

On May 2–3, black youth, urged on by King and others, took to the streets of Birmingham by the thousands, marching for their civil rights. The first day, the police chief, Eugene "Bull" Connor, had nearly 1,000 of them arrested. The next day, he went a step further and a step too far. He ordered his men to repel the marchers by turning loose vicious police dogs on them and by turning city fire hoses on them. This was a major mistake not only for humanitarian reasons but for public relations reasons. Television news crews captured the shocking scenes of trained German shepherds ripping the clothes and the flesh of defenseless marchers and of white policemen spraying African Americans with hoses that carried enough water pressure to peel the bark off trees. Although devastating to the marchers, these strong-arm law enforcement tactics were a gift to the larger movement. As a previously apathetic northern white public watched on television, read about the Birmingham events in the newspapers, and heard Governor George Wallace give his approval and threaten more of the same, the apathy began to turn to anger. No more would the South's race problems be its own; now they belonged to the nation, as thousands of white northerners, particularly college students, began to see their first life calling in going down to help free the oppressed.

In the meantime, the protest in Birmingham continued, resulting in bombings and riots by May 12. Beginning May 13 and lasting five days, the unlikely town of Cambridge, Maryland, became the focus of national attention. As white leaders negotiated with black protesters, the days dragged on, and patience waned. By June 10, the negotiations had collapsed, and rioting began that was serious enough to justify sending in the National Guard. The troops stayed in Cambridge nearly a month. No sooner had they left than the rioting broke out anew. Once again the town came under martial law, and not until Attorney General Kennedy intervened was a satisfactory compromise reached between blacks and whites.

As these events unfolded in northeastern Maryland, just down the road in the nation's capital, President Kennedy finally decided he could wait no longer to introduce his civil rights bill. On June 11, he went on national television and announced his plan for the most sweeping law for promoting racial equality in American history. Southern segregationists in Congress immediately attacked the bill, vowing the filibuster of all filibusters in the Senate, which they subsequently delivered. The bill stalled in Congress, therefore, for almost exactly one year.

At the same time as Kennedy showed the first glimmer of light at the end of the civil rights tunnel, down in Jackson, Mississippi, sit-ins and other protests were leading to bloodshed and murder. On June 12, the head of the Mississippi NAACP, Medgar Evers, died at the hands of an assassin while standing in front of his home in the presence of his wife and children. Once again, sympathy demonstrations were held in various cities and towns across the land. By this time, civil rights protests were going on in the North and West anyway, to bring an end to de facto school segregation and housing/employment discrimination. New York City, Philadelphia, Chicago, and Washington, D.C., among others, were affected. Within another month, and still only midway through the summer, about 750 demonstrations had been held in at least 180 different locations around the nation, and more than 14,000 protesters had been arrested.

On June 22, King and several other prominent civil rights leaders met with President Kennedy in the White House to discuss, among other things, the strategy to employ in trying to push the civil rights bill through Congress. There the 71-year-old A. Philip Randolph proposed to the president what had been his dream since 1941—to stage a march on Washington. He argued that it would draw at least 100,000 people and provide the strong show of support necessary to convince waffling congressmen to cast their lots in favor of the bill. Neither Kennedy nor the more conservative blacks in the room, such as Whitney Young and Roy Wilkins, were keen on the idea. King supported it, however, and at a speech in Detroit the next day he promoted it in front of a crowd estimated at 125,000. With that, there was no going back. Even if the president opposed it, there would be a march. Planning began for the March on Washington for Jobs and Freedom almost immediately. On July 2, the Big Six civil rights leaders—King, Randolph, Wilkins, Young, James Farmer of CORE, and John Lewis of SNCC—met in New York City to begin formalizing this march that was sure to be the climactic episode of the movement so far. The date they set was August 28.

As the planning continued throughout July and August, and as King shuttled back and forth across the country making speeches and leading rallies, the FBI began in earnest its secret surveillance of King and those around him. It was the height of the Cold War, and paranoia about domestic communism abounded. There were known communists and former communists in the ranks of the civil rights leaders, and virtually all integrationists were considered pinkos anyway. FBI Director J. Edgar Hoover would have liked nothing better than to bring King and his fellows crashing back to earth in shame just before their March on Washington. Despite efforts to that effect, neither King nor any of the Big Six could be proven to have any ties to the Soviets or the Cubans or other communist governments, although some of the obscure lieutenants in the movement could. King fired one of his righthand men for that reason, rather than risk having the man's communist connections become the ruination of the march.

On August 28, the march went on as scheduled. As hoped, it proved to be the high-water mark of the civil rights movement. Not an end in itself, the march was all about rallying the American people behind the civil rights bill. Even so, the march became just as important for its symbolism in history as the Civil Rights Act of 1964 became in substance. Even better than hoped, not merely 100,000 people showed up for it, but about twice that number, including blacks, whites, southerners, northerners, the old and the young, men, women, and miscellaneous foreigners. In addition, millions witnessed it firsthand on television. In an event that lasted only about seven hours from beginning to end, a plethora of celebrities and civil rights figures spoke, sang, and marched. The march culminated with King delivering his most famous oration, the "I Have a Dream" speech, which incited applause, cheers, and emotion not unlike what the biggest rock stars would receive from adoring fans today. When the one-day event was over, the Big Six met again with the president, who congratulated them on a job well done.

There was little time to bask in the afterglow of the march. Back in Alabama, on September 9, the Birmingham public schools were desegregated, against the wishes of the defiant Governor Wallace, with federal troops swarming the area. Complicating an already chaotic situation, on September 15, the Ku Klux Klan of Imperial Wizard Robert Shelton bombed the black Sixteenth Street Baptist Church, killing four young girls who had gone to Sunday School early that day. The sheer brutality and callousness of this act of terrorism shocked the nation and helped swell the ranks of white northern volunteers. No sooner had the American people finished mourning that tragedy than the most cataclysmic tragedy so far struck. On November 22, John F. Kennedy became the first president to be assassinated since 1901.

No one knew for sure at the time what to expect from his successor, Lyndon Johnson. A Texan with the stereotypical attributes of a southern good ole boy, Johnson had a long record in Congress that put him squarely in the moderate camp on social issues. Yet to expect him to pick up the torch of civil rights reform from the slain president and carry it into battle on behalf of African Americans seemed a bit of a stretch. Almost before the movement's rank and file had a chance to grow despondent over the prospect of failure, however, Johnson surprised everyone. In his first State of the Union address, on January 8, 1964, he showed his commitment to racial justice. Two months later, he appealed to the largest Christian denomination in America, the white Southern Baptists, to support the civil rights bill. Regardless of Johnson's position on racial issues, Kennedy's death made passage of the civil rights bill almost a certainty, since many congressmen would vote for it as a memorial to the former president. As Congress debated it, an Interreligious Convocation on Civil Rights convened in Washington, in which Protestant, Catholic, and Jewish leaders all demanded passage of the bill. Even so, it took eight months from the time of Kennedy's assassination for the House and the Senate to agree on a version of it to pass. On July 2, 1964, Johnson signed the Civil Rights Act of 1964 into law, and it immediately became the most important racial legislation passed since Reconstruction, nearly a century earlier.

The Civil Rights Act generated hope for better race relations in the future, but the reality of the present was still bleak in 1964. Earlier in the year, in Jacksonville and St. Augustine, Florida, demonstrations had led to race rioting, some of which occurred just one week before the signing of the Act; New York City blacks engaged in a boycott against the public schools, and within three weeks after the Act was signed, rioting broke out in Harlem and Rochester, New York; before the summer ended, riots had erupted in New Jersey and Pennsylvania; George Wallace of Alabama had made impressive showings in the Democratic primaries for president outside the Deep South, indicating that segregation sentiment was nationwide; several important civil rights cases had already gone through the federal court system, others were still in progress, and more were on the way, indicating that there were no signs that segregationists would be ready to give up the fight any time soon; and, most important of all, just 11 days before

Johnson signed the Act, three young men who were working to register black voters in Mississippi were reported missing, prompting one of the most massive manhunts in American history. When the bodies of the three civil rights volunteers were found, in Neshoba County, Mississippi, on August 4, the FBI began a murder investigation that yielded 21 arrests by the end of the year. The case would ultimately be a turning point against racial hate crimes in the American justice system.

The genesis of the case can be found in the Council of Federated Organizations' (COFO) Freedom Summer campaign to register black voters in Mississippi. COFO, a consortium of civil rights groups, including SNCC, CORE, and NAACP, had formed two years earlier. Led by the black activists Robert Moses, David Dennis, and Aaron Henry, COFO had called for white northern college students to come to Mississippi over their summer break to help with voter registration. By the summer of 1964, the campaign was in full swing, and about 1,000 white volunteers had signed up to participate. The Ku Klux Klan, however, intended to stop it with a countercampaign, and the infamous murders in Neshoba County were one result. Other results included two additional murders, at least 30 shootings, more than 30 bombings, 80 physical assaults, and the arrests of about 1,000 civil rights workers. Freedom Summer went on nonetheless, and many thousands of African Americans got registered to vote for the first time in their lives.

Even more important, COFO's activity led to the formation of the Mississippi Freedom Democratic Party (MFDP), an integrated version of the Democratic party that hoped to represent the state of Mississippi at the party's national convention in Atlantic City, New Jersey, August 24–27, in place of the traditional, all-white version of the party. Fannie Lou Hamer, an uneducated former sharecropper from the cotton fields of the Delta, spoke to the Credentials Committee at the convention and captured the nation's attention with her firsthand testimony, broadcast on television, of being beaten and jailed for trying to register to vote in Mississippi. Even so, the national party leadership, starting with Johnson at the top, did not allow the MFDP to displace the regular, all-white delegates but rather tried to compromise with them by giving them two at-large seats and calling them guests at the convention. Refusing the offer, Hamer and the MFDP delegates went home emptyhanded for the moment but ultimately succeeded in forcing the black voting rights issue to the forefront of the national party agenda for the coming year.

In November 1964, the Lyndon Johnson-Hubert Humphrey ticket won for the Democrats in a landslide. Running on a pledge to turn the United States into the "Great Society" through a war on poverty and an end to racial discrimination, Johnson would simultaneously begin waging a war against communism in Vietnam that would mitigate against the success of his Great Society ambitions. More immediately, though, the Great Society's first birth pangs came in Alabama, as Martin Luther King, Jr., began in earnest a black voting rights campaign in Selma. A town of about 30,000 sitting about 50 miles west of Montgomery, in Dallas County, in the heart of Alabama's Black Belt region, Selma had already been a main focus of SNCC's voting rights efforts for more than a year when King arrived. Kicking off the campaign on January 18 (two days before Johnson's inauguration), by February 3 more than 2,600 demonstrators—about half of whom were children—and King himself had been arrested. While King sat in jail, Malcolm X arrived in Selma to give a speech. In his typical fashion, he indicated that blacks would not long endure the violence of whites passively, but the time was coming when they would fight back. Within three weeks, he was dead, the victim of fellow Black Muslims in New York City who killed him, on February 21, out of jealousy over his repudiation of the Nation of Islam and his attempt to start a rival group, the Organization of Afro-American Unity. It was hardly a good beginning for the Great Society.

In the meantime, national attention remained focused largely down in Alabama. On February 10, the sheriff, James G. Clark, had 165 black children marched into the Dallas County countryside and left there, and six days later he punched a demonstrator in the face in front of television news cameras. On February 18, in the neighboring town of Marion, an Alabama highway patrol officer shot and killed Jimmie Lee Jackson in the midst of a nighttime march. To protest this killing, which resulted in no indictment, King decided to lead an integrated march from Selma to Montgomery, on March 7. When King canceled his plans for the march at the last minute, one of his lieutenants, Hosea Williams, decided to lead the march without him. Williams and about 600 marchers made it to the Edmund Pettus Bridge, at the edge of town, before being met by a bevy of state troopers and a local militia cavalry unit. At the direction of Governor Wallace, the law enforcement troupe ran down the marchers in a vile and violent display of power over the powerless. Captured by the television news crews, this event, which shocked the nation, became known as "Bloody Sunday."[34] Two days later, King arrived to lead a second attempt to cross the bridge. Again Wallace's minions waited. This time King did not force the issue but stopped his followers and had them join him in kneeling in prayer before turning around and heading back home. This prearranged outcome looked far better in the public eye, but devoted civil rights activists felt betrayed by King's compromise. Making matters much worse, after the show at the bridge, a white Boston preacher named James Reeb was beaten to death in Selma.

Such events were a public relations nightmare for the man in the White House trying to create the Great Society. He promptly called Governor Wallace to Washington for a conference, scheduled for March 13. After warning the governor that he would tolerate no more displays of brute force against civil rights demonstrators, Johnson went on national television two days later and announced his intention to sponsor a voting rights bill that would put an end to such problems once and for all. As if to spite the president, the next day in Montgomery, a group of renegade law enforcement officers armed with night sticks burst into a crowd of about 600 demonstrators and began swinging. The following day, March 17, Johnson sent to Congress the voting rights bill as promised, and a federal judge ordered Wallace to allow a peaceful march from Selma to

Civil rights demonstrators struggle on the ground as state troopers use violence to break up a march in Selma, Alabama, on what is known as Bloody Sunday on March 7, 1965. The supporters of black voting rights organized a march from Selma to Montgomery to protest the killing of a demonstrator by a state trooper and to improve voter registration for blacks, who are discouraged to register. AP Photo.

Montgomery to take place without interference. From March 21 to March 25, King led the four-day, 54-mile march, which ended in victory with more than 25,000 participants at the state capitol.

Immediately after this moment of jubilation, yet another murder rocked the movement. This time the victim was a white female volunteer from Detroit named Viola Liuzzo, who was driving marchers back to Selma in her own car on March 25. Although it is known that she was killed by Klansmen, justice has never been served in the case for lack of hard evidence against any particular shooter. On August 20, she was joined in the pantheon of civil rights martyrs by Jonathan Daniel, an Episcopal clergyman from New Hampshire, killed by a shotgun blast from a Klansman. Another minister, Richard Morrisroe, was also shot by the same man at that time, but he did not die. The trial ended in acquittal of the Klansman. When it seemed that no justice could be found in the Alabama courts, President Johnson called for a congressional investigation of the Ku Klux Klan designed to shut down the organization.

The remainder of the spring of 1965 seemed comparatively quiet. In July and August, however, significant demonstrations occurred in Bogalusa, Louisiana, and Americus, Georgia. By far the most important developments of the summer were the passage of the Voting Rights Act on August 6 and the Watts riot of August 11–16. Hailed as the coup de grace of Johnson's civil rights agenda, the

Voting Rights Act indeed put in place the legal machinery necessary to enforce the suffrage rights of African Americans in the South. Unfortunately, there was little time to savor the achievement, because out on the West Coast, in a poor section of Los Angeles called Watts, the most serious riot thus far of the 1960s erupted. The riot resulted in 34 people killed, 1,000 injured, 4,000 arrested, and an estimated $40 million in property damage. A routine arrest of a black motorist by white policemen sparked the bloody conflagration.

The Watts riot was an event thick with irony in that it came less than one week after the Voting Rights Act and barely a year after the Civil Rights Act, each of which was designed to bring the South into the national mainstream in terms of race relations. Now, in California, a state considered not merely in the mainstream but counted among the trend setters, it was discovered that race relations were not as rosy as everyone thought. The urban blacks of Los Angeles, it turned out, while better off than in some ways than their counterparts in the rural South, were still far from content. They had tasted just enough of American democracy and justice to know they were not living in a land of absolute equality, and they demanded more. Police brutality, both real and alleged, had not been covered by the Civil Rights Act, and it constituted a major problem for urban blacks. Sadly, what happened in California in this case did indeed set a trend for the rest of the nation, as similar race riots would soon rock major cities from one end of the country to the other. The only good news was that none of them happened for the rest of 1965.

The year 1966 brought hope that the American people had turned the corner and were heading toward better race relations in the future. The enforcement provisions of the Civil Rights Act and the Voting Rights Act indeed led to positive changes, some immediately and others after protracted litigation. Yet, important work remained to be done. Central Alabama continued to be a hotbed of voting rights activity, as Stokely Carmichael, the new national director of SNCC, worked diligently with Lowndes County residents in creating the first "Black Panther" party. Running seven black candidates in the November election, the party lost every race. Although the effort was unsuccessful in Alabama, Carmichael's fiery oratory and fighting spirit and the black panther emblem would soon go nationwide and have a far greater impact than he could have dreamed. Even more important work remained to be done outside the South. Sensing that it was now time to take the civil rights movement to the urban industrial North, Martin Luther King, Jr., planned a campaign to desegregate the Chicago area. Much to his dismay, he found that in some ways the racism of the urban North was more virulent than that of the rural South. Demonstrations there led to outbreaks of violence and helped contribute to one of the worst riots of the decade.

While King valiantly fought the housing and job discrimination of Chicago, down in Mississippi James Meredith took it upon himself to stage a one-man "March against Fear" from Memphis to Jackson to encourage black voter registration.[35] On June 6, the second day of his journey, not long after crossing the state line, he was shot by a lone gunman. Although not mortally wounded, he

Rev. Martin Luther King, Jr. stands with other civil rights leaders on the balcony of the Lorraine Motel in Memphis, Tennessee, on April 3, 1968, a day before he was assassinated at approximately the same place. From left are Hosea Williams, Jesse Jackson, King, and Ralph Abernathy. AP Photo.

was hospitalized with a serious injury. Upon hearing the news of the shooting, the very next day other civil rights leaders rallied to take up his march and finish it for him. King temporarily halted his northern campaign to go to Mississippi and lead the march, but Stokely Carmichael of SNCC and Floyd McKissick, the new director of CORE, vied with King for the top leadership position in the march. This jockeying for position among the three portended the eventual self-destruction of the civil rights movement. While King continued to be committed to leading his flock along the path of nonviolent resistance, Carmichael and McKissick both jettisoned the nonviolent approach in lieu of the Black Power approach. By the time the three and their fellow marchers reached the midway point, at Greenwood, Mississippi, they could be heard trying to outdo each other in competing shouts of King's "Freedom Now!" and Carmichael's "Black Power!"[36] It was now clear to everyone that King, despite his past successes and accolades, could no longer command the allegiance of the whole civil rights crowd.

It was equally clear that the Black Power slogan signaled the end of the non-violent and integrationist phase of the movement. A radical fringe of African

Americans had always advocated armed resistance to racial oppression, as evidenced by groups like the Revolutionary Action Movement and the Deacons for Defense, but never had they been in the mainstream. Carmichael, however, brought it into the mainstream. Black Power meant black separatism to many young African Americans—self-imposed racial segregation in which whites were deliberately excluded. To others it meant complete black nationalism—that the black race in America constituted a nation within a nation and, as such, should have its own land and territorial sovereignty—the same message that the Nation of Islam had preached for years. To all, it meant racial pride, encouraging young blacks to study their African heritage and to believe that "black is beautiful."[37] For his part, Carmichael meant it mainly as separatism and racial pride. He expelled all whites from SNCC, claiming that blacks must prove their self-sufficiency and demonstrate their willingness and ability to help themselves, rather than relying on the charity of generous, well-meaning whites. McKissick likewise led CORE to abandon a quarter-century of nonviolent protest in favor of the more militant Black Power approach. Essentially, both men and their organizations repudiated the leadership of King and followed the ghost of Malcolm X.

Once the Black Power train began rolling, it quickly achieved unstoppable momentum, captivating young urban blacks around the nation and leading them to increased radicalism in their protest against white oppression, both real and alleged. The summer of 1966 thus became the first "long, hot summer" of race riots.[38] Imitating the Watts riot of a year earlier were a host of similar disturbances, from San Francisco to New York and many points in between, including unlikely places like Des Moines, Iowa, and South Bend, Indiana. Just as important, the Black Power movement captured the minds of a couple of idealistic African Americans in Oakland, California, named Huey Newton and Bobby Seale, who used it to create the Black Panther Party for Self-Defense. Seeing police brutality as the most pressing problem facing urban blacks, they determined to hold the police in Oakland accountable. They carried weapons and followed the police, confronting them and getting involved in shootouts. Within a year, the Black Panthers had developed cult status among the black youth of America, and chapters sprang up all over the country. The explosive growth of this paramilitary group struck fear in the heart of law enforcement agencies, not the least of which was the FBI, which considered the Panthers the most dangerous organization in America in the late 1960s. Consequently, the FBI collaborated with local police departments in cities from coast to coast to shut down the Panthers one way or another, even if it meant murdering them in cold blood, and sometimes it did. The FBI's anti–Black Panther campaign continued into 1971.

By 1967, the nature of American race relations looked very different from the way it had looked at the beginning of the decade. Nonviolent protest was now passé, the problems of legal racial discrimination in the rural South had largely been solved through federal legislation and enforcement, the focus of racial justice became the ghettos of the northern cities, the Black Power movement had captured the attention of African American youth, and the hippies and anti–Vietnam War protesters had become thoroughly entangled with the racial integrationists of the civil rights movement. The Vietnam issue, acid rock music, the drug culture, the long-haired back-to-nature hippies, and the Black Power crowd all combined to make the late 1960s one of the most bizarre but fascinating periods of American history. As for the wedding of civil rights protesters with war protesters, the two made strange bedfellows in appearance, but it was a marriage in which pacifistic idealism united them. The most prominent civil rights pacifist, Martin Luther King, Jr., had become convinced by 1967 that leading the anti–Vietnam War movement was his next calling. It was one of several controversial decisions he made that further deteriorated the civil rights movement in the last three years of his life. On April 15, he led a demonstration of 100,000 in New York City, in which he marched from Central Park to the United Nations building and made an impassioned antiwar speech.

The most important development of 1967 historically was not a single event but a series of them that came in the form of race riots. Having reached its zenith in only a year's time, the Black Power philosophy turned the civil rights movement into a veritable racial revolution in America's cities. The summer of 1967, although referred to euphemistically by the hippies as the "Summer of Love," was more accurately a summer of hate. Race riots broke out in such large numbers and to such an alarming degree that people seriously wondered whether the United States would survive as a nation. The riots actually began before summer, when, in April, a group of black women in Boston calling themselves "Mothers for Adequate Welfare" chained themselves together inside the local welfare office, causing the police to have to forcibly remove them.[39] On May 11–13, Tampa exploded in rioting after a white policeman killed a black burglar. At the same time, Cincinnati experienced a riot serious enough to require National Guard intervention. On May 27–30, Buffalo became the next city embroiled in a racial ruckus.

July was by far the most destructive month, as Newark had a riot nearly as deadly as the 1965 Watts riot, and Detroit had one even worse. Nor was the rioting contained within those cities; in both cases, it spread to several neighboring towns in New Jersey and Michigan, respectively. Within a week after the riot had ended in Newark, the city hosted the first national conference on Black Power, in which about 1,000 delegates from 42 cities attended, at which no whites were allowed, and during which black nationalism—dividing America into two separate nations, one for blacks and the other for whites—became the mantra. In Cambridge, Maryland, on July 24, the day after the conference, another riot erupted, not surprisingly, when H. Rap Brown, who had replaced Stokely Carmichael as the head of SNCC in May, actually encouraged blacks to "burn this town down."[40] Altogether, before the summer had ended, 70 cities had been torn apart by riots, and 85 people had been killed.

Even before the last fire had been put out in July, President Johnson created the National Advisory Commission on Civil Disorders to find out the causes of the riots and to recommend ways to prevent future riots. The commission did its work with remarkable speed and dexterity, and it issued its report on February 29, 1968. Its conclusions seem oddly simple and predictable in retrospect but certainly came as new information to many white Americans who previously lived in a sort of isolated oblivion to the plight of urban blacks. In effect, the report said that unless and until whites and all levels of government in America truly began to give completely fair treatment to blacks in all walks of life, there was no hope of preventing such racial disturbances in the future.

Not all was bad in 1967, however. Two positive developments were the appointment of Thurgood Marshall to the U.S. Supreme Court, on June 13 (confirmed by the Senate on August 30) and the beginning of President Johnson's Model Cities Program, on November 16. Marshall, the former NAACP attorney and director of the Legal Defense and Educational Fund who had prosecuted the *Brown v. Board of Education* case, became the first African American Supreme Court Justice. The Model Cities program was one of Johnson's Great Society initiatives that involved pumping 311 million federal dollars into the ghettos of 63 cities in 1967 alone, with the promise of additional money for more cities later. The hope was obviously to change the economic dynamics and the housing problems of the inner cities and thus eradicate some of the factors that had led to the rioting earlier in the year. Another development of 1967 that indirectly aided the civil rights movement was the assassination of Lincoln Rockwell, the leader of the American Nazi party, on August 25, by a disgruntled former party member.

After the long, hot summer of 1967, once again hope sprang eternal that 1968 would be a better year for American race relations, but it was not to be. On February 8, after a SNCC group in Orangeburg, South Carolina, tried unsuccessfully to integrate the local bowling alley, a massacre of black students by state highway patrolmen occurred, resulting in three dead and 30 wounded. The officers claimed self-defense, and even though none of the students had fired a single shot, the patrolmen were acquitted. Meanwhile, Martin Luther King, Jr., turned his attention from antiwar pacifism to eliminating poverty in America. He began making preliminary arrangements for a campaign against poverty that would feature demonstrations in several places and culminate in a "Poor People's March on Washington."[41] In the month of March, he went to Memphis to help with a sanitation workers' strike. On the 28th, he led a procession through the downtown streets that got out of hand. A group of youth began vandalizing property and looting while shouting the Black Power slogan. Unable to bring the riotous behavior under control, King and his lieutenants feared for their own safety and left the streets for the motel. There they watched Memphis become the subject of negative national news coverage. It was the last offensive of his short life, and an unfitting end to it. A week later, on April 4, he was assassinated while standing on the balcony of the Lorraine Motel alongside several of his lieutenants. He had delivered his now-famous "mountaintop" speech the night before, in which he seemed to prophesy his own imminent death. His April 9 funeral in Atlanta became the largest memorial service ever held for a private American citizen.

News of King's murder spread like wildfire and immediately became the most incendiary event of the 1960s. Beginning on the day of his death, angry blacks in Washington, D.C., went on a four-day rioting spree that resulted in eight deaths. A three-day riot in Chicago ended with 11 killed. In Kansas City, six more people perished. Less deadly but equally scary riots broke out in about 40 other cities. Nor did the riots end after the furor over King's death had subsided. On July 23–27, in Cleveland, a five-day gunfight and standoff between police and Black Power advocates left 10 more dead. A week later, August 5–8, as the Republican National Convention met in Miami, three people were killed. At the end of the month, August 26–30, the Democratic National Convention in Chicago likewise attracted one of the most notable riots of the decade, as war protesters, civil rights demonstrators, Black Power advocates, and communist hippies all converged on the Windy City simultaneously.

Upon King's death, the leadership position in the SCLC passed to King's friend and fellow black pastor from Atlanta, Ralph David Abernathy. Amazingly, barely one month after King's funeral, Abernathy and King's widow, Coretta Scott King, took up the cause of the Poor People's Campaign, with the hope that they could influence Congress to pass new antipoverty legislation. On May 12, in Washington, D.C., they opened "Resurrection City," a shantytown of plywood, cardboard, and canvas spread over a 16-acre plot beside the Lincoln Memorial.[42] The campaign ended with a "Solidarity Day March" to the Capitol on June 19–20.[43] Poor planning, bad weather, and scant news coverage that reflected the American public's weariness with such events all contributed to the failure of the campaign.

The other major domestic news event of 1968 was only marginally related to the civil rights struggle. On June 5, while campaigning in Los Angeles for the Democratic nomination for president, Robert F. Kennedy was shot. He died the following day. Although his assassination was not a black-white issue, his loss was perhaps felt more by the millions of African Americans he had fought for as attorney general than by any other group. Prior to his assassination, Kennedy had been widely considered the most likely victor in the November election, but upon his death the Democrats settled for former Vice President Hubert Humphrey. The Minnesotan Humphrey would have almost certainly been more liberal on racial issues than the candidate who defeated him, Richard Nixon of California. The best news that came out of 1968 was that this year marked a small turning point in American race relations. After the summer riots, relative peace broke out across the land, and it continued, for the most part, into 1969.

The last year of the 1960s turned out to be more like the decade that followed it than the 10 years that preceded it. Although a few scattered racial skirmishes occurred, nothing remotely resembling the bloody clashes of previous years happened in 1969. Events involving Black Power advocates and the Black Panthers made the most sensational news stories. At the National Black Economic Development Conference, in Detroit, on April 26, James Forman presented the "Black Manifesto," which among other things, called upon white American churches and synagogues to pay $500 million in reparations to the black people of the

United States. On May 4, Forman disrupted the worship service at Riverside Church in New York City, reading aloud the list of demands contained in the manifesto. Although whites largely ignored the demands as preposterous, the reparations issue had been laid on the table for the coming years.

Later in 1969, Bobby Seale, the chairman of the Black Panthers, was implicated in the "Chicago 8" conspiracy to incite rioting at the Democratic National Convention of 1968. In the trial, which took place in October and November, Seale demanded the right to represent himself as his own attorney. When he refused to comply with court orders to be quiet, his repeated interruptions provoked Judge Julius J. Hoffman to hold him in contempt of court. In a bizarre spectacle, on October 29, Hoffman had Seale bound and gagged publicly. On November 5, he sentenced Seale to four years in prison. On December 4, a police raid on the Chicago headquarters of the Black Panthers resulted in the killing of two Illinois Panthers, Fred Hampton and Mark Clark, under suspicious circumstances. Four days later, a shootout occurred between police and the Panthers in Los Angeles.

With the exception of the events noted, the decade of the 1960s came to a close on a relatively peaceful note. African Americans had come a long way in a very short time. They had moved too far, too fast, for the taste of most whites, but in their own minds they had asked for nothing more than what had been rightfully theirs all along.

AMERICAN INDIANS

Compared with African Americans, all other minority groups in the United States in the 1960s seem to have been practically invisible. At least that was true until the second half of the decade. By then, the gains blacks had made in achieving equality under the law had begun to have coattails that other groups rode in carrying out their own civil rights movements. The oldest of all minority groups in the country was, of course, Native Americans. Suffering through a history just as troubling and tragic in its own way as that of African Americans, Indians in the 1960s still endured an unemployment rate 10 times the average of all other racial groups nationwide. Their life expectancy was also 20 years shorter, and their suicide rate was 100 times higher. For more than a century before then, the reservation system had served basically as a prison, locking them into lives of poverty and despair. Although the federal government had made an effort in the 1950s to get more Indians off the reservations and into the mainstream of American society, its programs to that effect (generally called the *termination* policy) had proved only partly successful. Thousands of Indians had left the reservations and moved primarily to major cities, but the transition was difficult for most. Moreover, the termination policy made Indians fearful that they would soon lose their identity by being absorbed and assimilated into corporate America.

In 1961, an American Indian Charter Convention met in Chicago, which 500 people representing 70 tribes attended, to discuss how to respond to the termination policy. The conference resulted in the formation of the National Indian Youth

Council (NIYC), which called for complete self-determination for all tribes and set the stage for specific civil rights protest actions in the coming months and years. When, in 1964, after the state of Washington had defied a federal court ruling upholding Indian fishing rights granted in decades-old federal treaties, NIYC members created the Survival of American Indians Association (SAIA), which staged "fish-ins" in Washington state.[44] The fish-ins led to ugly confrontations with local whites and law enforcement officers, but they drew the support of the famous actor Marlon Brando, which gave greater visibility and credibility to the cause.

Meanwhile, down in the San Francisco Bay area, many community groups had sprung up to help Indians make the transition from reservation life to urban life. They included the Intertribal Friendship House and the Four Winds Club, among others. These clubs helped the Indians of the Bay area coalesce into the most unified, effective, protest-oriented group of Indians in America. Their efforts culminated in the creation of the United Native Americans (UNA), in 1968, and several local colleges and universities adopted Native American studies programs. Not surprisingly, San Francisco became the focal point of the most important of the early Indian civil rights demonstrations. On March 9, 1964, a group of five Sioux made a public statement against their mistreatment at the hands of whites and their government by attempting an ill-fated takeover of Alcatraz Island, in San Francisco Bay. They claimed the land on the basis of an 1868 federal treaty with the Sioux tribe. Treaty or no treaty, the government authorities in possession of Alcatraz did not appreciate their presence on the island and summarily ran them off. A subsequent suit brought by the Sioux against the government in federal court yielded nothing.

In 1965, the Taos Pueblo tribe in New Mexico won a monetary settlement from the Indian Claims Commission as payment for the Blue Lake region, which the U.S. Forest Service had taken illegally. They did not want the money, though; they wanted their land back. In 1966 and again in 1968, bills were introduced in Congress to restore the Blue Lake area to the tribe, but they did not pass. It would remain for the Nixon administration to deal with this issue in the 1970s. Meanwhile, in 1966, as part of his broader civil rights agenda and war on poverty, President Johnson gave a speech to Congress emphasizing the need for better treatment of Indians. As a result, the Civil Rights Act of 1968 contained an "Indian Bill of Rights," which was supposed to protect individual Indians on reservations against the capricious use of power by their own officials. It actually just confused life on the reservations, however, creating disputes about who held jurisdiction over various matters. It was just one more indicator of how the wheels of reform turned slowly and painfully.

During this turbulent period of the late 1960s, young, urban Indians began to take matters into their own hands. Only after Johnson left office in 1969 did the National Council on Indian Opportunity (NCIO) that he had created become active in meeting with Indians in the San Francisco area. At an April 11 meeting, 37 Indians spoke before the NCIO, and some issued scathing indictments of the various levels of government for neglect of their people and abuses against them.

Within seven months, 25 of those speakers would stage another occupation of Alcatraz.

In the meantime, in 1968, important developments unfolded thousands of miles from San Francisco. In Minneapolis, four Chippewas formed a group that would ultimately become larger and more important than any other, the American Indian Movement (AIM). It would not take center stage, however, until the 1970s. In December 1968, a dispute among the Mohawks, the Canadian government, and the United States over tribal movement back and forth across the border stirred a controversy. The Mohawk reservation in upstate New York was and is located directly across the St. Lawrence River from the city of Cornwall, Ontario. When Canada tried to restrict the free movement of these Indian citizens of the United States across the border, the Mohawks blocked passage across the Cornwall International Bridge, claiming rights given them in treaties with Great Britain dating back to the 1700s. They were arrested. In 1969, Canada reversed its policy and recognized the tribal rights of the Mohawks.

Back in San Francisco, on November 9 and again on November 20, 1969, Indian activists calling themselves Indians of All Tribes staged more takeovers of Alcatraz Island. Although government authorities ran them off on the first attempt, just as they had done to the Sioux in 1964, on the second attempt the Indians came in larger numbers, and they came to stay. By far the most dramatic event of the Indian civil rights movement in the 1960s, the occupation dragged out until mid-1971. By then it had started a trend of Indians seizing government property. The "Red Power" movement was now here. It became fashionable for Indians to sport bumper stickers and lapel buttons with slogans like "Custer died for your sins."[45]

Unlike African Americans, whose main civil rights thrust came in the 1960s, the Indians' main thrust was still to come in the 1970s. Even so, Indian activists made substantial progress between 1960 and 1970. Thanks to a combination of Indian self-help and government help, the American Indian population increased from 552,000 to 827,000 over the decade.

HISPANICS

In the 1960s, Hispanics made up the second largest minority group in the United States, but they were still a distant second behind African Americans. Concentrated largely in the southwestern states from Texas to the Pacific coast, most of the 1.3 million Hispanics who immigrated to the United States legally in this decade ended up in California. In the 1960s, "Hispanic" and "Latino" first became popular and interchangeable ethnic labels for those living in the United States who had Spanish ancestry, had immigrated from a Spanish-speaking country, or still identified culturally with their family's Latin American roots. The terms thus referred to those who had come from Mexico, Central or South America, or any of the Caribbean islands and who might be among any number of separately identifiable nationalities. Of these many various Hispanic subgroups, the largest was Mexican American, with a population of about six million. The term "Chicano" came into vogue in the 1960s as a self-description of Mexican Americans, who were primarily urban youth and more often than not lived in southern California. Previously, "Chicano" had been a derisive term translating into English roughly as "clumsy one," but the new generation of the 1960s adopted it and turned it into popular slang. Technically, the term referred (and still refers) only to American citizens, not to Mexican guest workers, and certainly not to illegal aliens.

There were in fact many Mexican guest workers—called "Braceros"—in the United States in 1960. From 1942, when the Bracero program started, to 1964, when it ended, about six million Braceros had worked in the United States at one time or another. In the early 1960s, there were approximately 500,000 imported in any given year. They generally earned less than $500 annually, even though they were supposedly paid minimum wage after 1962. In 1964, Chicano leaders were instrumental in getting the Johnson administration to end the Bracero program. They believed Braceros kept the wages of Chicanos artificially low. The unintended consequence of ending the program was that it encouraged illegal immigration because landowners could pay the "wetbacks," as illegal workers were called, wages even lower than those the Braceros had accepted.[46] At the beginning of the decade, Chicano families earned on average a mere 62 percent of what white families in the United States earned, and that statistic had changed little by the end of the decade. Suffering, therefore, from many of the same racial and economic problems as blacks, Chicanos, not surprisingly, caught the wave of the civil rights movement in the late 1960s, as had American Indians. This Chicano movement for equality under the law, which later expanded to include other Hispanic groups, became popularly known as *La Raza* (my people). It meant an affirmation of the Mexican cultural ancestry, pride in one's current Chicano identity, and the uplifting of the whole Hispanic ethnic population politically, economically, and socially.

The genesis of *La Raza* can be found in two separate and distinct Chicano rights groups that emerged almost concomitantly in different geographic locations. In 1962, in the agricultural mecca of California's San Joaquin Valley, Cesar Chavez formed the National Farm Workers Association (NFWA), later called the United Farm Workers Union, to win better wages, working conditions, and benefits for migrant workers, the vast majority of whom were Chicanos. Because the NFWA started before the Bracero program had ended, by 1965, after it had ended, the need for better wages became an even greater problem and more urgent need. Chavez and his fledgling union thus joined in a strike begun by Filipinos against the grape growers of central California. Failing to effect much positive change for the first three years, in 1968 he went on a hunger strike (*heulga de hambre*) to draw attention to the plight of the migrant workers. It worked, and it also drew the attention of the likes of Robert F. Kennedy and Martin Luther King, Jr., among other prominent figures. Chavez called his movement not *La Raza* but *La Causa* (the cause), because, by the late 1960s, the former had taken on implications of violent rebellion, and he was absolutely committed to nonviolent protest.

Meanwhile, in 1963, in New Mexico, Reies Lopez Tijerina organized the *Alianza Federal de Mercedes* (Federal Alliance of Land Grants), later called the *Alianza de los Pueblos Libres* (Alliance of Free City-States) for regaining American territory taken from Mexico in the Mexican War of 1846–1848. It was a movement for creating a separate Chicano nation in the southwest. In 1967, Tijerina and his guerrilla fighters seized control of Kit Carson National Forest, in northern New Mexico. When some of the fighters were arrested and taken to jail, others raided the courthouse in Tierra Amarilla to set them free. In the ensuing altercation, one deputy was killed, fear spread throughout the white community there, and Tijerina became a Chicano hero. Despite the use of what seemed to white observers to be terrorist tactics, Tijerina rejected the "Brown Power" movement that he inadvertently helped launch. Chicano and other Latino youth took up where Tijerina left off in violent militance. In New York City, for example, the Puerto Rican Young Lords, a street gang that evolved into a brown version of the Black Panthers, seized a church to draw attention to the need for a free breakfast program for inner-city children. Puerto Ricans in New York City and Chicago likewise engaged in shootouts with the police in the late 1960s, just like the Black Panthers. A "Brown Beret" group also arose in 1968 to mimic the Panthers. The Mexican American Youth Organization (MAYO), a nationwide organization, became perhaps the most visible of the Brown Power groups.

In Colorado, in 1965, Corky Gonzales, a boxer and writer, founded the Crusade for Justice to bring better housing, jobs, education, and living standards to Hispanics in the Denver area. He and his followers became increasingly militant in the late 1960s, and he became one of the foremost spokesmen for Chicano separatism and nationalism. Having previously tried working within the system as an integrationist, he gave up and began espousing separation, which was precisely the same path that so many Black Power advocates had followed. By the end of the decade, he had evolved into the very embodiment of *La Raza*.

One issue among many that *La Raza* advocates espoused was that of getting better educational opportunities, facilities, and fair treatment for Latinos in public schools. They advocated that Hispanic studies courses be taught in the public schools and colleges and that textbooks be revised to include minority viewpoints. Another specific problem could be found in the Anglo-centric bias against the Spanish language that was prevalent in southern California. The Los Angeles school system, from the school boards to administrators and teachers, looked unfavorably on students speaking Spanish on school property, not only in class but even during recess. In 1968, in Los Angeles, about 10,000 students staged a "blowout" (walk-out) of five public high schools in protest against this and various other racist practices.[47] When the adult leaders of the blowout were arrested, others laid siege to the Los Angeles School Board office, staging a sit-in. The blowout and sit-in drew attention to the need for reform, and changes certainly began to be seen as the 1960s gave way to the 1970s. One reform, the Bilingual Education Act, outlawed discrimination against Spanish-speaking students. Meanwhile, Hispanic inner-city schools still suffered from the same poor physical facilities as did African American schools, and they had much higher drop-out rates than white-majority schools. Fixing these problems would prove more difficult.

Politically, changes came faster for Hispanics than for any other minority group. In 1961, Henry Gonzales of Texas became the first Mexican American elected to Congress. Two years later, Juan Cornejo of Crystal City was elected the first Mexican American mayor in Texas. The following year, Joseph Montoya of New Mexico became the first Mexican American elected to the U.S. Senate. By 1966, awareness of Chicano issues had developed at the nation's capital to the extent that President Johnson formed the Cabinet Committee on Mexican American Affairs. In 1968, with support from the Ford Foundation, the Mexican American Legal Defense and Education Fund was created in imitation of the NAACP's similarly named group for African Americans. Also proving that change was happening not just politically but in terms of white social awareness of Hispanics, as well, in 1969 Romana Banuelos became the first Mexican American to win Outstanding Businesswoman of the Year. This did not mean that Hispanic issues would cease to be completely invisible to white lawmakers. In 1969, when Senator Joseph Montoya tried to extend the life of the president's Inter-Agency Committee on Mexican-American Affairs, the bill he introduced to that effect got misfiled in the Foreign Affairs committee's docket. Such problems led some Hispanics to form their own political party in 1969–1970, called La Raza Unida (the people united).

Despite all the attention that Chicanos garnered, two other Hispanic groups are worthy of mention individually, as well. Puerto Ricans made up the second largest Latino group in the United States in the 1960s, with a population of about 1.5 million. The vast majority of them settled in or around New York City. By the end of the decade, they accounted for fully 10 percent of that city's population, with about 800,000 people out of eight million. Unfortunately, many of them found that their economic prospects were no better, and in some cases even worse, in New York than they had been in Puerto Rico. Interestingly, therefore, Puerto Ricans became unique among all ethnic groups in American history in that, during the 1960s, more of them left the United States to return to their homeland than came here as immigrants.

The other group worth mentioning are the Cuban Americans. When Fidel Castro overthrew the American puppet government of Cuba in 1959, a mass exodus of Cubans to the United States occurred over the next three years. By 1962, there were about 250,000 of the supposedly temporary visitors in south Florida. Although some later migrated to other parts of the country, the majority of the Cuban immigrants stayed in the Miami area permanently. Nor did the exodus stop after 1962, although the Cuban missile crisis of October that year halted it for a while. To help deal with the flood of Cuban immigrants that arrived on the shores of Florida daily, the Kennedy administration created the Cuban

Refugee Program under the aegis of the Department of Health, Education, and Welfare. Likewise, the Roman Catholic Church, which had only recently created the Diocese of Miami, helped the Cuban refugees through various charitable programs.

ASIAN AMERICANS AND OTHERS

Because of laws passed in the late 1800s and early 1900s that banned Asian immigration, in 1960 only about 900,000 people of Asian descent lived in the United States. During the decade, approximately 445,000 more immigrated here, accounting for barely more than 10 percent of the total immigration, and this figure includes Middle Easterners as well as Far Easterners. So diverse are the nationalities and ethnic groups that make up "Asian" Americans that it is difficult to generalize about them. Yet, there were so few of them collectively within the overall population of the United States that generalizations are necessary.

Although President Kennedy and Congress allowed 14,000 Chinese refugees into the country in 1961, not until the 1965 Immigration and Naturalization Act liberalized national policy did the number of Asian Americans begin to increase dramatically. The new law was phased in over three years, and not until 1968 did it fully take effect. It divided the world into eastern and western hemispheres. The eastern hemisphere countries got a quota of 170,000 visas per year, while the western hemisphere countries got only 120,000 per year. Within those broad parameters, each Asian country got a quota of 20,000 visas annually. The number could actually go much higher, however, because of certain factors, such as the possession of prized occupational skills, the presence of family members in the United States, and the occurrence of religious or political persecution in the home country. As a result, by 1970 the proportion of Asians immigrating had risen to more than one-quarter of the total of all immigrants.

Throughout the 1960s, Asian Americans were basically invisible in the mainstream of American society. Partly this happened because some ethnic groups tended to stick together in pockets rather than disperse and assimilate into the larger culture. Forty percent of all Filipino immigrants settled in California, for instance, and 35 percent of Chinese did. "Chinatowns" existed in San Francisco, Manhattan, and a few other places, and enclaves of various Asian groups—Koreans and Indians, for example—could be found scattered mainly in big metropolitan areas, such as in California and New York. Partly, too, they remained invisible because, unlike the other minority groups already mentioned, Asian Americans did not participate in the civil rights movement to any notable degree. Although there was plenty of poverty among Asian Americans, they did not suffer as a whole from quite the same level of economic disparity with whites as other minority groups did. Keeping in mind that generalizations are difficult, Asian American children tended to perform better in public schools, got admitted to prestigious colleges and universities at a much higher rate, and had more success in the business world thereafter than any other ethnic group. This was particularly true of Japanese and South Koreans. The exception was Filipinos, who came from such a heterogeneous background on their south Pacific island nation that they might speak any of several tribal languages and thus could barely assimilate with each other much less thrive in corporate America. Hence, many Filipinos became migrant farm workers in central California, some of whom allowed Cesar Chavez and the NFWA to unite with them on a strike in 1965.

Of the various notable Asian nationalities, China sent the largest number of immigrants to America in the 1960s, followed by the Philippines, Japan, Korea, and India. Vietnam did not even make the list. Few Americans could have readily found Vietnam on a globe prior to military escalation there in 1965, and virtually no Vietnamese or other Indo-Chinese people lived in the United States before that. During the war, a few hundred Vietnamese began to trickle in each year in the late 1960s. Not until the late 1970s, however, did the American floodgates open for them. Other Asians, including Middle Easterners, generally came in such small numbers as to be negligible within the overall population.

LAW AND GOVERNMENT

During the 1960s, more important developments that affected American race relations came out of Washington, D.C., than at any other time in the nation's history. They can be categorized in six ways: constitutional amendments, civil rights legislation, executive orders, federal agencies and programs, election and appointment of minorities, and court rulings.

CONSTITUTIONAL AMENDMENTS

The Twenty-third Amendment, adopted in 1961, gave Washington, D.C., the right to cast electoral college votes in presidential elections equal in number to that of the least populous state. Since the nation's capital had a large minority population, the thought was that it would increase black voting strength and give minorities generally a greater say-so in electing the president. The Twenty-fourth Amendment, adopted in 1964, outlawed poll taxes as a voting requirement in federal elections. Again, this measure was designed primarily to help enfranchise black southerners who could not afford to pay the tax and to send minorities in general the message that the federal government was interested in protecting their right to vote.

FEDERAL LEGISLATION

The first law Congress enacted in the 1960s to reform American race relations was the Civil Rights Act of 1960, which passed despite the longest continuous filibuster in Senate history. President Eisenhower signed it on May 6. It made interference with any federal court order involving desegregation of public schools a specially punishable crime. It also dealt with black voting rights by authorizing federal judges to appoint disinterested referees to mediate disputes between would-be voters and state or local election officials. Although the law was a step in the right direction for civil rights proponents, it left much to be desired.

Four years later, the Johnson administration and the Eighty-sixth Congress followed with the single most significant civil rights law ever passed, the Civil Rights Act of 1964. Signed on July 2, it dealt with all of the various issues that had surfaced during the movement up to that point through sit-ins, voter registration drives, and racial hate crimes. It outlawed racial discrimination in all government-owned facilities, such as schools, parks, libraries, and recreation areas. It also outlawed racial discrimination in privately owned facilities that were deemed indispensable for accommodating the public, such as establishments that sold food, lodging, and gasoline. It also exempted all potential voters with a sixth-grade education or higher from taking state literacy tests as a qualification for voting. Just as important, it set up enforcement mechanisms through the Justice Department. Specifically, it authorized the U.S. attorney general to sue state and local government agencies that discriminated on the basis of race. It led to many important federal court rulings that ultimately were responsible for making true racial reform happen.

Although the Civil Rights Acts of 1960 and 1964 both dealt with minority voting rights, President Johnson and Congress still found it necessary to pass the Voting Rights Act of 1965 because of the dust-up with the MFDP at the Democratic National Convention in Atlantic City in 1964. Signed on August 6, the new law authorized the Civil Service Commission to appoint disinterested federal registrars to register minorities in counties where there had been recent complaints of racial discrimination. It, and the court cases that arose immediately because of it, led to a dramatic turnaround in the southern states that were the most egregious offenders against black voting rights. Mississippi, for instance, saw a tenfold increase in the number of black voters between the 1964 election and the 1968 election.

The last piece of major racial reform legislation to come out of the Johnson years was the Civil Rights Act of 1968, signed on April 11. Its most important provision outlawed discrimination in housing, including the selling, renting, or financing of a home. Contained in Title VIII, also called the Fair Housing Act, this attempt to desegregate the residential districts of cities and towns all across America met with violent opposition from some whites. It also caused the white flight to the suburbs that had been under way for years to increase, and it created new racial problems that the Nixon administration would have to deal with in the coming years.

EXECUTIVE ORDERS

Supplementing these civil rights laws were a series of executive orders, beginning with President Kennedy's EO 10925. Signed on March 6, 1961, it created the Equal Employment Opportunity Commission (EEOC) and introduced the concept of "affirmative action" in government hiring. It dealt specifically with companies that received federal contracts, requiring them to demonstrate to the satisfaction of the EEOC a good-faith effort to increase the number of minorities on their payrolls. It also empowered the attorney general to sue companies that did not comply. Kennedy followed it up with EO 11063, on November 20, 1962, which outlawed racial discrimination in government housing, and EO 11114, on June 22, 1963, which extended the EEOC's affirmative action program specifically to unionized construction companies building government projects.

President Johnson did not issue as many executive orders affecting race relations, perhaps because he did not need to, thanks to the success of his legislative agenda. On September 24, 1965, however, he did issue EO 11246, setting up the machinery for enforcing the Civil Rights Act of 1964. Likewise, President Nixon did not issue many executive orders involving civil rights, perhaps because he favored a more conservative approach on many racial matters. On August 8, 1969, however, he did issue EO 11478, extending the EEOC's affirmative action program to all federal government agencies—a major step forward for a president noted for his opposition to certain other civil rights reforms.

FEDERAL AGENCIES AND PROGRAMS

As far as setting up federal programs goes, President Kennedy took the initiative almost immediately after stepping into office. On February 2, 1961, he started the distribution of Food Stamps to the needy. Placed under the Department of Agriculture, the Food Stamp program was not aimed specifically at helping minorities, but, considering the disproportionate rate of poverty among minorities, it always helped a greater percentage of them than whites. Whether Kennedy would have done more if he had been given more time is unclear. As it was, his successor Lyndon Johnson singlehandedly did more to try to improve life for minorities than any other president in history. After authorizing the continuation of the Food Stamp program, Johnson turned his attention to helping the poor get the skills necessary to avoid needing federal welfare. Through the Economic Opportunity Act of 1964, signed on August 20, he created the Job Corps, which provided free vocational and academic training to disadvantaged teens and young adults to help them be successful in the workforce. At the same time, he created VISTA (Volunteers in Service to America) to be a partner agency with the Job Corps. It allowed talented and conscientious Americans who possessed skills and leadership abilities to share in training the less fortunate. It was often called a domestic version of the Peace Corps. In 1965, Johnson followed with two more education initiatives. Project Head Start was designed to provide disadvantaged preschool children with government day care, health care, food, and kindergarten education. Upward Bound, meanwhile, was designed to target disadvantaged high school students and help guide them to college or to successful careers in the workforce.

All of these programs fell under the umbrella of Johnson's Great Society agenda, and specifically his "War on Poverty." Along with Johnson's introduction of Medicare and Medicaid, federally subsidized student loans, and increases in the minimum wage and social security benefits, these programs had the noblest of intentions, and all potentially benefited minorities disproportionately. They also had unintended consequences, including an explosive growth of the federal budget, major increases in the size of the federal bureaucracy, and greater federal intrusiveness into the lives of private citizens, among others. They did not constitute the whole of Johnson's racial reform agenda, however. Additionally, the Elementary and Secondary Education Act of 1965 sought to improve standards in low-performing public schools, most of which were in districts where racial minorities constituted the majority of the student populations. Likewise, the Bilingual Education Act of 1968 was designed specifically to help Hispanic students with limited English language skills make the grade. The Immigration and Naturalization Services Act of 1965, meanwhile, made the United States an inviting place for even more minority groups.

Finally, Johnson created the Model Cities program in 1966 to try to improve life in the ghettos where race rioting was so prevalent. His administration devised the initial "Philadelphia Plan," using the fourth largest city in the United States as a testing area to try to make a "Model City" through government construction projects under the affirmative action program. Quite complex and controversial, the plan had to be shelved in 1968 because of opposition to unreasonable racial "quotas" in hiring. It remained for the Nixon administration to repackage or reject the Philadelphia Plan, and it chose the former. In 1969, the plan was reworded to say that construction companies did not have to show a *higher number* of minorities hired, just a *percentage* that was compatible with the overall ratio of minorities-to-whites in the area. This time the plan held up to scrutiny and continued into the early 1970s. President Nixon's final contribution to reforming the racial landscape in the 1960s was to create the Office of Minority Business Enterprise. Signed on March 5, 1969, this act offered federal grants and low-interest loans to minority entrepreneurs who applied for venture capital to start up new businesses.

ELECTION AND APPOINTMENT OF MINORITIES

Among the appointments of minorities to powerful government positions in the 1960s, none was more high profile or important than that of Thurgood Marshall to the Supreme Court, in 1967, by President Johnson. President Kennedy had previously appointed him the first African American federal judge, in 1961. Marshall had earned these honors through his groundbreaking efforts heading the NAACP's Legal Defense and Education Fund team, which won the *Brown v. Board of Education* case in 1954. Not quite as prominent, but still important, was Johnson's appointment of the first African American to a cabinet position, Robert C. Weaver, Secretary of Housing and Urban Development, in 1966. Several blacks made history in the 1960s through election to high office. Among them were Edward Brooke of Massachusetts, who in 1966 became the first African American elected to the U.S. Senate since Reconstruction. The following year, Carl Stokes of Cleveland and Richard Hatcher of Gary, Indiana, became the first black mayors of American cities, and in 1968 Shirley Chisholm of New York became the first black woman ever elected to Congress. Many other blacks were elected to southern state legislatures and local government offices or appointed to lower-level federal positions in the late 1960s. Nor were blacks the only minority group so represented. Hispanics also made inroads into the federal government. Henry Gonzales from Texas became the first Hispanic congressman, in 1961, and Joseph Montoya of New Mexico became the first Hispanic U.S. senator, in 1964.

COURT RULINGS

The final aspect of federal government involvement in racial reform in the 1960s can be found in the courts. Literally hundreds of federal cases resulted from the various aspects of the civil rights movement. Dozens of them resulted in Supreme Court rulings and/or lower circuit court rulings that together rearranged the social and political landscape of the United States. Although the overwhelming majority of them involved African American litigants, most came eventually to apply across the board to every minority group. These cases, too numerous to discuss in detail, can be broadly categorized in three ways: desegregation suits, voting rights suits, and miscellaneous others. Within each category are multiple subcategories.

Within the first category, school desegregation problems resulting from the 1954 *Brown v. Board of Education* decision continued to produce spinoff cases throughout the 1960s. In 1961, in *United States v. Louisiana*, the Court reinforced the Brown ruling, specifically in light of efforts in the New Orleans area to stop it. Two years later, in a case arising in Tennessee, *Goss v. Knoxville Board of Education*, the Court said that white students could not change schools to avoid becoming minorities in their current school. In 1964, the Court ruled, in *Griffin v. County School Board of Prince Edward County*, that the state of Virginia could not keep a public school closed in order to prevent its integration, while its *Calhoun v. Latimer* ruling called for more deliberate speed in integrating schools in the Atlanta area. Four years later, in *Green v. County School Board*, the Court disallowed the practice of allowing students in Virginia to choose the public school they wished to attend.

In 1969, the ruling in *Alexander v. Holmes County Board of Education* effectively put an end to all stalling tactics that Mississippi had attempted since 1954 and required that it integrate its public schools immediately. This case served as the opposite bookend to the *Brown* case nationwide, in that one started the integration of public schools and the other finished it. Finally, in the same year, the ruling in *United States v. Montgomery County School Board* required public schools in Alabama to make a good-faith effort through affirmative action to increase the proportion of minority teachers so that it reflected the racial makeup of each school district.

On the issue of desegregation of public accommodations and facilities, the *Boynton v. Virginia* ruling of 1960 required integration of interstate transportation carriers, such as buses, trains, and planes. This case led to the Freedom Rides of 1961. Once the sit-ins started, in 1960, many suits were brought by both proponents and opponents of integration that challenged the other's point of view. In 1961, in *Burton v. Wilmington Parking Authority*, the Court ruled that a privately owned restaurant located on the grounds of a public parking garage in North Carolina could not refuse to serve customers on the basis of their race. In the same year, in *Garner v. Louisiana*, the Court held that peaceful sit-ins did not disturb the peace and thus could not be considered illegal. The following year, in *Bailey v. Patterson* and *Turner v. Memphis*, the Court ruled that public transportation terminals and the various businesses located within them in Jackson and Memphis could not refuse to serve customers on the basis of their race. In 1963, several rulings came down that effectively upheld the rights of those engaged in sit-ins or other direct-action protests: *Peterson v. Greenville* in South Carolina, *Lombard v. Louisiana* in New Orleans, *Johnson v. Virginia* in Richmond, *Wright v. Georgia* in Savannah, and *Watson v. Memphis* in Tennessee. The next year brought *Heart of Atlanta Motel v. United States* from Georgia and *Katzenbach v. McClung* from Alabama, which required integration of lodging and eating establishments. In 1966, the Court ruled, in *Evans v. Newton*, that a public park in Macon, Georgia, could not deny black patrons access on the basis that the land had been donated to the city by a deceased white man who bequeathed it with the understanding that it be used for whites only. The ruling in *Brown v. Louisiana* in the same year said that the public library in the town of Clinton could not segregate its patrons on the basis of race. The next year brought *Reitman v. Mulkey*, in which the Supreme Court overturned a California law that gave sellers of real estate sole discretion in deciding to whom they would sell. In 1968, in *Jones v. Mayer*, the Court upheld the Fair Housing Act's prohibition against racial discrimination in housing. Finally, in the following year, in *Daniel v. Paul*, the Court outlawed racial discrimination in private-club memberships, and in *Hunter v. Erikson* it said federal housing laws could not be circumvented by local referendums designed to keep minorities out of communities or neighborhoods.

On voting rights, the 1961 *Gomillion v. Lightfoot* ruling said a municipality could not redraw its city limits in order to exclude blacks from voting in city elections. Three years later, the Court ruled, in *Anderson v. Martin*, that a Louisiana law requiring a candidate's race to be stated on the ballot was unconstitutional. In 1965, in *Harman v. Forssenius*, the Court held that states could not substitute other discriminatory voting requirements for the recently outlawed poll tax, while in *Louisiana v. United States* it ruled that requiring voters to pass an understanding clause test was unconstitutional. The next year, the Court decided, in *Harper v. Virginia State Board of Elections*, that no alternate type of poll tax could be used, while in *Katzenbach v. Morgan* it ruled that voters did not have to be able to read or speak English in order to qualify to vote. This case resulted in thousands of Puerto Ricans in New York City getting the franchise immediately.

Among the many miscellaneous other rulings affecting American race relation in the 1960s, one of the most important was *Hamm v. Rock Hill*, in 1964, in which some 3,000 separate pending suits involving sit-ins were uniformly dismissed because they all concerned substantially the same thing—peaceful and quiet protest against segregation in public facilities. The Court said all such protests were legal and that suits brought against participants in those protests must be dropped. Two cases arising in Mississippi in 1965 and 1966 in the wake of the infamous murders in Philadelphia—*United States v. Mississippi* and *United States v. Price*—resulted in rulings that gave the Justice Department the power to sue state and local government officials for willful failure to protect the civil rights of people under their jurisdiction. Perhaps the most revolutionary ruling of all came in 1967 in *Loving v. Virginia*, when the Court overturned a state law prohibiting interracial marriage. Not all rulings were favorable to civil rights advocates, however. *Cox v. Louisiana*, in 1965, and *Adderly v. Florida*, in 1967, both placed limitations on civil rights demonstrations, distinguishing between those that disturbed the peace or otherwise disrupted the flow of orderly business and those that did not.

MEDIA AND MASS COMMUNICATIONS

The civil rights movement and television were inextricably linked. How much so, or to what extent, is the question. The answer is undoubtedly more than most people would think. At the time the movement began, in the mid-1950s, television was in its infancy. Many cities had only one TV station, affiliated with one of the three big networks: NBC, ABC, or CBS. For residents, newspapers and radio were still the news media of necessity, if not of choice. Some cities had two TV affiliates, but only the largest cities had all three. Within a decade, by the mid-1960s, most states had at least one city large enough to carry all three. Interestingly, color television began to replace black-and-white ones in the mid-'60s, just as the civil rights movement was kicking into high gear, making skin color more of a factor that ever before for the cameras.

Because of the competitiveness of the news business, sensationalism had been a problem long before television came along. In the 1890s, for instance, yellow-press journalism (the deliberate reporting of half-truths and lies) from the two most respected newspapers in New York contributed to the United States' going to war with Spain. In the 1950s, when the civil rights movement began, such tabloid journalism generally was not to be found among the major TV news media. By the 1960s, however, there was no doubt that covering racial disturbances would improve ratings, and the more sensational the stories covered, the higher the ratings a network could expect. The venerable CBS reporter Howard K. Smith lamented the fact that the cameras loved negative news, because positive news tended to be boring. The nonviolent protests of the early 1960s were interesting enough, but when the Black Power movement came along, the cameras naturally gravitated in that direction. Violence and militancy were clearly more sensational and tantalizing to viewers than were peaceful demonstrations. This partly accounts for the demise of Martin Luther King, Jr., as the leading spokesman for the civil rights movement—he was old news by 1966, and he was boring in comparison with the Black Panthers.

The Black newspaper columnist William Raspberry complained that the problem with news coverage of such black extremism was that flamboyant activists such as Stokely Carmichael, Eldridge Cleaver, and Rap Brown did not represent the attitudes and opinions of the vast majority of African Americans. Whitney Young of the National Urban League likewise berated the media for covering only the *bad* news. His organization, which did not engage in violent demonstrations or use revolutionary rhetoric, could not get any meaningful press coverage in the late 1960s. Mayor Richard Daley of Chicago even speculated that, other than the Watts riot of 1965, which was truly spontaneous, the race riots that followed from 1966 through 1968 were all created by television. In other words, if there had been no TV coverage, there would have been no riots. While such an assertion contains more than a grain of truth, it is not altogether accurate. The Detroit riot of 1967 dragged on for days despite the best efforts of authorities in Michigan to suppress news coverage of it.

Television reporting undoubtedly increased, inflamed, and dramatized the riots of the late 1960s. In the most egregious cases, when the actual news stories were not sensational enough on their own, TV reporters deliberately tried to aggravate the situation to make it more newsworthy. In 1967, for example, in Cambridge, Maryland, a town where racial violence had previously flared up in 1963, black demonstrators conferred with TV news producers to find the optimal time to stage their next protest to get maximum TV exposure. Then TV reporters presented their coverage to the unwitting public as that of a spontaneous event.

Sensationalism was not the only abuse inflicted on the American public by TV reporters. An equally disturbing problem was that of using TV coverage to promote a given sociopolitical agenda. Ever since Orson Welles's *War of the Worlds,* broadcast in 1938, demonstrated the influence that a radio program could have over human behavior, the potential for using the mass media to promote sociopolitical agendas was just waiting to be tapped. Television could tap the potential even better than radio. In 1963, President Kennedy invited an ABC TV crew to make a special documentary about the desegregation of the

University of Alabama, an event he staged with the cooperation of Governor Wallace. The result was the program "Crisis: Behind a Presidential Commitment," which aired October 21, 1963, four months after the event. Kennedy hoped the program would increase support for his civil rights agenda by showing the contrast between his liberal humanitarianism and egalitarianism and Wallace's conservative racism and segregationism. In 1967, the Ford Foundation, which promoted liberal social causes, funded the Public Broadcast Laboratory's first-ever program, "Day of Absence." The show was about a southern town where all the black residents just left. The whites were dismayed to discover that the town could not function without blacks, because they possessed valuable skills and often performed different jobs than whites. The obvious message was that whites should appreciate and value African Americans and their contributions to the welfare of the nation.

Television was the medium that had by far the greatest opportunity to manipulate popular perception of racial issues in the 1960s. Movies did not catch up, nor did literature, until the 1970s. These and other media tended to respond to changes already under way rather than help create them.

Cultural Scene

American culture and society changed as dramatically in the 1960s as in any other decade in the nation's history. This was largely a result of the infusion of baby boomers into the colleges, the workforce, and the military. They brought a youthful restlessness into the decade that simply could not be satisfied with the bland, placid lifestyle of the 1950s. They wanted action, energy, movement, and change. Sometimes there were legitimate reasons for their desires, but other times they seem to have wanted something new merely for the sake of having something new. Virtually no aspect of American culture or society went untouched by this rebellious mentality. It affected fashion, literature, music, art, film, television, and sports, among other weightier things, such as religion, the civil rights movement, the Vietnam War, and America's Cold War ideology.

SPORTS

Essentially, the major thrust of change in the early 1960s was toward integration of African Americans into previously all-white or nearly all-white venues. Change came faster in some venues, such as sports, than it did in others, such as television. In athletic competitions, blacks had already made many inroads in earlier decades, so continuation and increase were the keys in the '60s. Most whites, except for the most hardened racists, appreciated seeing the best athletes in any given arena, regardless of their race. In the professional sports of boxing and basketball, blacks had already shown a great propensity for dominance, but they solidified their hold on both through the exploits of Cassius Clay (later Muhammad Ali) in the ring and Wilt Chamberlain on the basketball court, among many others. As a player for the Boston Celtics from 1960 to 1966, Bill Russell helped turn that franchise into a basketball dynasty, and in 1967 he became the first black coach in any integrated professional American sport, whereupon he continued to lead the Celtics to championships. In other professional sports, such as baseball and football, blacks as a whole had not yet been given full opportunity to prove their dominance, but the potential was clearly there. Jackie Robinson, the first black player to integrate major league baseball (which he did in the 1940s), also became the first African American inducted into the major league Hall of Fame in 1962. Players such as Frank Robinson, who won baseball's triple crown and the American League Most Valuable Player Award in 1966, and Jim Brown, who ran over would-be tacklers in the National Football League as nobody had ever done and seized the all-time rushing title by the end of the decade, merely offered a glimpse of what was to come in those sports going into

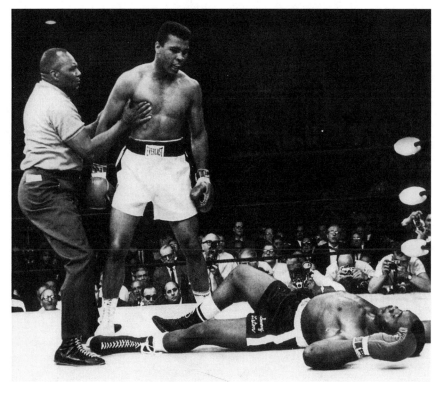

Muhammad Ali (a.k.a. Cassius Clay) decks Sonny Liston in the first round of their 1965 rematch to retain his title as heavyweight champion of the world. Courtesy of Photofest.

the 1970s. Even the perceived country-club sport of professional tennis did not go untouched by integration, as Arthur Ashe in 1968 became the first black to win the U.S. Open Championship. Nor were blacks the only minorities to make their athletic talents known in the 1960s. In 1968 Lee Trevino became the first Hispanic to win a major professional golfing title when he won the U.S. Open tournament.

Amateur (collegiate and Olympic) sports likewise became fertile ground where black athletes could display their physical prowess in the 1960s. Thanks to them, the United States routinely won medals—too many to list—in track and field events and in boxing, among other sports. Some of those who became famous for their Olympic exploits include Wilma Rudolph, a runner who won the 1962 Zaharias Award for best female athlete in the world; Cassius Clay (Muhammad Ali), Joe Frazier, and George Foreman, who won heavyweight boxing gold medals in 1960, 1964, and 1968 respectively; and Ralph Boston and Bob Beamon, world record holders in the long jump.

Extending gloved hands skyward in racial protest, U.S. athletes Tommie Smith, center, and John Carlos stare downward during the playing of the Star Spangled Banner after Smith received the gold and Carlos the bronze for the 200 meter run at the Summer Olympic Games in Mexico City on October 16, 1968. Australian silver medalist Peter Norman is at left. AP Photo/FILE.

In collegiate sports, Ernie Davis in 1961 became the first of many black football stars to win the Heisman Trophy for best all-around player. A string of talented black basketball players helped the UCLA Bruins build a dynasty in the 1960s, but perhaps none was more important than Lew Alcindor (later Kareem Abdul-Jabbar), who would eventually become the all-time scoring leader in the National Basketball Association in the 1980s.

Several important sporting news events transcended the world of athletics and crossed over into politics in the 1960s. In 1966, Ruben "Hurricane" Carter, a black professional boxer, was arrested in New Jersey for murder. A year later, an all-white jury convicted him on testimony provided by an ex-con who was copping a deal with prosecutors to save his own skin. This apparent miscarriage of justice was symptomatic of how the American legal system often dealt with physically imposing black men accused of a crime. The case went largely unnoticed by mainstream America for nearly a decade before the singer Bob Dylan and others began drawing attention to it. Meanwhile, in 1967, an even more sensational news story broke involving Muhammad Ali. When Ali, the heavyweight champion of the world, was drafted by the U.S. Army to go to Vietnam, he refused to serve. As a recent convert to the Muslim religion, Ali claimed that he was a conscientious objector. The court disagreed, fined him, and sentenced him to prison for five years. He did not actually serve time but was barred from boxing for three years. He won both an appeal in court and a championship bout against Joe Frazier in 1971. Perhaps even more scandalous was Tommie Smith and John Carlos's conduct at the 1968 Olympic games track and field medal ceremony. They wore black socks, with no shoes, and one black glove, which they raised high on fisted hand as they bowed their heads during the playing of the "Star Spangled Banner." They claimed to be making a statement in favor of "Black Power," but the Olympic rules committee could not appreciate it, and both men were barred from further competition.

MUSIC

After sports, the next most integrated venue of the 1960s was music. Why this was so depended largely on three factors—the musical taste of the individual who controlled his or her own radio dial, the fact that there were so many stations for listeners to choose from, and the quality and novelty of innovative new styles, composers, and performers. In the field of classical and opera, Marian Anderson had been world-renowned for 30 years when the black vocalist gave her farewell performance at Carnegie Hall, in New York City, in 1965. Waiting to take her place was her protégé, Leontyne Price, who had already sung at the New York Metropolitan Opera in 1961. In 1968, Henry Lewis became the first black conductor of a major symphonic orchestra, the New Jersey Symphony. In jazz and easy-listening music, blacks had long been staples, having pioneered those artistic forms decades earlier. The pianist Duke Ellington continued to perform at the top of his game into the late 1960s, starring as the feature attraction in three television programs in 1967 alone. Two years later, President Nixon honored him with the White House Medal of Freedom for his illustrious career and exemplary citizenship. Ellington's contemporary, the trumpeter, vocalist, and songwriter Louis Armstrong, likewise continued to score hits with racially mixed audiences right up to his death, with "Hello, Dolly!" and "What a Wonderful World."

Other black artists to make big impressions on white audiences by singing "white"-style music were the blind pianist Ray Charles and the country singer Charley Pride. Although Ray Charles already enjoyed success as a traditional rhythm and blues artist, in 1962 and 1963 he crossed over with *Modern Sounds in Country & Western Music*, volumes I and II. His "modern country" still sounded like rhythm and blues, but the semifalse labeling grabbed a huge white audience that would not have latched on to "black" music so readily. Stranger still, perhaps, Charley Pride became a legitimate singer of white-sounding country music and was such a hit that he headlined at the Grand Ole Opry in Nashville in 1967.

These types of racial crossovers in music were not new, of course. Rock and roll in the 1950s had been nothing more than white artists performing black music, and in the early 1960s the Beatles became the most commercially successful group of all time with songs that mimicked black American rhythm and blues, only with an unmistakable British accent, on their first few albums. Elvis Presley continued to churn out soulful rhythm and blues–sounding hits in the '60s just as

Jimi Hendrix playing at Woodstock, 1969. Courtesy of Photofest.

he had in the '50s. Although race-mixing in making music was not new, it still had to be handled delicately by white performers and promoters. Consider the case of "The Twist," a dance song originally recorded by the black group the Sensational Nightingales, which first scored a hit in 1960. The white television disc jockey Dick Clark, who hosted *American Bandstand* on Saturday mornings and the *Dick Clark Show* in prime time, would not allow the Nightingales to perform the song because they were too sexually sensual in their stage presence. He wanted the song on his show, however, so he arranged for a more wholesome-looking black artist, Chubby Checker, to perform it. Thanks to this performance, both "The Twist" and Checker became mainstream American household names.

Far more common, however, were black artists who made no pretenses of trying to sound or look white. They just performed their own style and hoped whites would buy into it. By the mid- to late 1960s, they were not disappointed. Motown Records, a black-owned company out of Detroit that featured Little Stevie Wonder, the Supremes, the Four Tops, Smokey Robinson and the Miracles, and a dozen other equally legendary artists, was the biggest producer of "soul" music in the decade. A dozen more black artists, including James Brown, Otis Redding, Aretha Franklin, and Wilson Pickett, scored huge commercial successes by signing with conventional white-owned labels while performing soul music. All owed their tremendous sales to the white listening public, who cared less and less about the color of the artist and more and more about the quality of the music each year that went by. Many of their songs have since become icons of American music, as recognizable to the average person on the street as the national anthem. The ultimate indication that black music had now been fully embraced by mainstream America came in 1967 when the Fifth Dimension, a black pop group, won the Record of the Year Grammy for "Up, Up and Away." Two years later, they won again for "Aquarius/Let the Sunshine In."

Other interesting musical developments included the growing popularity of the Latin style. Going back to the '50s with Desi Arnaz and Ritchie Valens, American audiences began embracing Latin music. In 1963, the bossa nova–flavored "The Girl from Ipanema" by Stan Getz and Astrid Gilberto became a number one hit. Shortly thereafter, Herb Alpert and the Tijuana Brass began an extremely successful career playing, oddly enough, instrumentals. Highlighted by a Record of the Year Grammy for "A Taste of Honey," this southern California group, which had its own record label, A & M, sold more records in 1966 than any other artist in the world, even outselling the Beatles by a two-to-one margin.

Perhaps the most notable change that music brought about in American culture in the 1960s was not merely the growing acceptance of integrated bands but the fashionableness of it. By 1968, three of the top rock groups in the United States had black front men with white or partially white supporting casts—the Jimi Hendrix Experience, which won the Billboard Artist of the Year Award, Sly and the Family Stone, and the Buddy Miles Express. At the same time, a white blues diva from Texas named Janis Joplin became the most electrifying individual performer since the debut of Elvis Presley more than a decade earlier by sounding even more soulful and sensual than most African American singers. The year 1969 brought even more integrated and crossover performers to prominence, including the Allman Brothers Band, from Georgia, and Three Dog Night, from California. This final year of the '60s arguably marked the zenith of rock music because of the immortal three-day Woodstock festival of August 15–18, near Bethel, New York. Although the audience and the performers were predominantly white, a spirit of racial integration and harmony pervaded the event.

MOVIES

The motion picture industry integrated at a slower pace than music but still managed to push the boundaries of acceptability with regard to racial issues. As with music, this occurred largely because individual ticket buyers could choose the movies they wished to see. The historic theme of a southern white woman falsely accusing a noble black man of assaulting her, thus turning white townsmen into a lynch mob, became the basis for the 1962 thriller *To Kill a Mockingbird*, whose message was that racial moderation is more likely to result in justice being served than is a knee-jerk reaction. A year later, Sidney Poitier became the first African American to win the Best Actor Oscar for his role in *Lilies of the Field*, showing that Hollywood was now open to accepting blacks as equals. By far the most provocative racial theme in film in this decade came in 1967 in *Guess Who's Coming to Dinner?* about an interracial relationship between a white girl and a black man, which, not surprisingly, creates strife in the couple's families.

TELEVISION

Change came slower in television than in any other medium, perhaps because viewers had different channels from which to choose. Advertisers could not afford to risk sponsoring a controversial program that might offend viewers, thus provoking them into changing the channel or turning off the set. Consequently, not until 1965 did the first African American get a starring role in a television series—Bill Cosby in *I Spy*. In both television and movies, Hispanics and American Indians were, by contrast, heavily portrayed in "Westerns," although often in negative stereotypes and in roles subordinate to those of white stars. Not until the 1970s did these patterns change noticeably.

LITERATURE

The development of African American literature largely paralleled the issues and tactics of the civil rights movement, going from conciliatory integrationist rhetoric to the militant Black Power philosophy as the 1960s progressed. Among the serious nonfiction publications of the decade, James Baldwin's *The Fire Next Time* (1963) was perhaps the most poignant. It essentially warned in advance that the nonviolent strategy might soon be abandoned in favor of a more confrontational style of protest if blacks did not begin to see racial reform in the near future. How right he was. Within two years, a young black journalist named Alex Haley had begun to make a reality the transition that Baldwin envisioned by publishing *The Autobiography of Malcolm X*. Published just after the assassination, the book offered the clearest view into the mind of the revolutionary Black Muslim yet seen, capturing the attention of whites and kindling a fire in the minds of young African Americans. Although Martin Luther King, Jr., continued to publish commercially successful books (*Why We Can't Wait*, in 1964, and *Where Do We Go from Here*, in 1967), his writings, like his nonviolent strategy, seemed to pale in comparison with the more militant or shocking nonfiction works coming out in the mid- and late 1960s. Besides, his basic ideology was and is summed up concisely in his "Letter from Birmingham Jail" and his "I Have a Dream" speech in 1963, making his books somewhat redundant.

Firsthand accounts of the civil rights movement and other memoirs made important literary contributions in the 1960s. James Meredith wrote of his experiences integrating Ole Miss in 1962 in his *Three Years in Mississippi* (1966), although one of his professors and acquaintances there, James Silver, preceded him by two years in writing about the event in *Mississippi: The Closed Society*. Anne Moody gave us one of the most moving memoirs of what it was like growing up in the Deep South before and during the civil rights years in her *Coming of Age in Mississippi* (1968), which won the American Library Association Book of the Year Award. Eldridge Cleaver, meanwhile, wrote his best-seller *Soul on Ice* in prison and published it shortly after returning to society in 1967. Its shock value, derived from its discussion of black masculinity and sexually taboo subjects, was unrivaled to that point in time.

What came to be known as the "Black Rage" genre of literature also became prevalent in and after 1967. Stokely Carmichael and Charles V. Hamilton sought to define and explain the Black Power philosophy with a book of that name. Although they tried in the book to tone down the militance that others saw in the term, most other Black Power advocates did not accept it. Instead, they revved up the rhetoric ever more with books like *Black Fire* (1968), by LeRoi Jones and Larry Neal; *Black Rage* (1968), by William M. Grier and Price M. Cobb; *Look Out Whitey! Black Power's Gon' Get Your Mama!* (1969), by Julius Lester; and *Die! Nigger, Die!* (1969), by H. Rap Brown.

Not all black literature was so politically weighty, however. Black historians and social scientists had long written quality works, but they began to be more accepted in the mainstream of their fields in the 1960s, thanks to the civil rights movement. John Hope Franklin, E. Franklin Frazier, Benjamin Quarles, and Louis Lomax are just a few of the many who fit this category. Likewise, dozens of white counterparts began to explore the black experience historically, generating an even greater acceptance in the mainstream. August Meier and Elliott Rudwick, Howard Zinn, Leon Litwack, and David Brion Davis are just a few of them. The 1960s brought a few important works of fiction, such as the black poet Gwendolyn Brook's award-winning children's book *The Bean Eaters*, in 1960 and the black playwright Lorraine Hansberry's Broadway play-turned-motion picture, *A Raisin in the Sun*, in 1961. The venerable poet and fiction writer Langston Hughes also continued to publish right up to his death in 1967.

Besides African Americans, no other minority group really enjoyed much literary success in winning over white audiences in the 1960s. Most of their works tended to be ethnic in nature and thus mainly appealed to their own ethnic group. Corky Gonzales, the Denver Chicano activist, for example, wrote "I Am Joaquin," a poem about rejecting Anglo values and culture in favor of Hispanic ones. Such works had little impact on white audiences. The same was true with ethnic newspapers and scholarly journals. Both Hispanics and American Indians published them in the late 1960s, but with their own ethnic readers in mind.

FASHION

Fashion and apparel, and the rebellious mentality that fostered changes in them in the 1960s, served as indicators of how dramatically different a new generation could be from its predecessors. Starting innocuously (by later standards), mop-top hairdos for boys and miniskirts and bikinis for girls started the steady erosion of the standards of earlier decades. By the late 1960s, the hippie subculture had pervaded all racial groups and genders equally. Long hair, unshaven male faces, and informal attire characterized the last three years of the decade. The Black Power movement brought Afros, cornrows, and dashikis, among other things, into vogue for African Americans. For American Indians, long hair and informal dress had been standard on reservations all along, but these styles became mainstream in the late '60s. Other ethnic groups mainly chose to imitate rather than innovate in fashion and apparel. The youth culture of the 1960s was also characterized by an increase in drug usage, sexual promiscuity, crime, and other similarly negative activities, and these knew no racial or ethnic boundaries. It seems that the liberation given to this new generation of Americans by the civil rights movement and the hippie subculture brought with it a destructive sense of licentiousness. It would be easy to write this off as an unintended consequence, except for the fact that so many millions of youth came to understand that they were engaging in self-destructive behavior in time to stop it but embraced it and continued it anyway.

INFLUENTIAL THEORIES AND VIEWS OF RACE RELATIONS

The "Moynihan Report" became one of the biggest topics of racial controversy in the 1960s. Written by Daniel Patrick Moynihan, a New York Democrat working as the assistant secretary of labor in the Johnson administration, the 1965 position paper was officially called *The Negro Family: The Case for National Action*. Moynihan, a social scientist with a Ph.D., prepared the 78-page report not for public reading but merely to help President Johnson formulate a plan to wage the "War on Poverty," which he had already declared. Johnson was scheduled to give an address called "To Fulfill These Rights" at Howard University in Washington, D.C., on June 4, 1965, in which he would discuss the problem of poverty among African Americans and offer potential solutions. The "Moynihan Report" became the basis of the speech and of the controversy that followed.

The problem the report addressed was well known and indisputable: African Americans suffered the highest poverty rate of any group in the country. The controversy stemmed from Moynihan's explanation of why this was so. Whereas the traditionally accepted answer was simply that racial discrimination caused black poverty, Moynihan argued that a secondary cause was the breakdown of the black family. He did not deny that the root of the problem could be found in slavery and in the subsequent generations of Jim Crow racism, but that root, he said, had grown a stem that in turn had added branches. His argument went like this: blacks, especially in the urban ghettos, had a higher rate of broken homes and single-parent homes, out-of-wedlock births, unemployment, drug addiction, crime, and practically every other negative demographic category. The lack of two-parent households featuring a strong father-husband served as the catalyst (root) for all these other problems (branches). What had caused this breakdown of the traditional family model among blacks was the fact that slavery and racial discrimination had basically emasculated the male, or at least undercut his role as provider for the family. Since the advent of federal welfare, the black man's role had been reduced even further. There was in fact no place left for him other than to be a procreator. The solution to black poverty, therefore, was not to continue providing welfare indefinitely but rather to find ways to restore and strengthen the black man's masculinity and sense of responsibility to his family. This would give him a purpose, would create stable black families with two adult wage-earners, and would double the chances that black children would grow up with positive role models and adult supervision. Thus, poverty, vice, and crime among blacks would decrease. How could this be done? Moynihan offered one potential way that proved the most controversial: encourage black male youth to enter the armed forces. The training would give them self-discipline and self-respect, he said, which would be valuable assets to them as they later became husbands and fathers.

This report and its conclusions, which Moynihan supported with statistical evidence, seemed innocuous at first, because they showed that the Johnson administration at least cared enough about the problem to address it and offer a plan to combat it. They were in fact little more than reiterations of what the black social scientists and commentators E. Franklin Frazier and Kenneth Clark had long written and stated publicly. Not surprisingly, Martin Luther King, Jr., of the SCLC, Roy Wilkins, of the NAACP, and Whitney Young, of the NUL, all embraced the president's speech, which was based on the report. As time went on, however, critics began to arise to question the "Moynihan Report."

These critics could be found among the news media, in academia, in federal agencies that dealt with civil rights and welfare, and among lesser-known black leaders. Essentially, their criticism focused on the fact that, while nobly intentioned, the "Moynihan Report" shifted the responsibility for fixing a problem that generations of racism had caused from the federal government to blacks themselves. More specific criticisms came in three varieties: (1) the report insulted decent, hard-working black men by stereotyping black men generally as unwilling to function or as incapable of functioning in the role that white society expected of them, and it did so during the civil rights movement—the very time in it history that black men were finally standing up en masse to fight racial oppression; (2) it insulted single black mothers and breadwinners, devaluing the role of the black woman in the family unit, saying essentially that she would almost automatically raise dysfunctional children unless there was a father present, and it did so just as the feminist movement was getting under way; (3) it insulted intellectually gifted and ambitious black youth by recommending that black youth in general prepare for military service, because without it they would not likely develop the necessary work ethic and personal standards to succeed in a white-dominated society, and it did so just as the Vietnam War was cranking into high gear.

These criticisms first made their way around the "cocktail party" circuit of nation's capital, then filtered out into the press and academia. Just as the general public was beginning to hear the first of them, the infamous Watts riot of August 1965 erupted. It immediately caused a cacophony of "what caused this riot?" to be sounded all across America. The convenient and immediate answers could be found, so it seemed, in the "Moynihan Report." Blacks should blame themselves for burning down their own city, the argument went, and it all started with a single dysfunctional black family. This instantaneously caused the criticism to grow loud and prolonged, forcing President Johnson eventually to call the hastily planned and sloppily conceived "To Fulfill These Rights" conference at the White House, in November 1965. The conference basically tried to undo the damage done to Johnson's carefully cultivated image as a civil rights crusader. It served at least to deflect some of the criticism just long enough to allow other issues to arise and consume the nation's attention. Otherwise, it was a largely forgettable little event amid the many bigger, more important racial events of the 1960s.

The report, meanwhile, was like the proverbial genie that had been let out of the bottle. It provided fodder for social scientists to argue over from that time to the present. It also put the previously unknown Daniel Patrick Moynihan on the political map. President Nixon would soon tap him as a moderately conservative Democratic ally and put him to work in his administration in the 1970s, whereupon Moynihan would again make negative headlines for his usage of the term "benign neglect" to describe Nixon's policy of federal assistance to poor African Americans. Thereafter, Moynihan would go on to a distinguished career representing New York in the U.S. Senate, serving as an ambassador to India and the United Nations, and authoring many books.

RESOURCE GUIDE

SUGGESTED READINGS

Sit-ins

Carson, Clayborne. *In Struggle: SNCC and the Black Awakening of the 1960s.* Cambridge, MA: Harvard University Press, 1981.

Chafe, William A. *Civilities and Civil Rights: Greensboro North Carolina and the Black Struggle for Freedom.* New York: Oxford University Press, 1980.

Raines, Howell, ed. *My Soul is Rested: Movement Days in the Deep South Remembered.* New York: Putnam, 1977.

Wolfe, Miles. *Lunch at the Five and Ten: The Greensboro Sit-Ins.* New York: Stein and Day, 1970.

Freedom Rides

Arsenault, Raymond. *Freedom Riders: 1961 and the Struggle for Racial Justice.* New York: Oxford University Press, 2006.

Farmer, James. *Lay Bare the Heart: An Autobiography of the Civil Rights Movement.* New York: Arbor House, 1985.

Meier, August, and Elliott Rudwick. *CORE: A Study in the Civil Rights Movement, 1942–1968.* New York: Oxford University Press, 1973.

James Meredith and the Integration of Ole Miss

Meredith, James. *Three Years in Mississippi.* Bloomington: Indiana University Press, 1966.

Silver, James. *Mississippi: The Closed Society.* New York: Harcourt, Brace and World, 1964.

March on Washington

Bass, Patrick Henry. *Like a Mighty Stream: The March on Washington, August 28, 1963.* Philadelphia: Running Press, 2002.

Branch, Taylor. *Parting the Waters: America in the King Years, 1954–1963.* New York: Simon and Schuster, 1988.

Gentile, Thomas. *March on Washington: August 28, 1963.* Washington, D.C.: Self-published, 1983.

Levine, Daniel. *Bayard Rustin and the Civil Rights Movement.* New Brunswick, N.J.: Rutgers University Press, 2000.

Pfeffer, Paula. *A. Philip Randolph: Pioneer of the Civil Rights Movement.* Baton Rouge: Louisiana State University Press, 1990.

Rosenberg, Jonathan, and Zachary Karabell, *Kennedy, Johnson, and the Quest for Justice: The Civil Rights Tapes.* New York: W. W. Norton, 2003.

Schlesinger, Arthur, Jr. *A Thousand Days: John F. Kennedy in the White House.* Boston: Houghton Mifflin, 1965.

Freedom Summer in Mississippi

Mars, Florence. *Witness in Philadelphia.* Baton Rouge: Louisiana State University Press, 1977.

Stubbs, Stephen H. *Mississippi's Giant Houseparty: The History of the Neshoba County Fair.* Philadelphia, Mississippi: Dancing Rabbit Press, 2005.

Watts Riot

Sears, David O., and John B. McConahay. *The Politics of Violence: The New Urban Blacks and the Watts Riot.* Boston: Houghton Mifflin, 1973.

Martin Luther King, Jr., and the Chicago Freedom Movement

Branch, Taylor. *At Canaan's Edge: America in the King Years, 1965–1968.* New York: Simon and Schuster, 2006.

Garrow, David J. *Bearing the Cross: Martin Luther King Jr., and the Southern Christian Leadership Conference.* William Morrow, 1986.

Washington, James M., ed. *A Testament of Hope: The Essential Writings and Speeches of Martin Luther King, Jr.* San Francisco: Harper San Francisco, 1990.

Newark and Detroit Riots of 1967

Kerner, Otto, et al. *The Report of the National Advisory Commission on Civil Disorders.* New York: Bantam Books, 1968.

Cesar Chavez

Bruns, Roger. *Cesar Chavez: A Biography.* Westport, Conn.: Greenwood Press, 2005.

Gillon, Stephen M. *The American Paradox: A History of the United States Since 1945.* Boston: Houghton Mifflin, 2003.

Levy, Jacques E. *Cesar Chavez: Autobiography of La Causa.* New York: W. W. Norton, 1975.

Taylor, Ronald B. *Chavez and the Farm Workers.* Boston: Beacon Press, 1975.

Indians on Alcatraz

Johnson, Troy R. *The Occupation of Alcatraz Island: Indian Self-Determination and the Rise of Indian Activism.* Urbana: University of Illinois Press, 1996.

Johnson, Troy R., et al., eds. *American Indian Activism: Alcatraz to the Longest Walk.* Urbana: University of Illinois Press, 1997.

Contemporary Accounts of the Civil Rights Movement

Baldwin, James. *The Fire Next Time.* New York: Dial Press, 1963.

King, Martin Luther, Jr. *Why We Can't Wait.* New American Library: 1964.

———. *Where Do We Go from Here?* Boston: Beacon Press, 1968.

Moody, Anne. *Coming of Age in Mississippi.* New York: Dell, 1968.

Sobel, Lester A., ed. *Civil Rights, 1960–1966.* New York: Facts on File, 1967.

Stang, Alan. *It's Very Simple: The True Story of Civil Rights.* Boston: Western Island, 1965.

The Black Power Movement

Brown, H. Rap. *Die! Nigger, Die!* New York: Dial Press, 1969.

Carmichael, Stokely, and Charles V. Hamilton. *Black Power.* New York: Vintage Books, reissued 1992.

Cleaver, Eldridge. *Soul on Ice.* New York: Dell, 1968.

Grier, William M., and Price M. Cobb. *Black Rage.* New York: Basic Books, 1968.

Haley, Alex, ed. *The Autobiography of Malcolm X.* New York: Grove Press, 1965.

Jones, LeRoi, and Larry Neal. *Black Fire.* New York: William Morrow, 1968.

Lester, Julius. *Look Out Whitey! Black Power's Gon' Get Your Mama!* New York: Grove Press, 1969.

"Moynihan Report" Controversy

Rainwater, Lee, and William L. Yancey. *The Moynihan Report and the Politics of Controversy* Cambridge, MA: M.I.T. Press, 1967.

Blacks in Sports

Ashe, Arthur, Jr. *A Hard Road to Glory: A History of the African American Athlete since 1946.* New York: Warner Books, 1988.

Bass, Amy. *Not the Triumph but the Struggle: 1968 Olympics and the Making of the Black Athlete.* Minneapolis: University of Minnesota Press, 2004.

Carter, Rubin. *The Sixteenth Round: From Number 1 Contender to #45472.* New York: Penguin Reprint, 2005.

Hartmann, Douglas. *Race, Culture, and the Revolt of the Black Athlete: The 1968 Olympic Protests and Their Aftermath.* Chicago: University of Chicago Press, 2004.

Hirsch, James S. *Hurricane: The Miraculous Journey of Rubin Carter.* Boston: Mariner Books, 2000.

Media and Mass Communications

Erik Barnouw. *Tube of Plenty: The Evolution of American Television,* rev. ed. New York: Oxford University Press, 1982.

Woll, Allen L., and Randall M. Miller. *Ethnic and Racial Images in American Film and Television: Historical Essays and Bibliography.* New York: Garland, 1987.

FILMS/VIDEOS

Nonfiction

Eyes on the Prize: American Civil Rights Years, 1954–1965, and *Eyes on the Prize II: American at the Racial Crossroads, 1965–1985* (exec. prod. Henry Hampton, Blackside, Inc., for Public Broadcasting Service, 1987 and 1990). Companion to the Juan Williams book of the same name, it is the best documentary to date covering the whole civil rights movement. Highly recommended.

The Hurricane (prod. Armyan Bernstein, dir. Norman Jewison, for Universal Studios, Touchstone Pictures, 1999). A sympathetic portrayal of the Ruben Carter story that viewers should watch with a critical eye.

Mississippi Burning (prod. Fred Zollo, dir. Alan Parker, for Orion Pictures, 1988), A partly fictionalized account of the Freedom Summer killings in Philadelphia, Mississippi.

X (prod. Marvin Worth, dir. Spike Lee, for Warner Brothers Pictures, 1992). An accurate biographical film of the life of Malcolm X. Recommended.

Fiction

A Raisin in the Sun (dir. Daniel Petrie, Columbia Pictures, 1961).
Guess Who's Coming to Dinner? (dir. Stanley Kramer, Columbia Pictures, 1967).
Lilies of the Field (pro./dir. Ralph Nelson, United Artists, 1963).
To Kill a Mockingbird (dir. Robert Mulligan, Universal Pictures, 1962).

WEB SITES

Ruben "Hurricane" Carter

Deal, Cal. "Hurricane Carter: The Other Side of the Story." http://www.graphicwitness.com/carter (accessed August 25, 2007).

The Greensboro Sit-Ins

NRinteractive, "Greensboro Sit-Ins: Launch of a Civil Rights Movement." 1998, http://www.sitins.com (accessed August 25, 2007).
International Civil Rights Center & Museum, "They Opened One Door for All." http://www.sitinmovement.org (accessed August 25, 2007).

Martin Luther King, Jr.

The Martin Luther King, Jr., Research and Education Institute, http://www.stanford.edu/group/King/ (accessed August 25, 2007).

The Black Power Movement

Hiltz, Virginia and Mike Sell. "Black Arts Movement." 1998, http://www.umich.edu/~eng499/ (accessed August 25, 2007).

The Watts Riot

Reitman, Valerie and Mitchell Landsberg. "Watts Riot, 40 Years Later." August 11, 2005, http://www.latimes.com/news/local/la-me-watts11aug11,0,7619426.story?coll=la-home-headlines (accessed August 25, 2007). Government Documents Department and the Doheny Electronic Resources Center at the University of Southern California, "Violence in the City: An End or a Beginning?" http://www.usc.edu/libraries/archives/city instress/mccone/contents.html (accessed August 25, 2007).

NOTES

1. NRinteractive, "Greensboro Sit-Ins: Launch of a Civil Rights Movement." 1998, http://www.sitins.com (accessed August 25, 2007).

2. Ibid.

3. John Hope Franklin and Alfred A. Moss, Jr., From Slavery to Freedom: A History of African Americans, 8th ed. (Boston: McGraw Hill, 2000), 530.

4. Alan L. Berger, "American Fuehrer: George Lincoln Rockwell and the American Nazi Party," Holocaust and Genocide Studies 17(1) 2003:180–85, http://hgs.oxfordjournals.org/cgi/content/citation/17/1/180 (accessed August 25, 2007).

5. "USA—A Divided Union 1941–80: Key Question—What was the 'New Frontier' of John F. Kennedy?" http://www.learnhistory.org.uk/usa/newfrontier.htm (accessed August 25, 2007).

6. Chris Nammour, "The March on Washington for Jobs and Freedom." http://www.pbs.org/newshour/extra/features/july-dec03/march_8-27.html (accessed August 25, 2007).

7. Abbeville Press, "The Civil Rights Movement, The March on Washington, 1963: 'We Stood on a Height,'" http://www.abbeville.com/civilrights/washington.asp.

8. Gary Younge, "I Have a Dream." The Guardian. August 21, 2003, http://www.guardian.co.uk/Columnists/Column/0,5673,1026385,00.html

9. Samuel Francis, "The King Holiday and Its Meaning." http://www.martinlutherking.org/articles.html (accessed August 25, 2007).

10. "Speech prepared for the March on Washington, August 1963." February 10, 2006. http://www.hartford-hwp.com/archives/45a/641.html (accessed August 25, 2007).

11. Taylor Branch, *Parting the Waters: America in the King Years, 1954–1963* (New York: Simon and Schuster, 1988), 874.

12. International Information Programs, "John Lewis Leads Commemoration of March on Washington." July 25, 2003, http://usinfo.state.gov/scv/Archive/2005/Aug/15-620146.html (accessed August 25, 2007).

13. Jack E. White, "Aug. 28, 1963." March 31, 2003, http://www.time.com/time/magazine/article/0,9171,1004520,00.html (accessed August 25, 2007).

14. The Martin Luther King, Jr., Research and Education Institute, http://www.stanford.edu/group/King/ (accessed August 25, 2007).

15. T. David Mason and Jerry A. Murtagh. "Who Riots? An Empirical Examination of the 'New Urban Black' versus the Social Marginality Hypotheses." January 10, 2005, http://www.springerlink.com/content/w6252x3441564x62/ (accessed August 25, 2007).

16. Otto Kerner et al. *Report of the National Advisory Commission on Civil Disorders* (New York: Bantam Books, 1968), 226.

17. Center for Urban Research and Learning, Loyola University Chicago, "40 Anniversary." May 8, 2004, http://www.luc.edu/curl/cfm40/ (accessed August 25, 2007).

18. Jeff Kelly Lowenstein, "Resisting the Dream." http://www.chicagoreporter.com/ (accessed August 25, 2007).

19. Kerner, *Report*.

20. Scott Sherman, "A Turbulent Life." http://www.dissentmagazine.org/article/?article (accessed August 25, 2007).

21. Kerner, *Report*, 57.

22. Kerner, *Report*, 64.

23. Kerner, *Report*, 64, photo no. 32, between pp. 318–319.

24. New Urban Dictionary, Pig. Blind=http://www.urbandictionary.com/define.php?term (accessed August 25, 2007).

25. Library of Congress, "America's Story, Meet Amazing Americans, Activists and Reformers, Cesar Chavez." http://www.americaslibrary.gov/cgi-bin/page.cgi/aa/activists/chavez (accessed August 25, 2007).

26. Williford-Sosnowsky, Julia. "Walter P. Reuther Library, La Causa Exhibit." March 2005, http://www.reuther.wayne.edu/exhibits/fw/thecause.html (accessed August 25, 2007).

27. U.S. National Park Service, "Alcatraz Island." May 1, 2007, http://www.nps.gov/alcatraz/ (accessed August 25, 2007).

28. Bay City Guide.com, "Top Ten Attractions: Alcatraz." 2007, http://www.sanfranciscoonline.com/top_ten_attractions/tt_alcatraz.html (accessed August 25, 2007).

29. Carlton, Cleet. "Golden Gate Photo—Alcatraz, the Rock Gallery." 1999, http://www.goldengatephoto.com/sanfran/alcatraz.html (accessed August 25, 2007).

30. United Native America, "Bureau of White Affairs." 2004, http://www.unitednativeamerica.com/bureau/index.html (accessed August 25, 2007).

31. Milton Greenberg, "The Negro in America," *Collier's 1964 Year Book: Covering the Year 1963* (New York: Crowell-Collier), 46.

32. Center for Media and Democracy, "April 1963: "Freedom Walk" from Chattanooga, Tennessee to Jackson, Mississippi." August 16, 2005, http://www.sourcewatch.org/ (accessed August 25, 2007).

33. Greenberg, "Negro in America," 47.

34. U.S. National Park Service, "We Shall Overcome." August 2001, http://www.cr.nps.gov/nr/travel/civilrights/al4.htm (accessed August 25, 2007).

35. Freeman, Jo. "The Meredith Mississippi March–June 1966." http://www.jofreeman.com/photos/meredith.html (accessed August 25, 2007).

36. Public Broadcasting Service, "Eyes on the Prize." 2006, http://www.pbs.org/wgbh/amex/eyesontheprize/ (accessed August 25, 2007).

37. Beck, Ernest. "Black Is Beautiful and It's History, Too." March 9, 2005, http://www.columbia.edu/cu/news/05/03/black_artists.html (accessed August 25, 2007).

38. Haymes, Don. "The Long Hot Summer." http://www.mun.ca/rels/restmov/texts/race/haymes43.html (accessed August 25, 2007).

39. Time Magazine, "Blue Hill Blues." (June 16, 1967) 2007, http://www.time.com/time/magazine/article/0,9171,843932,00.html?iid=chix-sphere (accessed August 25, 2007).

40. David Burner, *Making Peace with the '60s* (Princeton, N.J.: Princeton University Press, 1998), 63.

41. Charles D. Lowery and John F. Marszalek, eds., *The Greenwood Encyclopedia of African American Civil Rights: From Emancipation to the Twenty-first Century, 2nd ed.* (Westport, Conn.: Greenwood Press, 2003), 413–14.

42. Lowery and Marszalek, eds., 432.

43. Maron L. Waxman et al., eds., *1969 Year Book: Covering the Year 1968* (New York: Crowell-Collier, 1969), 421.

44. Dodge, John, The Olympian. "Years After the Boldt Decision." February 9, 2004, http://www.citizenreviewonline.org/feb2004/years.htm (accessed August 25, 2007).

45. Vine Deloria, *Custer Died for Your Sins: An Indian Manifesto* (New York: Macmillan, 1969).

46. Pearson, Kim. "Wetback." 2004, http://kpearson.faculty.tcnj.edu/Dictionary/wetback.htm (accessed August 25, 2007).

47. "The Making of MEChA." http://studentorgs.utexas.edu/mecha/archive/research.html (accessed August 25, 2007).

1970s

TIMELINE

1970

February 2	Sixteen Black Panthers are put on trial in New York City for plotting to bomb public buildings.
March 3	Whites in Lamar, South Carolina, attack busloads of black schoolchildren on their way to their newly integrated school.
May 1	Nearly 15,000 youths at Yale University stage a demonstration in support of Black Panthers on trial in New Haven, Connecticut.
May 15	Two black students are killed at Jackson State College, Mississippi, by state troopers.
May 23	Ralph Abernathy, the leader of the Southern Christian Leadership Conference, heads a "march against repression" that ends at the state capitol in Atlanta with 10,000 participants.
May 29	The murder conviction of the Black Panther leader Huey Newton is overturned by an appeals court.
June 19	Black Panthers, at the Lincoln Memorial in Washington, D.C., announce plans for a "Revolutionary People's Constitutional Convention."
July 8	President Richard M. Nixon issues a Special Message to Congress on Indian Affairs.
July 10	The IRS revokes the tax exemptions of all racially segregated private schools in the United States.
August 5	The Black Panther leader Huey Newton is released from prison, ending the "Free Huey!" campaign successfully.

August 7	Jonathan Jackson leads a holdup and attempted kidnapping in a San Rafael, California, courtroom in an effort to free a black defendant; the attempt results in a deadly shootout and the prosecution of the Black Panther activist Angela Davis as an accomplice.
August 31	Philadelphia police raid Black Panther offices and make highly publicized arrests of members.
September 5–7	Black Panthers hold constitutional convention in Philadelphia and draft a communist constitution for the United States.
September 17	The black entertainer Flip Wilson debuts his *Flip Wilson Show* on NBC television.
October 13	Angela Davis is captured by authorities in New York City.
November 27	Black Panthers' scheduled constitutional ratification convention in Washington, D.C., fails to materialize.
December 4	The Latino labor leader Cesar Chavez is sentenced to jail in California for organizing a lettuce boycott.

1971

January 5	Angela Davis is arraigned on charges of conspiracy in the Jonathan Jackson case.
January 22	The 13 members of the Congressional Black Caucus from the House of Representatives boycott President Nixon's State of the Union message.
February 26	The Black Panther leaders Huey Newton and Eldridge Cleaver disagree in a television debate on the direction of the party, effectively destroying the party.
March 25	President Nixon meets with the Congressional Black Caucus and listens to their grievances.
April 20	U.S. Supreme Court rules, in *Swann v. Charlotte-Mecklenburg Board of Education*, that forced busing of students from one school district to another to achieve racial balance is acceptable.
May 18	President Nixon issues a statement rejecting most of the proposals of the Congressional Black Caucus.
June 11	The last Indians on Alcatraz are removed by government officials.
June 28	The U.S. Supreme Court overturns the conviction of the black boxer Muhammad Ali for draft evasion in 1967.
August 14	Taos Pueblo Indians in New Mexico celebrate Congress's decision to award them the Blue Lake region they had asked for.

August 25	The Black Panther and Soledad Brother George Jackson kills five people in an attempt to escape from prison before being gunned down himself.
August 30	Ten school buses are bombed in Pontiac, Michigan, by whites protesting cross-town busing order of federal courts.
October 8	"Angela Davis Day" is held in New York City as part of the "Free Angela!" campaign.

1972

February 23	Angela Davis is released on bail.
February 28	Angela Davis's trial begins.
March 8	Congress gives the Equal Employment Opportunity Commission the power to enforce compliance with all civil rights hiring laws.
March 10–12	The first National Black Political Convention is held, in Gary, Indiana, resulting in the creation of the National Black Assembly.
March 16	President Nixon makes an address calling on the federal courts to halt cross-town busing.
April 12	Benjamin L. Hooks becomes first black appointee to the Federal Communications Commission.
May 16	The National Association for the Advancement of Colored People (NAACP) withdraws from the National Black Assembly, citing its separatist agenda.
June 4	Angela Davis is acquitted by an all-white jury in California.

1973

February 27	The American Indian Movement (AIM) begins siege of Wounded Knee.
May 8	AIM ends siege of Wounded Knee.
May 29	Tom Bradley is elected the first black mayor of Los Angeles.
July 2	The National Black Network begins operations with 38 radio stations nationwide.

1974

January 21	U.S. Supreme Court rules in *Lau v. Nichols* that school districts must provide bilingual education or offer remedial classes in English where needed.
March 15–17	The second Black National Political Convention is held, in Little Rock, Arkansas.

April 8	The black professional baseball player Hank Aaron breaks Babe Ruth's home-run record, hitting number 715.
June 21	Federal court orders the city of Boston to begin integrating its public schools.
August 27	A black inmate, Joan Little, kills her white jailer in North Carolina and escapes.
September 12	School starts in Boston, causing a racial uproar as integration begins.
September 16	A federal court dismisses charges against AIM leaders for Wounded Knee II.
September 19	Rioting occurs in Boston because of integration problems at Hyde Park High School.
October 7	Rioting occurs in Boston again over school integration problems.
October 9	President Gerald R. Ford publicly declaims the federal court rulings requiring cross-town busing.
December 11	Rioting occurs in Boston yet again over integration problems.

1975

May 17	NAACP marches in Boston in support of cross-town busing to integrate schools.
June 13	The city of Jackson, Mississippi, opens integrated public swimming pools for the first time.
July 28	Congress extends the Voting Rights Act for seven years, adding protection for Spanish-speaking and other non-English-speaking minorities.
August 15	Joan Little is acquitted of murder charges in a highly publicized case.
September 6–7	Riots erupt in Louisville, Kentucky, over forced busing.
October 24	Racial violence erupts at South Boston High School.
December 9	A federal court gives federal authorities jurisdiction over Boston public schools.

1976

October 4	U.S. Agriculture Secretary Earl Butz resigns under pressure after making racially insensitive remarks about African Americans.
October 25	A black activist, the Reverend Clennon King, announces his intentions to integrate the Plains Baptist Church, in Georgia,

| | the church attended by the Democratic presidential candidate, Jimmy Carter. |
| October 31 | The Reverend Clennon King attempts to integrate the Plains Baptist Church but is denied admission. |

1977

January 19	Outgoing President Ford pardons Tokyo Rose for treason in World War II.
January 31	Federal court orders the merger of the University of Tennessee-Nashville with Tennessee State University to achieve integration.
February 22	U.S. Supreme Court begins deliberations on *University of California Regents v. Bakke*, a case alleging reverse discrimination (the favoring of minorities over whites) in college admissions.
March 10–11	Hanafi Muslims in Washington, D.C., take 134 hostages, with one person killed and 19 wounded, before surrendering to police.
June 13	James Earl Ray, the convicted assassin of Martin Luther King, Jr., is captured after a prison escape in Tennessee.
June 27	The U.S. Supreme Court rules against forced busing in *Dayton Board of Education v. Brinkman*.
August 29	Black leaders meet in New York City to discuss ways to deal with black urban poverty.

1978

February 11	AIM begins "The Longest March" from Alcatraz to Washington, D.C.
July 17	AIM ends "The Longest March" on the steps of the U.S. Capitol.
July 18	AIM leaders meet with Vice President Walter Mondale and Secretary of the Interior Cecil Adams.

OVERVIEW

The 1970s had the dubious distinction of being the decade to follow the revolutionary 1960s. It is hard to imagine that any other decade could have measured up to that time of dramatic change in terms of race relations reform. The '70s did not bring much in the way of new initiatives but rather focused on carrying out the reforms begun in the '60s. The new decade was basically the testing period of all the civil rights laws, court rulings, and societal changes that the prior decade had generated. The '70s saw a white backlash against new initiatives, such as forced busing of students across cities and counties to achieve integrated public schools and, to a lesser extent, affirmative action programs. At the same time, however, whites fully embraced racially integrated entertainment media and venues, such as television, movies, music, and sports. The '70s was thus a decade of contradictions.

Unlike the 1960s, which began mildly with simple sit-ins and ended militantly with Black, Brown, and Red Power movements, the 1970s began with revolutionary rhetoric and actions by groups such as the Black Panthers and the American Indian Movement and ended with barely a whisper of racial tension. At least four reasons can be identified that explain this reversal. First, as the racial justice that Martin Luther King, Jr., and fellow nonviolent activists espoused began to come to fruition in the '70s, the advocates of revolution and rebellion largely lost their credibility and thus most of their audience. Second, the FBI's program to put radical organizations out of business also contributed to the demise of the militant movement; many of the most visible and vocal militants were silenced by prison, exile, or death. Third, some of the militant groups imploded through their own internal power struggles. Fourth, perhaps as important as any other factor, the American public had grown weary of racial violence and bloodshed by the mid-1970s. Indeed, by then Americans of all colors were largely ready and willing to take a break from racial issues. The late '70s were, therefore, as much as anything else, a time of healing.

KEY EVENTS

1970: THE RISE AND FALL OF THE BLACK PANTHERS

The Black Panther party (BPP) rose meteorically in the late 1960s to become the most prominent race-based organization in America. A group with an ephemeral existence, the BPP came crashing down to earth in 1971, the victim of both an FBI campaign to destroy it and self-destruction. During its brief time in the national and even international spotlight, it captured attention like no other civil rights group ever had, if it can be called a "civil rights" group at all. It defied description in its own day and still puzzles historians and social scientists today. Much about it is shrouded in mystery and controversy, partly because in the common perception it was, and still is, seen as a reverse-racist Black Power organization, roughly the inverse of the Ku Klux Klan, and partly because its members' and supporters' version of events differs so sharply in many cases from police reports and FBI records. Separating fact from fiction and half-truth about the BPP is thus difficult but must be the starting point of any discussion about the group's place in history.

To begin, the name of the group must be dissected and clarified. Although the BPP was primarily "black" in its leadership, membership, and purpose, it was not racially exclusionary but rather welcomed anyone who agreed with its ideology, regardless of race. That ideology was tantamount to communism, although a particular poor, urban, minority version of it that had no direct equivalent anywhere else in the world. It might be more accurately described as "communalism" or "communitarianism" than communism, because it focused on taking care of the people in the black ghetto communities through a free breakfast program for children, as well as providing legal aid and medical care for those who could not otherwise afford them. Nonetheless, the ideology was absolutely pro-Marxist, anti-free-market-capitalist and anti-imperialist, which puts the BPP about as far left politically as any group in America before or since. Claims that it engaged in terrorist activity designed to overthrow the government in true Leninist-communist fashion in several cases could not be substantiated in court. Despite having the word "party" in its name, the BPP was never a party in the political sense, although it was politically active, running a member, Eldridge Cleaver, for president of the United States on the Peace and Freedom party ticket in 1968 and sponsoring a constitutional convention in 1970 to draft a new constitution for the United States.

The origin of the BPP is one of the few aspects of its history not in dispute. Two young black men named Huey P. Newton and Bobby Seale created "The Black Panther Party for Self-Defense," almost on a whim, while attending Merritt Junior College, in Oakland, California, in October 1966. In many ways, the two were typical of the new urban blacks who had come of age in the post–World War II American industrial cities. They had experienced the early civil rights movement in the South only vicariously but had become socially and politically conscious through the preaching of Malcolm X about the time of Malcolm's assassination. They watched the transformation from nonviolent resistance in response to racism as espoused by Martin Luther King, Jr., to Black Power as advocated by Stokely Carmichael. They were unusually intellectual, despite their lack of education, and they needed an exciting new cause to live for in order to be fulfilled. They had read the black Algerian psychologist Frantz Fanon's *Wretched of the Earth,* the Chinese head-of-state Mao Tse Tung's *Little Red Book,* the Argentine-born, Cuban rebel Che Guevara's *Guerrilla Warfare*, and various other pro-communist, anticolonialist books. They found their cause in the unlikely wedding of Black Power with racially integrated communism. Ironically, the two chose an unoriginal name for their organization, since black voters in Lowndes County, Alabama, had called themselves the "Black Panthers" nearly two years earlier and a competing group calling itself the Black Panther Party of Northern California already existed at that time.

After deciding upon the name, Newton and Seale dubbed themselves the "Minister of Defense" and the "Chairman" of the party, respectively, then drew up the "Black Panther Party Platform and Program," sometimes called the "Ten Point Program," which they divided into two parts: "What We Want" and "What We Believe." Basically, the platform reiterated the same concerns that all previous civil rights groups had voiced for years, thus making it nothing special. How Newton and Seale went about implementing it, however, was quite extraordinary. Their implementation of point seven of the platform became their launching pad to fame. It stated, "We want an immediate end to POLICE BRUTALITY and MURDER of black people." In Oakland, in 1966 and 1967, they did all in their power to make that objective a reality. They followed police cars when they came into black neighborhoods or when the policemen seemed to be harassing an African American anywhere in the city so they could be witnesses to any brutality or discrimination that might occur. They carried firearms with them as they did it, threatening to use them to defend their helpless black neighbors against the evil "pigs." This behavior, coupled with their stylish black leather apparel and black berets, irritated the police while greatly impressing the black denizens of Oakland, especially the youth. When, on April 1, 1967, a black man named Denzil Dowell died at the hands of the police, the BPP began printing *The Black Panther* newspaper, in which they covered the victim's story sympathetically; then they staged an antipolice rally in which they recruited followers.

The event that really put the BPP on the map, however, came a week after the first edition of *The Black Panther* was printed. On May 2, 1967, Seale and 29 other members caused a media spectacle by marching into the California State Assembly while the legislature debated a bill against allowing citizens to carry firearms in public—a bill aimed at stopping the nascent BPP from continuing its antipolice activity. Seale and the leaders were arrested for disturbing the peace, although they had technically violated no law. Meanwhile, Newton, the mastermind of the group, manned the office in Oakland and missed the chance to seize the spotlight. He would soon have other chances, however. On October 28, 1967, he was involved in a shootout with the Oakland police that resulted in a dead policeman and left Newton with four bullets in his abdomen. As he recovered and awaited trial, the BPP grew by leaps and bounds. On February 17, 1968, the BPP merged with the Student Nonviolent Coordinating Committee (SNCC), if only temporarily. The merger did not last long because the leaders of SNCC—Stokely Carmichael, H. Rap Brown, and James Forman—had become absolutely antiwhite in ideology, steering SNCC to become a narrowly focused black nationalist/black separatist organization, while the Panthers professed a big-tent ideology that was open to racial integration, women's rights, homosexual rights, and basically any left-wing issue (although not every member agreed with every one of these tenets).

When Martin Luther King, Jr., was assassinated, on April 4, 1968, race riots broke out in cities all over the country, but not Oakland. The BPP kept the black residents there under control, not wanting to give the white police any excuse to shoot them down in the streets. Ironically, two days later, the Oakland police raided the BPP office anyway, killing a 17-year old member, Bobby Hutton, and wounding "Minister of Information" Eldridge Cleaver. An ex-con who had spent nine years in prison, Cleaver had recently published his best-selling book *Soul on Ice*, which he wrote before joining the BPP but which became a sort of BPP manifesto nonetheless. With his book propelling his fame, he ran for president on a minor-party ticket. Before the election, however, he was sentenced to 60 days in jail for his role in the fracas with police in April, and he fled the country. On the same day he was sentenced, September 27, 1968, Huey Newton's two-month-long trial ended with his being sentenced on a manslaughter conviction. The public outcry against the conviction and sentence brought even more notoriety to the BPP, as supporters waged a two-year campaign to "Free Huey!" The "Free Huey!" campaign did as much as anything else to grow the BPP, because it garnered the support of many whites in Hollywood ("Friends of the Panthers") and coverage from news media all over the world. BPP chapters sprang up not only

Huey P. Newton, national defense minister of the Black Panther Party, raises his clenched fist behind the podium as he speaks at a convention sponsored by the Black Panthers at Temple University's McGonigle Hall in Philadelphia Saturday, September 5, 1970. He is surrounded by security guards of the movement. The audience gathered was estimated at 6,000 with another thousand outside the crowded hall. AP Photo.

throughout the United States at the time but internationally as well, from Japan to Australia and from Scandinavia to southern Africa. In 1970, Huey was indeed freed, and charges against him were eventually dropped.

At the same time, Seale was prosecuted along with seven other leftists for conspiring to cause riots at the Democratic National Convention in Chicago, August 26–29, 1968, bringing even more publicity to the BPP. The fall 1969 trial became a media circus, the low point of which was Seale being ordered bound and gagged after his repeated demands that he be given the right to dismiss his court-appointed lawyer and defend himself. Although he was convicted, the verdict was overturned on appeal. No sooner did that trial end than Seale was again in court in 1970, this time in New Haven, Connecticut, accused of conspiring in the May 21, 1969, murder of a party member, Alex Rackley, who was suspected of being an FBI informant. Seale escaped conviction once again, thanks to a hung jury.

Beginning August 25, 1967, FBI Director J. Edgar Hoover had authorized COINTELPRO (an acronym for Counter-Intelligence Program), an anticommunist task force of the FBI, to target Black Power groups and similar militant groups such as the Puerto Rican Young Lords and the Brown Berets, for surveillance and infiltration. From 1968 to 1971, the Panthers became the main focus of COINTELPRO activity, as the FBI, working in conjunction with local police departments, conducted nearly 300 separate actions against them. Some of these actions involved raids and shootouts, but others involved disseminating propaganda about them to the media, getting the IRS to investigate them for tax evasion, and getting them into turf wars with other black nationalist groups, such as US (United Slaves), in Los Angeles. Although these actions resulted in several assassinations of party members by either law enforcement personnel or rival militant groups, the membership and support for the group actually reached an all-time high in the midst of the COINTELPRO war against the BPP. This was undoubtedly a result of all the publicity generated by shootouts and trials, but it was also due to excellent organizational leadership at the hands of David Hilliard, the BPP chief of staff, who had run a tight ship while the big three—Newton, Seale, and Cleaver—were in jail, on trial, in the hospital, and/or in exile (Cleaver stayed in exile in Algeria for seven years).

The zenith of the BPP came in 1970, when several notable events occurred. On June 19, 1970, the BPP staged a demonstration on the steps of the Lincoln Memorial in Washington, D.C., at which they announced plans to hold a "Revolutionary People's Constitutional Convention" in Philadelphia on September 7, 1970. They chose June 19 for the meeting because it was the anniversary of Lincoln's issuance of the Emancipation Proclamation. The convention was designed to draft a new constitution for the United States, one that would embody the egalitarian ideals expressed in the Declaration of Independence that "all men are created equal" and that all have a right to "life, liberty, and the pursuit of happiness." Likewise, the BPP hoped to make the words in the current U.S. Constitution about establishing justice and securing the blessings of liberty a reality for blacks and other minorities for the first time.

Meanwhile, Huey Newton got out of prison on August 5, showered with adulation from thousands who had participated in the "Free Huey!" campaign. The campaign had essentially deified Newton as the black messiah, and the teaming thousands who had never met him, seen him, or heard him speak considered him their leader and prepared to rally around him at Philadelphia a month later. A week before the convention, on August 31, 1970, the Philadelphia police raided all three BPP offices in the area, arresting 14 members. They forced six of the Panthers to strip naked, while newspaper reporters snapped photos of their bare buttocks. The pictures, obviously intended to humiliate and discredit the party, were plastered on front pages everywhere the next day.

If the police intended to stop the Philadelphia convention, they failed. Members and supporters of the BPP arrived at Temple University in the "City of Brotherly Love" on the weekend of September 5–6 just as scheduled to listen to "power to the people!" speeches and to participate in constitution writing. The star attraction, however, was Huey Newton. As he walked to the podium, the din of the crowd fell to a whisper, and the audience of about 6,000 fixed their eyes on him as if he were a god. Yet, as he began speaking, the crowd was immediately taken aback, surprised by his lack of oratorical ability. Could this be the great leader they had been following all this time—this man with a high-pitched, nasal voice, who spoke in abstractions and made sophisticated analytical arguments about history and politics that went over the heads of the common people? The disappointment could not have been greater.

Apparently, the disappointment was mutual, as Newton remarked that the people had gotten hung up on Cleaver's simple slogans and increasingly black-separatist philosophy and had never really plumbed the depths of the integrationist-communist ideology he believed in. Newton was supposed to leave the convention hall and go make another speech to a crowd of perhaps 3,000 waiting in a Philadelphia church. He never showed, however, preferring to jilt his adoring disciples in favor of partying with friends. The next day, the constitution making happened just the same. The thousands broke into groups, some as many as 500 strong, made up of men, women, and children. They tossed ideas back and forth, debated civilly, argued minimally, and in the end drafted a constitution that was communist—economically socialist but socially inclusive of all groups of people, including women and homosexuals, and politically democratic. Conspicuously missing from it were all traces of capitalism, racism, religion, male chauvinism, and sexism—in short, most things that have traditionally divided people into warring factions.

Thereafter, the BPP planned to hold a ratification convention on November 4 (later changed to November 27) in Washington, D.C., at Howard University. Although more than 7,000 people showed up to participate, the event never materialized. Because of some problem involving the use of Howard's facilities, and because Newton had second thoughts about the whole idea of writing a new constitution, the ratification convention was postponed and never rescheduled. Subsequently, Newton disavowed the constitutional convention, lapsed into paranoia and drug addiction, and began closing down the various party chapters around the country and refocusing on Oakland exclusively. These actions, combined with the FBI's ongoing divide-and-conquer propaganda strategy, contributed to widening the rift between Newton and his faction of the BPP in Oakland and Cleaver and his faction, in Algeria and New York. The rift became permanent and irreparable on February 26, 1971, when the two met on a San Francisco television program via satellite and got into an argument about the direction of the BPP. They basically excommunicated each other from the party. With the continued assassinations of party members, attributed mainly to the Newton and Cleaver feud but provoked by the FBI, by the end of 1971, there was almost nothing left of the party that J. Edgar Hoover had once called the most dangerous organization in America.

1971: THE STRANGE CASE OF ANGELA DAVIS AND THE SOLEDAD BROTHERS

At the time of her media-circus trial, in 1971–1972, Angela Davis represented the logical culmination of all New Left ideologies and movements of the 1960s. She was a Black Power advocate, a radical feminist, and an unashamed member of the Communist party. She hated the government of the nation of her birth and citizenship, the United States, and extolled the supposed virtues of the Soviet Union, Maoist China, Ho Chi Minh's Vietnam, and Castro's Cuba. She believed her own country was a fascist, imperialist, white-supremacist, and male-chauvinist state incapable of reform and unworthy of redemption. She hoped for the overthrow of the U.S. government and the American way of life, and she did her small part to try to make it happen. She became literally the poster girl for the New Left in the early 1970s, the supposed victim of a justice system stacked against her. Charged with conspiracy to aid in a jailbreak and of being an accomplice to murder, with a mountain of evidence against her, she became the focal point of one of the trials of the century.

Born in Birmingham, Alabama, in 1944, Davis grew up in a middle-class family and attended public school there until recruited by representatives of Elizabeth Irwin High School in New York City, a private academy seeking intellectually gifted black students. There she received her first exposure to and indoctrination in communist ideology. After graduating, she matriculated at Brandeis University, in Massachusetts, where she studied French and philosophy and eventually became the student disciple of the radical scholar Herbert Marcuse. Traveling abroad in the early 1960s as part of her program of study, she earned a scholarship to study at the Sorbonne in Paris. While there in 1963, she witnessed a pro–North Vietnam rally and became attracted to the communist cause in the former French Indochina. At the same time, back in the United States, her hometown of Birmingham became the focus of international media attention as Martin Luther King, Jr., led marches there and as the Ku Klux Klan waged its most infamous campaign of terrorist activity there. She could only watch news coverage from thousands of miles away, mourn for her black neighbors back home, feel ashamed amid the racially liberal French, and vow to return someday to help correct the problems of the American South.

After graduating with honors from Brandeis, Davis worked for a while on a master's degree in Germany, where she witnessed a communist May Day celebration in East Berlin, which impressed her greatly. Before completing her degree, however, she transferred to the University of California at San Diego, where her mentor, Marcuse, had taken a job. There she participated in a hostile takeover of the university's administrative offices aimed at getting a minority-studies program implemented. Successful in that objective, she joined a black Marxist club called Che Lumumba. Upon finishing her degree, she returned to Germany to begin her doctoral program. Before completing her Ph.D., however, she was recruited in 1969 by the administration of the University of California at Los Angeles (UCLA) to teach philosophy. Before even giving her first lecture there, her status as a member of the Communist party was leaked to the press, and the university terminated her contract. Allowed to teach while appealing the decision, Davis lived in a fishbowl of attention and scrutiny from colleagues, administrators, the media, and the public. Students, meanwhile, seemed to like her as a person and value her as a teacher. After a California court ruled in her favor, the university subsequently reinstated her. In 1970, however, upon urging from Governor Ronald Reagan, the California Board of Regents dismissed her for making incendiary speeches and promoting radical activist causes. Although the case attracted local attention, Davis was not yet an international celebrity.

On the day the Regents fired her, Davis was engaged in picketing for the release of the "Soledad Brothers" from a state prison just south of San Francisco. The self-proclaimed Soledad Brothers included George Jackson, John Cluchette, and Fletta Drumgo, who were charged with killing a white prison guard. George Jackson, the leader of the group, was a communist and a Black Panther who had spent a decade in jail for petty crimes. From a decent, middle-class family, he had attended private school but had gone to prison rather than college. He was soon to be the author of two books about his life in prison, in which he philosophized about race relations in America. His philosophy can be summarized as "whites are evil, capitalism is bad, and blacks who do not rebel against both are Uncle Toms." Davis became attracted to Jackson not only intellectually and ideologically but personally and physically, as well. She believed the deck of the American justice system had been stacked against him from birth merely because he was black. Therefore, he could not possibly be truly "guilty" of any crime. If he had rebelled against the "pigs," it was justifiable homicide. This line of reasoning, essentially the same one the Black Panthers had used with some success in their earlier trials, would become the basis for Davis's own defense the following year.

Davis befriended George Jackson's younger brother Jonathan, who was only 17 at the time, and made him her bodyguard and constant companion in 1970. On August 7, Jonathan Jackson sneaked weapons into a Marin County courtroom in San Rafael, California, and held the judge, jury, and prosecution at gunpoint in order to free his black friend James McClain, who was accused of assaulting

Angela Davis raises her fist in a radical salute as she enters court for a bail hearing in San Rafael, California, on June 14, 1971. Her attorney, Howard Moore, Jr., is at right. Davis was tried and acquitted on charges of supplying weapons for the failed 1970 escape attempt of prisoners from the Marin County courthouse. In that escape attempt, a judge and several prisoners were killed. AP Photo.

a white police officer. Jackson, McClain, and two other accomplices took Judge Harold Haley, Assistant District Attorney Gary Thomas, and three women jurors hostage, leading them outside into a getaway van. Having taped a shotgun under the chin of Haley, the criminals expected the police not to fire on them. They were mistaken. When police opened fire, Haley's head was blown off, and Thomas took a bullet in the back that left him paralyzed. Jackson and McClain, meanwhile, were killed. Although Davis was not on the scene of the crime, and although it was not proven that she had foreknowledge of the plot, three of the four guns used in the shootout were registered in her name. Indeed, Davis had already begun arming herself, as was the Black Panther custom, before ever meeting Jonathan Jackson, indicating that she anticipated violence. Circumstantial evidence thus placed her squarely in the plot, although she claimed her ownership of weapons was purely for self-defense.

The FBI promptly put her on its Ten Most Wanted list. Davis became a fugitive, running and hiding from authorities for the next two months. On October 13, 1970, she was captured in New York City. She was then extradited to California to stand trial in the same courthouse where the Jonathan Jackson shootout had occurred. Although she initially requested the same communist defense attorney (John J. Abt) that Lee Harvey Oswald, the assassin of John F. Kennedy, had asked for prior to his murder at the hands of Jack Ruby, in 1963, she ultimately defended herself with the help of a different lawyer. The arraignment, which occurred on January 5, 1971, started the media spectacle that became her case. Because she was a known communist, her case even attracted the attention of academic and political leaders in the Soviet Union. When 14 Soviet citizens sent a letter of support for Davis to President Richard Nixon, in a strange bit of Cold War strategy, Nixon invited them to the United States to witness the trial firsthand so that they would believe in the fairness and impartiality of American justice.

Not only did Soviet communists rush to her side, but white liberals and black civil rights leaders in America did so, as well. The Presbyterian Council on Church and Race, a predominantly white organization, donated $10,000 to her defense in what turned out to be an extremely controversial move that contributed to a schism within the Presbyterian denomination. The former Beatles leader John Lennon and his wife, Yoko Ono, as well as the Rolling Stones, performed songs in her honor. Coretta Scott King, Ralph Abernathy, Jesse Jackson, and Roy Wilkins all became apologists for her. A "Free Angela!" movement thus bubbled up throughout America that mimicked the "Free Huey!" campaign of the Black Panthers a couple of years earlier. Its apex was the celebration of "Angela Davis Day" in Central Park a year after she was captured there in New York City. On February 23, 1972, after 16 months in detention, Davis was freed on bail; the "Free Angela!" campaign had finally raised enough money—more than $100,000—to allow her to leave jail. The trial started five days later.

While Davis's case dragged on, her friend George Jackson still sat in San Quentin prison in California, planning his escape. On August 21, 1971, Jackson killed three prison guards and two white trustees as he attempted a breakout. His plan ended abruptly in failure. As he scaled a fence, a guard in a watchtower put a bullet through the top of his head that went all the way down his back and came out the other end. Despite the fact that Davis had kept company with such revolutionaries as the Jackson brothers, with all the positive publicity that came from the "Free Angela!" campaign, her trial resulted in an acquittal. Interestingly, the jury was composed of eleven whites, one Hispanic, and no blacks. After the trial, a white juror, Ralph De Lange, was heard to say that by setting Davis free, he hoped to send a clear message to the world that white Americans now understood and sympathized with the plight of black Americans. In other words, the verdict had nothing to do with the merits of the case in his opinion; it was purely symbolic, designed to show how far the United States had come since the beginning of the civil rights movement. Whether he was right or wrong in his assessment of the verdict, four other jurors joined him and Davis in a public celebration of the acquittal that day. Some observers, such as the Reverend Jesse Jackson, believed that the verdict proved the case was so flimsy it never should have been brought to court, while the majority of white Americans considered it a miscarriage of justice. Either way, De Lange's statement echoed loud and clear that times were changing.

1973: THE AMERICAN INDIAN MOVEMENT AND THE WOUNDED KNEE STANDOFF

On February 27, 1973, while the freezing cold winds still whistled across the vast open plains of South Dakota, a group of militant American Indians stormed the town of Wounded Knee on the grounds of the Pine Ridge Sioux Reservation, and held it for 71 days.

The leaders of the group represented the American Indian Movement (AIM), and they chose Wounded Knee as center stage for the occupation because it had been the site of the last great Indian massacre in U.S. history, back in 1890. AIM had a list of complaints to which they hoped to draw attention, ranging from corruption in the tribal government to neglect of the Pine Ridge reservation by the U.S. government. The activists got their wish. "Wounded Knee II," as it became known, grew into one of the biggest media spectacles of the 1970s, as the ensuing showdown with government forces—U.S. marshals, FBI agents, the National Guard, and tribal police—resulted in, according to one estimate, 5 million rounds of ammunition being fired. All three major television networks covered it extensively, and it became the third most documented event of the decade, behind only the Vietnam War and the Watergate scandal. The price for all the attention, however, was unfortunately high. Two Indians were killed, 12 were wounded, and 600 were arrested (although none were convicted).

Chippewas, led by the ex-convicts Dennis Banks and Clyde Bellecourt, had founded AIM in 1968 in Minneapolis. Although the organization was not directly the catalyst behind the Alcatraz occupation of 1969–1971, AIM's support of such militant tactics made it the most visible of the various Indian activist groups in the 1970s. In November 1970, on the 350th anniversary of the Pilgrims' landing at Plymouth Rock, in Massachusetts, AIM seized the ship *Mayflower II* to remind white Americans which racial group was here first and what debt they owed to the indigenous people. AIM continued its radical ways, staging an occupation at Mount Rushmore in the Black Hills of South Dakota in 1971 and an occupation/desecration of the Bureau of Indian Affairs (BIA) office in Washington, D.C., a year later. In October 1972, AIM issued its "Trail of Broken Treaties 20-Point Position Paper," which it sent to President Nixon. Then, at the beginning of 1973, the group occupied Custer County Courthouse, just five miles from Mount Rushmore, before moving down the road about 50 miles to Wounded Knee, on the Pine Ridge reservation. Although grievances against the reservation system, the BIA, racial discrimination against Indians off the reservation, and all levels of the white man's government had been building for years, the immediate cause of AIM's South Dakota campaign in 1973 can be traced to corruption in the tribal council of Pine Ridge. The elected leader of the reservation was an

Indian named Dickie Wilson. He polarized the population with his overly friendly cooperation with the federal government and his allegedly preferential treatment of family and friends even as he neglected or abused the rest of the Indians. AIM first sought to end his tenure by impeaching him. When that failed, it tried removing him by armed rebellion.

Internal politics on Indian reservations has always been an enigma for whites observing from a distance. Blending aspects of traditional tribal customs and culture with white values, BIA requirements and expectations, and modern technology, governance of Indian reservations was and is complex. Often the Indians have been torn between clinging to the old and embracing the new, hopelessly caught in the middle of the clash of cultures. Compounding the problem was race-mixing between Indians and whites, which produced a new generation whose members often had natural advantages over the pure blood Indians in their ability to communicate and assimilate and who ultimately become leaders among the Natives. Such was the case at Pine Ridge in 1973, but none of this constituted anything new. Going back more than 200 years, when French explorers dubbed the Indians of the region "Sioux" (even though those Natives called themselves "Lakota" or "Dakota"), there had been such cultural confusion. Over the course of time, the Natives mostly came to accept the Sioux label but kept their traditional subtribal identities, of which there were several, alive among themselves. There were Santee Sioux, Teton Sioux, Oglala Sioux, and even smaller subdivisions among these groups. The Sioux collectively were among the last Indians to be conquered by the United States government and military forces and to be confined to reservations. By the late twentieth century, they had mostly fallen victim to all the same socioeconomic problems that ran rampant on all reservations: unemployment, lack of usable education, alcoholism and drug addiction, depression, and suicide.

Into this cocktail of misery was thrown the allegedly corrupt administration of Dickie Wilson, a Sioux who received the full support of the BIA despite the problems his leadership caused. The first complaint against him was that he claimed to be a supporter of AIM but then sold out the group by giving information to the federal authorities about its leaders' plans and whereabouts. Next, he ran the reservation as his own personal fiefdom, using his office to embezzle and extort money. In blatant and egregious cases of nepotism, he hired his relatives to work in various capacities on the reservation. Then he sold off tribal lands to the federal government, pocketing the money and getting in the good graces of the feds, defying the well-known desire of his people to keep their land. Finally, he crushed anyone who dared question his decisions or oppose his rule. To intimidate his opponents, he ran a tribal police force called the Guards of the Oglala Nation, which opponents mocked as the GOON squad. The GOONs did Wilson's bidding, beating up and, when necessary, murdering opponents.

To end these abuses, AIM arrived on the scene on February 27, 1973, and, along with 300 local Indians, staged an occupation of the town of Wounded Knee. At least 75 different Indian tribes were represented in the ancestry of the occupiers. They used the Sacred Heart Catholic Church in the center of town as their headquarters. The main spokesman for the occupiers was Russell Means, a founding member of AIM who later became a movie star by playing Indian roles. Soon after beginning the occupation, AIM created the Independent Oglala Nation as a rival government to the Wilson regime and called for the federal government to honor the 1868 Fort Laramie Treaty, which promised the Black Hills region to the Sioux in perpetuity. Although government agents came in supposedly to negotiate, all they really did was demand that AIM lay down their weapons and submit to government authority. When AIM refused such demands, government forces surrounded the town, cut off all roads and access points to the reservation, prohibited suppliers from bringing food in, and turned off the electricity in Wounded Knee, hoping to starve and freeze the occupants out. Sporadic shooting back and forth resulted in two Indians, Frank Clearwater and Buddy Lamont, being killed. Other AIM supporters were reportedly lynched by the GOONS. AIM held out through three blizzards and for more than two months but ultimately had to surrender or starve.

Although the leaders of Wounded Knee II faced charges in federal court, none were convicted. Partly this was due to growing sympathy for the Indians among

On March 10, 1973, more than one week after seizing Wounded Knee, South Dakota, and starting a standoff with federal authorities, members of the Oglala Sioux tribe march to the cemetery where their ancestors were buried following the 1890 massacre at the site. Third-in-line is Carter Camp, one of the leaders of the American Indian Movement (AIM). Members of the AIM were calling the government's withdrawal that day from the village outskirts a victory. AP Photo.

the general public, which was largely generated by media portrayals of the red man as the helpless victim of white oppression and as underdogs in a fight they could not win. Russell Means later acknowledged the heavy media coverage of the occupation as the only reason the federal authorities did not perpetrate another massacre of his people at Wounded Knee as they had done in 1890—it would not have played well on television. In addition to that, President Nixon's restraining influence on federal authorities at Wounded Knee also helped preserve lives. Indeed, Nixon had a more magnanimous policy toward the Indians than any of his recent presidential predecessors. The Nixon administration might have been more inclined to negotiate with AIM on some level and possibly make some concessions had it not been for the Watergate scandal, which was just beginning to become a major distraction in early 1973. Conversely, the trials of AIM leaders, which occurred as the Watergate scandal was being fully exposed, might have resulted in some convictions had it not been for the lack of credibility of the Nixon administration in prosecuting anyone else for alleged crimes at that time. The ultimate irony, in fact, is that none of the Indians went to jail for federal offenses, yet several officials in the Nixon administration did, while others lost their government jobs.

Even though the Wounded Knee II trials ended in 1974, the AIM saga was just beginning. AIM members and the FBI engaged in a deadly shootout in 1975, resulting in the conviction of Leonard Peltier of AIM for murder in a case that has attracted nationwide attention ever since. In addition, some 60 Indians around the Pine Ridge reservation disappeared under mysterious circumstances between 1973 and 1976, allegedly at the hands of Wilson's GOONS. Whether Wilson was responsible or not, residents voted him out of office in 1976, ending what AIM called his "reign of terror." In 1978, AIM achieved its coup de grace with its "Longest Walk," a march on Washington, D.C., that began in San Francisco. In the years since, movies have been made and books have been written about AIM's crusade for Indian justice. Yet, for all the attention such actions received temporarily, they have been all but forgotten by mainstream America as time has marched on.

1974: THE BOSTON BUSING CONTROVERSY

Since the days of the American Revolution 200 years earlier, Boston had prided itself on being the cradle of liberty. Moreover, since the days of the Abolition movement 150 years earlier, this hub of New England had enjoyed a smug sense of racial enlightenment. One of the main seats of education and high culture in the United States, this city built by the Puritans could not have thought of itself in the 1960s as anything less than a paragon of progressive race relations. As white Bostonians watched civil rights events unfold in the Deep South, they felt largely insulated from such problems. An occasional march or minor riot in their own midst did little to shake their faith in their own collective goodness. They were simply a cut above white southerners in their own minds—that is, until the forced-busing issue cropped up in 1974. School integration, it turned out, received precisely the same reception among white Bostonians as a whole as it did among whites in Birmingham. A cold, hard reckoning took place, as the people of Boston were exposed before the eyes of the world as being made of the same flesh and blood as everybody else in America, North and South alike.

The genesis of the school integration issue in Massachusetts dates back to the early 1950s. Even before *Brown v. Board of Education*, black Bostonians noticed the same kind of inequities between predominantly white schools and their own that black southerners typically complained about. There were disparities in the quality of facilities, the size of classes, the number of teachers and administrators, the age of textbooks, and the amount of money spent on resources generally—$340 per white pupil but only $240 per black pupil. Twelve of the 13 predominantly black schools in Boston did not meet city or state health and safety standards and had no funds allocated to fix the problem. There were few black teachers and no black principals. Worse, no efforts to recruit minorities were being made by the Boston School Committee or the state of Massachusetts. When the NAACP confronted the Massachusetts Commission against Discrimination with these findings, it basically ignored them and reported that no legal segregation existed in the Boston school system. Technically this was true, but de facto segregation was rampant in Boston, just as it was in most major northern cities in the 1960s. Although African Americans made up just 16 percent of the city's population, by 1970 more than 80 percent of black elementary school students attended "black" schools in "black" neighborhoods and suburbs.

As early as 1963, it became obvious to black parents that the all-white Boston School Committee had no intention of upsetting the racial status quo. They took matters into their own hands, therefore, and organized a "Stay-Out-for-Freedom" boycott, in which about 3,000 black high school students participated. A year later, a second boycott spilled over from the schools into the city, and about 20,000 people participated. Then, in April 1965, Martin Luther King, Jr., led a march through town that drew about 25,000 to Boston Common. One result of these actions was that the state legislature passed, on August 18, 1965, the Racial Imbalance Act, which was designed to force majority-white schools to take affirmative action-type steps to adjust the ratio of blacks to whites in their student bodies. The following school year, a black parent group started Operation Exodus, a privately funded busing/car pooling effort to get black students on the south side across town to majority-white schools. An organization called METCO, which had funding from the federal government and the Carnegie Corporation, had taken over the effort by the early 1970s, busing some 2,500 students to 38 different schools daily.

None of these early busing efforts led to any major racial altercations, partly because private initiative had started and largely sustained them and partly because fewer than half of all black students participated and those who did were so widely scattered that they posed no threat to the overall racial balance of any one predominantly white school. Two changes occurred between 1971 and 1974, however, that upset the hitherto acceptable arrangement. First, an organization called the Black Student Union emerged in 1971, demanding the right of pupils to dress in African dashikis if they so chose and staging protests to force the School Committee to change the curriculum to offer black studies courses. This group also demanded that more black teachers and administrators be hired and that other similar measures be taken to improve the quality of life and education in the schools. Second, when these demands fell on deaf ears, the following year the NAACP filed suit against the Boston school system in federal court. The judgment, which came on June 21, 1974, favored the NAACP and coincided with a state supreme court order also requiring the Boston School Committee to develop a plan to adjust the racial inequities.

The plan that resulted called for 23 of the 65 area schools to bus students across town, beginning at the start of the fall semester in September. The black-majority schools were paired with the nearest white-majority schools to keep the distance of the busing to a minimum. Roxbury High, a heavily black suburban school, was thus paired with South Boston High, an almost exclusively white school. Only three blacks had attended South Boston High in the previous decade. The school, and the area of South Boston in general, was predominantly Irish Catholic and had a reputation as tough, streetwise, and working class. Both students and parents alike in South Boston let everyone know in no uncertain terms that they did not want blacks in their school. Even more important, though, the students did not want to be bused to Roxbury. Nor did their parents want them to be bused there. A group of parents led by Louise Day Hicks, a former teacher and current School Committee member, organized ROAR (Restore Our Alienated Rights) to protest the busing plan. Not only did ROAR protest the plan, but so did the Boston Teachers' Union and the Boston Police Patrolmen's Association. On the eve of the start of the fall term, ROAR and some of its political allies in the Massachusetts state legislature issued a "Declaration of Clarification" that explained why they opposed busing. "It is against our children's best interest," they said, "to send them to school in crime-infested Roxbury. . . . There are at least one hundred black people walking around in the black community [there] who have killed white people during the past two years."[1]

Despite the opposition, the plan was carried out according to the court order. On the first day of class, September 12, mobs of whites surrounded South Boston schools waiting to hurl epithets and stones at the busloads of black students. At the elementary school, nine children were injured, and 18 buses were damaged. At the high school, in addition to more of the same, whites also held bananas and yelled, "Monkeys get out!" and "Niggers go home!" Anticipating such violence, the vast majority of the black students feared to attend school that first day. Only 40 out of 941 who were supposed to attend South Boston High got on a bus that day to go. Most of the white students stayed out in protest of the forced integration, with only 25 out of 1,604 attending that first day. In Roxbury, by contrast, more that 400 out of 453 black students showed up for school the first day, but only 40 whites out of 523 got on a bus to go there. It was probably fortunate that so many skipped school the first day; it kept the violence to a minimum. A week later, however, on September 19, rioting broke out at Hyde Park High and spilled over into the surrounding community. It was serious enough that all classes had to be canceled the next day.

Although some of the schools in Boston managed to integrate peacefully, most teetered on the brink of exploding for months. White parents sought redress at the hands of their elected officials, but the politicians either were powerless to change the court order or agreed with it, even at the risk of incurring the wrath of their constituents. U.S. Senator Edward Kennedy of Massachusetts, for example, became the butt of parents' criticism for approving the court order and busing plan. When he tried to make a public statement on the issue, they taunted him, threw tomatoes and eggs at him, and forced him to seek shelter inside a nearby office. They shattered the window of that office. Meanwhile, they picketed the home of Judge Arthur Garrity, who had issued the ruling. They also turned their anger against Cardinal Humberto Medeiros, the Archbishop of Boston, who had refused to allow students to enroll in the private Catholic schools to avoid integration of the public schools. They even turned against the police, who, although largely sympathetic to their cause, were forced to do their duty and enforce the busing plan.

All this tension over the school situation turned Boston at large into a racial powder keg. On October 7, a black man was attacked by a white mob in South Boston and beaten severely. A television news crew that happened to be in the area to cover the ongoing school busing protest caught the beating on tape. The mob then turned violently on the news reporters and cameramen. That same day, riots broke out at three different Boston high schools. To try to quell the violence, President Gerald R. Ford made a public statement on October 9, saying that he sympathized with the whites in Boston who opposed forced busing. The next day, Mayor Kevin White of Boston likewise came out publicly against forced busing. These statements by important public officials encouraged whites to continue resisting, thus prolonging the agony of the inevitable change. Black leaders such as Coretta Scott King and Angela Davis, however, showed up in Boston thereafter to stage rallies in support of school integration and forced busing. Consequently, by December, the racial tension was still high in Boston. On December 11, a white student at South Boston High was stabbed by a black man who was not a student there. Fellow white students went on a rampage in retaliation, attacking buses, police cars, and black people alike. Whites in South Boston were "dreaming of a white Christmas," as they put it.

As 1975 began, the tension did not diminish. On May 17, the NAACP staged a march attended by 15,000 supporters of integrated schools in Boston. For every participant, however, there were easily three white Bostonians who continued to oppose it vehemently. By the start of the fall semester in 1975, the situation had grown so tense that even the white police officers in Boston did not want to get involved. They staged a "sick-out" on the first day of school. They soon were forced back to work, of course, but they also received backup help from the National Guard. After all such efforts had failed to yield peace and safety for school children, on December 9, Judge Garrity removed control of the Boston public schools from the School Committee, fired eight school administrators who he considered the catalysts, and placed the schools under control of the court. The white response to these measures was to firebomb the local NAACP office. Even so, at this point, white opponents realized this was the beginning of the end of their fight to prevent desegregation. They would not regain control of their own schools at the local level for 10 years.

The results of this social experimentation in Boston were mixed. On the one hand, black students generally scored higher on standardized tests after integration than before, more blacks got teaching and administrative jobs in schools, and blacks and their white integrationist allies had their faith in the American justice system either confirmed or restored. Whites, on the other hand, began to vacate the city for the suburbs at a higher rate than ever before, and there are now no majority-white public schools left in Boston. This indicates that the way white southerners had resisted integration of their public schools a decade earlier was not an aberration; it was an all-too-common reaction to a life-changing, world-altering situation that was forced on them against their will. Whether right or wrong, moral or immoral, it was all too common. Some whites who initially opposed court-ordered integration, however, came eventually to see the benefits of it. It forced them to get to know a group of people, African Americans, they otherwise never would have wanted to, needed to, or had the opportunity to get to know. That turned out to be a positive educational experience for them in the long run.

1976: THREE KINGS AND A PRESIDENT

Three "Kings" were key players in the 1976 presidential race: Leslie, Clennon, and Martin Luther King. The election pitted the incumbent, Gerald R. Ford, Jr., whose birth name before adoption was Leslie King, Jr., against the former Georgia governor James E. Carter, Jr., who preferred to be called "Jimmy." The choice, on paper at least, seemed quite a contrast. Ford, a Michigan Republican with a long career as a Washington "insider," had served as House Minority Leader until 1973, when President Nixon appointed him to the vice presidency after Spiro T. Agnew's resignation amid a tax evasion scandal. A year later, because of a much bigger scandal, the Watergate coverup, Ford was automatically elevated to the presidency when Nixon resigned. Thus, Ford became the only Commander-in-Chief in American history to have never been elected either president or vice president. Ford had served two years and almost three months as the nation's chief executive officer when the presidential election rolled around, on November 2. Ford's record was spotty. The economy was in recession, the energy crisis was at full throttle, and the Vietnam War had ended in disgrace. Worse, the Watergate scandal and the seeming corruption of the Republican party weighed like millstones around Ford's candidacy, especially since it appeared that Ford might be complicit in the corruption because of his pardon of Nixon. He had little in the way of a record to run on in terms of leadership on racial issues.

Jimmy Carter, meanwhile, seemed like a breath of fresh air. No Washington insider, he was as unlikely a candidate to win the presidency as one might find. A south Georgia farm boy who had gone off to the Navy and studied nuclear engineering in the 1940s and 1950s, Carter had returned home to the sleepy little town of Plains to run his family's peanut farming business and to run for local and state offices. Having no connections with anyone in the Washington establishment, he brought a candidacy that seemed squeaky clean when measured by Ford's. Upon inspection, his record was not absolutely pure, but it still seemed extremely so by contrast. Through the civil rights struggles of the 1960s, Carter developed a reputation as a racial "moderate" in Georgia, rather than a staunch segregationist. While certainly no crusader for racial justice, he walked a step or two ahead of most of his peers in Georgia with his racial views. Winning the governorship of the Peach State in 1970, Carter amassed a mixed record on racial issues while residing in and presiding from Atlanta. He appointed more blacks to government posts (more than 100) than any of his predecessors, but critics pointed out that most of the jobs were of the low-level, advisory type that carried little power. He also signed a state resolution making January 15, 1973, the first "Martin Luther King, Jr., Day" and had paintings of King and two other blacks hung in the state capitol alongside dozens of Georgia's white leaders of renown. Despite such positive changes, so unclear was his record on race relations as governor that black leaders in Georgia divided over supporting his presidential candidacy in 1976. Andrew Young and Martin Luther King, Sr., publicly supported Carter, for instance, while the noted state legislator and civil rights activist Julian Bond vehemently opposed him.

At stake in the election for minorities was the legacy of Martin Luther King, Jr., who had dreamed that one day blacks and whites would join hands across the racial divide in peace and amity. Which candidate would best help make the dream come true? The answer did not look clear, and thus the black vote was not a slam dunk for either man. As the election approached, into the political fray stepped a strange figure who hoped to steer the black vote away from Carter and toward Ford. It was the Reverend Clennon King of the Interdenominational Divine Mission Church in Albany, Georgia. A civil rights activist with a checkered past, this King was in many ways the antithesis of the more famous Reverend King (MLK). In 1958, Clennon became the first African American to attempt to integrate the University of Mississippi (four years before James Meredith did it successfully), for which state authorities locked him away in a mental institution. In 1960, he ran for president of the United States on the Afro-American party ticket and invited Richard Nixon to be his running mate. Thereafter, he spent time in a California prison for failure to support his family financially, although his conviction was later overturned. He tried unsuccessfully to become a citizen of Jamaica before coming back to the United States and again running for president in 1972. Because of these factors, many observers have concluded that King may have been somewhat mentally unbalanced.

On October 25, 1976, one week before the election, Clennon King announced publicly that he intended to travel 45 miles north from Albany to Carter's hometown of Plains and attempt to become a member of his Southern Baptist Church the next Sunday morning. It was an obvious publicity stunt designed to draw attention to the fact that Carter attended an all-white church that barred blacks and thus to show that Carter was hypocritical on racial issues and could not be trusted as president. The truth was that the Plains Baptist Church had indeed passed a resolution in 1965 barring "Negroes" from membership, but Carter voted against it. King kept his word and arrived the next Sunday morning, which just happened to be Halloween, with an entourage of three other blacks. It might have looked, to observers who watched black men approach the front doorstep of an all-white church in south Georgia with hands outstretched, like some kind of bizarre trick-or-treat prank, except that it was too serious be considered child's play.

King arrived in time for the worship service only to find that the church's morning service had been canceled. The 254-member church's 12 active deacons had heard of his plans and unanimously decided to thwart them. As King approached the church, they turned him away. Pastor Bruce Edwards opposed the deacons' decision and invited King to come back for the evening service or next Sunday's morning service. King decided against doing either, having made his point. Another black man, however, Roger Sessoms of North Carolina, did show up for the evening service, taking a seat directly in front of Jimmy Carter, who, interestingly, had a black Secret Service agent shadowing him everywhere he went, including church. Carter, the pastor, and some members welcomed Sessoms. Others did not.

Although the disturbance that Sunday had no bearing on the outcome of the election, the repercussions for the church itself were huge. Pastor Edwards faced possible dismissal from his own church for his stance. In a subsequent referendum, the congregation voted 107 to 84 to keep Edwards and 120 to 66 to rescind the 1965 resolution barring blacks from membership. The minority wielded more power, however, than the vote would indicate, since the deacons and some of the most faithful attendees and tithe-givers were among them. Consequently, in a strange twist, about half of the congregation discussed the possibility of breaking off and forming a new church that would welcome people of all races in the event that the segregationists should somehow override the vote. Eventually, the church would indeed split, although not directly a result of this issue, but more because Carter's fame created problems for the tiny church, such as jealousy among members and political differences of opinion that led to theological disputes. In the meantime, at the next Sunday service, with news reporters on the scene, a crowd of 500 people gathered in the muddy parking lot, dividing into two camps—one for keeping segregated churches, one for integrating them. In a sort of perverse reincarnation of Civil War sentiments, they competed by singing "Dixie" and "The Battle Hymn of the Republic." It made great theater, but it continued to eat away at the church like a cancer. Within a few more weeks, attendance and tithes/offerings had dwindled, Edwards stepped down under pressure, and the church faced an uncertain future.

Beyond the localized and immediate problem of this one church, this episode symbolized the dilemma that white southerners in general faced in the late 1970s. Since the federal government had forced the integration of all public facilities, white southerners debated whether they should now cling desperately to segregation in their churches. After all, churches were the last remaining institution that, because of the First Amendment, was untouchable by the long tentacles of government regulation. Many decided, however, that they should bow to public pressure, catch up with modern life in America, and voluntarily accept integration, in even their private religious sphere. To remain segregated in church would preserve their pride intact and keep the religious convictions of their forefathers unadulterated by changing times. To embrace the integration of their churches would prove they were not bigots and buffoons and in some cases would salve their consciences. In Carter's estimation, the churches of the deep South represented the last stronghold of pre-civil-rights-movement racism in America, and he for one favored integration over tradition.

The media and the American public outside the Deep South used this episode to learn about the history and contemporary views of the Southern Baptist Association of Churches (also called the Southern Baptist Convention), of which the Plains Baptist Church was a member. Although it was founded in 1845, in Augusta, Georgia, and had developed into the largest Protestant denomination in the United States, with some 35,000 local churches scattered through all 50 states and in various countries around the world, it had managed to keep a low profile for generations. Quietly, it had gone about the business of domestic evangelism and foreign missions, rarely playing any open role in national politics. The president of the Southern Baptist Convention in 1976, James L. Sullivan of Nashville, spoke out freely about the dilemma of racial segregation in religion. He strongly supported integration as the denomination's official policy, but he added that the churches were local entities that made their own decisions about such matters. He opposed Clennon King's attempt to integrate the Plains Baptist Church, saying that it was clearly an insincere gesture that had nothing to do with religion and everything to do with politics. For starters, King had tried to embarrass and pressure the church into accepting him as a member, said Sullivan. More important, he was already a minister of another church, was not a Baptist, and did not reside close enough to the church to be able to participate in its services regularly even if he did join.

Perhaps the logic of that explanation satisfied the press, or perhaps there were more pressing issues to cover regarding the president-elect, such as what he would do to fix the broken economy and how he would heal the wounded pride of a once mighty nation after Vietnam. Whichever the case, public attention turned away from this blip on the radar screen of Carter's presidency. Soon, every time the media converged upon Plains, Georgia, it would be to mock Jimmy's homey redneck brother Billy or to cover some other familial matter. Former president Gerald Ford, alias Leslie King, accepted defeat graciously and faded into the background, playing the role of ex-leader of the free world with dignity. Clennon King, meanwhile, faded back into the obscurity from whence he had come but appeared on the public scene occasionally in later decades in equally bizarre situations. Later in life, he announced to the world that people had made a huge mistake in setting up Martin Luther King as some kind of Superman while considering Clennon King some kind of super-nutcase. Just as the comic book Superman had his "Bizzaro" alter ego who lived in "Bizzaro World," so too, it seems, MLK had his.

VOICES OF THE DECADE

BOBBY SEALE

Bobby Seale co-founded the Black Panther Party for Self-Defense with Huey P. Newton, in 1966. In 1970, he published a book that served as an autobiography of both himself and the Black Panthers. In this excerpt, he describes how the Panthers came into being and expresses one of their most important ideas—that, contrary to popular misconception, they were not a reverse-racist organization. They were, however, a Marxist organization, as can be seen here.

One day Huey said, "It's about time we get the organization off the ground, and do it now."

This was in the latter part of September 1966. From around the first of October to the fifteenth of October, in the poverty center in North Oakland, Huey and I began to write out a ten-point platform and program of the Black Panther Party. . . .

When we got all through writing the program, Huey said, "We've got to have some kind of structure. What do you want to be," he asked me, "Chairman or Minister of Defense?"

"Doesn't make any difference to me," I said. "What do you want to be, Chairman or Minister of Defense?"

"I'll be the Minister of Defense," Huey said, "and you'll be the Chairman.". . .

With the ten-point platform and program and the two of us, the Party was officially launched on October 15, 1966, in a poverty program office in the black community in Oakland, California. . . .

The Black Panther Party is not a black racist organization, not a racist organization at all. We understand where racism comes from. Our Minister of Defense, Huey P. Newton, has taught us to understand that we have to oppose all kinds of racism. The Party understands the imbedded racism in a large part of white America and it understands that the very small cults that sprout up every now and then in the black community have a basically black racist philosophy.

The Black Panther Party would not stoop to the low, scurvy level of a Ku Klux Klansman, a white supremacist, or the so-called "patriotic" white citizens organizations, which hate black people because of the color of their skin.

The ruling class . . . are the ones who help to maintain and aid the power structure by perpetuating their racist attitudes and using racism as a means to divide the people. But it's really the small, minority ruling class that is dominating, exploiting, and oppressing the working and laboring people.

All of us are laboring-class people, employed or unemployed, and our unity has got to be based on the practical necessities of life, liberty, and the pursuit of happiness, if that means anything to anybody. . . . So let me emphasize again—we believe our fight is a class struggle and not a race struggle.

From Bobby Seale, *Seize the Time: The Story of the Black Panther Party and Huey P. Newton* (New York: Random House, 1970), pp. 59, 62, 69–70, 72.

DAVID HILLIARD

Although the Black Panthers' Marxist dogma made them in many ways anti-American from the beginning, by 1970 the group had evolved into a revolutionary force intent upon replacing the existing power structure of the United States by rewriting the Constitution. This evolution can be traced to the fact that, by this time, no longer did local police departments work alone to destroy the Black Panthers in their vicinity; the FBI and the Nixon administration had begun a campaign to destroy the group nationally. This war against the Panthers, which involved frequent shootouts with law enforcement agents, prison sentences imposed on them, and funerals for their members, led the Panthers to the conclusion that no hope remained that their race could ever get a fair shake in America. Here are excerpts from their "Call for a Revolutionary People's Constitutional Convention, September 7, 1970, Philadelphia, PA," which had been delivered orally by a group leader, David Hilliard, at the Lincoln Memorial in Washington, D.C., three months earlier.

"Message to America." Delivered on the 107th Anniversary of the Emancipation Proclamation at Washington, D.C., Capitol [*sic*] of Babylon, World Racism, and Imperialism, June 19, 1970 by The Black Panther Party.

As oppressed people held captive within the confines of the Fascist-Imperialist United States of America, we Black Americans take a dim view of the position that we, as a people, find ourselves in at the beginning of the 7th decade of the Twentieth Century . . . we see clearly that a well-planned, calculated Fascist Genocidal Conspiracy is being implemented against our people.

Black people within the domestic confines of the U.S.A. have reached another crossroad. This is a time for the most serious decisions that we, as a people, have ever been called upon to make. The decisions that we make in our time, the actions that we take or fail to take, will determine whether we, as a people, will survive or fall victims to genocidal extermination at the hands of the FASCIST MAJORITY. . . .

The United States of America is the Number One exploiter and oppressor of the peoples of the whole world. . . . The empty promise of the Constitution to "establish Justice" lies exposed to the world by the reality of Black Peoples' existence. . . . The Constitution of the U.S.A. does not and never has protected our people or guaranteed to us those lofty ideals enshrined within it. . . . We were held in slavery under the Constitution. . . . We have had Human Rights denied and violated perpetually under this Constitution . . .

We feel that, in practical terms, it is time for Black people as a whole to address their attention to the question of our National Destiny.

Black people can no longer either respect the U.S. Constitution, look to it with hope, or live under it. . . . We repudiate, most emphatically . . . the Constitution of the United States. . . .

If we are to remain a part of the United States, then we must have a new Constitution that will strictly guarantee our Human Rights to Life, Liberty, and the Pursuit of Happiness, which is promised but not delivered by the present Constitution . . . if we cannot make a new arrangement within the United States, then we have no alternative but to declare ourselves free and independent of the United States. . . .

WE THEREFORE, CALL FOR A REVOLUTIONARY PEOPLE'S CONSTITUTIONAL CONVENTION, TO BE CONVENED BY THE AMERICAN PEOPLE, TO WRITE A NEW CONSTITUTION THAT WILL GUARANTEE AND DELIVER TO EVERY AMERICAN CITIZEN THE INVIOLABLE HUMAN RIGHT TO LIFE, LIBERTY, AND THE PURSUIT OF HAPPINESS! . . .

We are from 25 to 30 million strong, and we are armed. . . . Before we accept Genocide, we will inflict Total Destruction upon Babylon. . . .

In Philip S. Foner, ed., The Black Panthers Speak (Philadelphia: J. B. Lippincott, 1970), pp. 267–71.

HENRY L. ADAMS

The American Indian Movement (AIM) began among Chippewas in Minnesota in 1968 as a "Red Power" imitation of the Black Power movement. Having previously staged demonstrations in California, Nebraska, and South Dakota that drew national attention, AIM was about to seize and occupy the headquarters of the Bureau of Indian Affairs in Washington, D.C., when it issued its "Manifesto" calling for radical reforms in Native American-U.S. government relations. Henry L. Adams, an AIM member, wrote the document.

An Indian Manifesto for Restitution, Reparations, Restoration of Lands for a Reconstruction of an Indian Future in America: The Trail of Broken Treaties

We need not give another recitation of past complaints nor engage in redundant dialogue of discontent. Our conditions and their cause for being should perhaps be best known by those who have written the record of America's action against Indian people. In 1832, Black Hawk correctly observed: You know the cause of our making war. It is known to all white men. They ought to be ashamed of it.

The government of the United States knows the reasons for our going to its capital city. Unfortunately, they don't know how to greet us. We go because America has been only too ready to express shame, and suffer none from the expression—while remaining wholly unwilling to change to allow life for Indian people. We seek a new American majority—a majority that is not content merely to confirm itself by superiority in numbers, but which by conscience is committed toward prevailing upon the public will in ceasing wrongs and in doing right. For our part, in words and deeds of coming days, we propose to produce a rational, reasoned manifesto for construction of an Indian future in America. If America has maintained faith with its original spirit, or may recognize it now, we should not be denied.

Press Statement issued: October 31, 1972. From the archives link on the AIM Web site: http://www.aimovement.org/.

RUSSELL MEANS

Russell Means was one of the first members of AIM. He became perhaps the best-known spokesman for the group through his Hollywood acting career. In his 1995 autobiography, he explains why AIM staged the occupation of Wounded Knee, South Dakota, from February 27 to May 8, 1973.

In early 1973, Pedro Bissonnette and other leaders of the Oglala Sioux Civil Rights Organization at Pine Ridge had been telling us about the terrible beatings and intimidation inflicted by Dick Wilson's goons. We didn't know why Wilson had turned against his people, but many on the reservation and in AIM thought he had been bought off by white ranchers. They were rich, politically powerful men who paid next to nothing to lease vast areas of the reservation for grazing. The tribal council, at least theoretically, could have ended that cozy arrangement. That theory, however, never quite explained why Wilson got so much support from the feds. . . .

On Pine Ridge, the government desperately wanted to maintain control of the Sheep Mountain Gunnery Range, an area amounting to about an eighth of the reservation. During World War II, the land had been "lent" to what became the U.S. Defense Department. It was supposed to revert to tribal control after the war. While prospecting it secretly, the feds discovered large deposits of uranium and molybdenum, essential to making high strength steel alloys. After Wilson became tribal president, he agreed to the permanent transfer of the gunnery range to the feds. In return, he received their unrestricted support. Giving away Sheep Mountain violated our treaty. Wilson, on orders from his white masters, knew that traditional Lakota people would never permit the transfer. Because those people and AIM supported each other, he set out to destroy AIM and to crush all resistance.

From Russell Means, *Where White Men Fear to Tread: The Autobiography of Russell Means* (New York: St. Martin's Press, 1995), pp. 249, 250.

JESSE JACKSON

A Baptist preacher born and raised in South Carolina, the Reverend Jesse Jackson moved to Chicago in 1966 to work with Martin Luther King, Jr., in the Northern Freedom Movement campaign. He became one of King's lieutenants and upon King's death styled himself as the heir apparent, much to the chagrin of the Reverend Ralph Abernathy. After a rift with Abernathy and the Southern Christian Leadership Conference (SCLC), Jackson formed his own organization, called People United to Save Humanity (PUSH). His fame grew in the early 1970s enough to make him indeed appear to the general public to be the main "leader" of African Americans. Here, in a 1974 interview with the black journalist Barbara Reynolds, he discusses black leadership issues.

I was born to lead. But some things disturb me. For example, black people have a way of praising the dead but crucifying the living. Many people today are praising King but they crucified him publicly, which I think set the climate for his assassination. In many cases, I will be asked to a city to help with a particular problem and I will have to spend half my time trying to keep down jealousy. People sometimes hold this misplaced notion that I am trying to come in to take over. . . .

None of our problems is the result of the lack of black leadership. It's the lack of white leadership. Black leaders don't have the power to save our people. By and large, black leaders can only raise hope so as to keep our people from giving up. White leaders have the power. . . .

It is possible to have one spiritual leader. . . . So I see nothing wrong in embodying the spiritual and moralistic qualities of this nation. And with white national leadership sinking this proves more and more that a black man can symbolize the moral principles of a nation.

From Barbara A. Reynolds, *Jesse Jackson: The Man, the Movement, the Myth* (Chicago: Nelson-Hall, 1975), pp. 401–2.

RALPH ABERNATHY

In 1989, the Reverend Ralph Abernathy, former president of the SCLC, published his autobiography. In it he confessed to contributing to the downfall of the SCLC and of the civil rights movement as a whole through his less-than-spectacular leadership. In the excerpts here, he tells how he came to realize that he had failed.

> The story I am about to tell is one I have never told anyone before. . . . But it needs to be told in order to round out the history the Southern Christian Leadership Conference (SCLC). My pride or vanity matters little at this point when measured against the demand of history to have the whole truth.
>
> In the summer of 1976, I received a letter from Chauncey Eskridge, who at that time was serving as chief fund raiser for the SCLC. The tone of what he had to say was somber, even grim. The organization was in financial difficulties. It had been a long time since we had won a dramatic victory on the national scene or attracted the attention of the national press. The civil rights movement was no longer as fashionable as it once had been. The battles still to be fought were smaller, more complicated, and did not play so well on the evening news. Watergate had been a better show than anything we had managed to stage.
>
> So I wasn't really surprised to read what Chauncey was saying. . . . "Mr. President," he said, "we appreciate everything you've done for the organization and the movement, but, well, we feel you've outlived your usefulness. We feel we have to have a change."
>
> As he said this I remained expressionless, but I felt a sudden stab of pain. . . .
>
> What hurt was my growing awareness that I had failed the SCLC, an organization that I helped to found, that I had nurtured over the years, that had been left in my keeping by my dear friend, who had somehow known he would soon be dead. I had loved the organization from the very beginning, before it had even come into being, when its only existence was in my mind and in Martin's, a shared dream waiting to be fully conceptualized.
>
> From Ralph David Abernathy, *And the Walls Came Tumbling Down: An Autobiography* (New York: Harper and Row, 1989), pp. 579–82.

RACE RELATIONS BY GROUP

AFRICAN AMERICANS

For all the problems blacks faced in the 1960s, they at least had the benefit of liberal Democrats in the White House for eight years, a liberal majority in

Congress and on the U.S. Supreme Court, strong leadership from Martin Luther King, Jr., for the first half of the decade, and a large number of sympathetic white Americans. In the 1970s, they had none of those benefits. The moderately conservative presidencies of Richard Nixon and Gerald Ford made the continuation of advances in civil rights more difficult, as did the changing ideological composition of the Supreme Court. No black leader of the caliber of King arose to replace him, although many, such as Ralph Abernathy and Jesse Jackson, tried. The Black Power movement and the advent of radicals such as the Black Panthers killed the sympathetic feelings of most white Americans. The "silent majority" of Americans, as Nixon called them, favored a sort of *detente* in civil rights activism just as they did in the Cold War.

President Nixon did not oppose all civil rights initiatives that came up for consideration in the early 1970s, but he did favor a more moderate, cautious approach. On March 24, 1970, Nixon issued an 8,000-word statement on civil rights. His position, generally speaking, could be called one of minimal compliance, although his civil rights adviser, Daniel Patrick Moynihan, inadvertently coined the negative-sounding term "benign neglect" to describe it.[2] The news media, and hence black leaders, latched onto the benign neglect term and never let Nixon live it down. Whether one chooses to call Nixon's policy benign neglect or minimal compliance, the policy was simply that the president disapproved of initiatives that seemed to benefit the black race at the expense of some whites, as in the case of cross-town busing to achieve integrated schools. To him, it was basically a form of reverse racism, and he believed that such measures would create more problems than they solved. Yet he strongly favored initiatives that benefited the poor without regard to their race, and he favored continuing those laws and plans begun under Presidents Kennedy and Johnson that seemed genuinely fair to all races. On June 24, 1970, at the White House, Nixon met with the Mississippi State Advisory Committee on Civil Rights, an interracial group that he impressed with his commitment to improving race relations in the South. About two months later, he met with Louisiana's similar state advisory committee in New Orleans and urged the members to find peaceful solutions to their state's racial problems. He even elicited the help of America's most famous preacher, Billy Graham, who echoed that sentiment. He met with five other state advisory committees, as well, and in 1972 he proposed that Congress increase funding to minority schools.

President Nixon had created the Office of Minority Business Enterprise (OMBE) in 1969, and it played a central role in his civil rights policy throughout the early 1970s. It made possible the building of 60 of the 100 largest black-owned businesses in America by 1974. Nixon also recognized the newly minted Congressional Black Caucus by meeting with its delegation in 1971, thus giving it the credibility it needed to become a force in Washington. In another unprecedented move, Nixon designated October 1, 1972, as the first "National Heritage Day" and led the Republican party to create some 1,000 local "Heritage Councils" to show his support for ethnic and cultural minorities. Although aimed more at the smaller and less visible minority groups than at African Americans, these councils provided benefits across the board to every group. For all these reasons, Nixon deserves to be remembered as a decent president on civil rights issues. His record on civil rights, however, like his record on most other issues, has been negatively skewed in the popular perception by the Watergate scandal and his subsequent resignation, and his accomplishments are often forgotten or ignored. Then, too, the fact that he took a moderately conservative approach on certain issues, such as forced busing, annulled whatever good he may have done, at least in the minds of most blacks and their white liberal allies. The NAACP, for example, bitterly opposed Nixon and attacked his policies as antiblack. Ralph Abernathy of the SCLC expressed optimism about Nixon's commitment to civil rights until the two met one-on-one in the White House. Abernathy left disappointed.

President Gerald Ford took office on August 9, 1974, amid some of the worst circumstances imaginable: Watergate, impeachment, Nixon's resignation, the inglorious end of the Vietnam War, and a growing economic recession. The only person ever to hold the job of president without being elected to either the presidency or the vice presidency, Ford was ill prepared for the position into which circumstances thrust him. That, plus the fact that he had barely more than two years to do the job of president, makes his paltry record on civil rights understandable. His most memorable public statement involving a black-white racial problem came at the height of the cross-town busing controversy in Boston. On October 9, 1974, Ford stated controversially that, in effect, he sympathized with the whites who had had the busing plan forced on them against their will by an overactive judge. The statement merely reinforced white resistance to the court order and busing plan.

By the time the presidential campaign of 1976 rolled around, the poor economy, which adversely affected Americans of all races, made life especially hard for blacks. While the national unemployment rate stood at 8 percent, the average for black adults was 12 percent, and for black teens it was a whopping 30 percent. Such problems would have favored the challenger rather than the incumbent in any other election, but black voters faced a dicey choice in this one. The challenger, Jimmy Carter, looked on the surface to be the opposite of a man who would be interested in promoting black civil rights. The former governor of Georgia, Carter was a true Deep South country boy, a Southern Baptist, and one not held in unanimous admiration by blacks from his own state. Some black Georgians supported him, while others did not, and his record on civil rights issues as governor seemed spotty. Compounding the problem for Carter, in the week before the election, a black Republican minister from Albany, Georgia, named Clennon King tried to expose him as a hypocrite. Carter attended a segregated church in his hometown of Plains. When King showed up there for a Sunday service, he found the church doors locked and the service canceled. This incident drew a great deal of negative media attention, but Carter managed to squeak out a close victory nonetheless, as 85 percent of African American voters chose him over Ford.

Carter, the first genuinely and completely southern president since before the Civil War, appointed two blacks to cabinet positions, put more blacks on the federal judiciary than had all previous presidents combined, and reorganized several federal agencies that dealt with civil rights issues to make them more efficient. Carter's Justice Department also vigorously pursued civil rights cases in court. Even so, at the midway point in Carter's presidency, Vernon Jordan, director of the National Urban League, blasted the federal government in the annual "State of Black America" report for its apathy in addressing the needs of African Americans. Carter's civil rights record suffered from a combination of the problems that plagued Nixon and Ford. He had the misfortune of being in office for only four years, and they just happened to be four years when the nation's collective attention was focused on many other problems, pushing civil rights issues to the back burner. The economy, enduring recession in all its many manifestations, and the Iran-hostage crisis, distracted both Carter and the American people from dealing with domestic racial problems, while the silent majority of whites felt uncomfortable pushing ahead with civil rights, anyway.

An embarrassment for the administration that involved events in the Middle East resulted from Carter's appointment of a black fellow Georgian, Andrew Young, as U.S. ambassador to the United Nations. Young made some controversial statements and engaged in some unconventional behavior for an ambassador. In the summer of 1979, a scandal surfaced because Young had violated government policy by holding secret talks with the Palestinian Liberation Organization (PLO), a Muslim group that had long been considered a front for terrorists bent on the destruction of Israel. Young hoped to secure better relations with the Muslim nations and to help end the constant fighting in the Middle East, but the American public did not appreciate his actions. In August, he resigned under scrutiny, and Carter, while mainly supportive of Young, distanced himself from the scandal by accepting the resignation. Black supporters of Young, however, came out in large numbers in New York City to protest the resignation, which they perceived as actually a firing by Carter. A month later, other black leaders, such as Jesse Jackson and Joseph Lowery of the SCLC, took it upon themselves to visit the PLO's leader, Yasser Arafat, in Lebanon, offering their support to the Palestinians against the U.S. government's official support of Israel. Such maverick actions by these black leaders did nothing to help Carter's slim chances of reelection in 1980.

Throughout the 1970s, African Americans largely found leadership in sources other than the U.S. presidents or the federal government. To a certain extent, they looked to themselves and to their own communities for grass-roots support. Although the SCLC floundered under the leadership of Ralph Abernathy, SNCC and CORE committed virtual suicide by following Rap Brown and Roy Innis's Black Power movement. Plenty of other civil rights and black activists groups, however, carried on undeterred. The two oldest organizations, the NAACP and the National Urban League, plodded ahead, although without the level of success they had enjoyed in the 1960s. Meanwhile, Jesse Jackson, the self-styled protégé of Martin Luther King, Jr., created People United to Save Humanity (PUSH) in December 1971, primarily to do the work he believed the SCLC was failing to do under Abernathy's guidance. Jackson developed a reputation as a polarizing figure, however, who, unlike King, could not bring whites into his camp in large numbers. Actions such as his attempt to convince African Americans to boycott the Bicentennial celebration in July 1976, saying blacks had nothing to celebrate, just did not appeal to a majority of people of any color. Other black organizations that formed in the 1970s but had limited degrees of influence included the Coalition of Black Trade Unionists (1972), and the National Black Feminist Organization (1973).

The 1970s produced little in the way of a continuous struggle for racial justice by any notable civil rights group that would make for a compelling narrative like that of the previous decade. Instead, these years yielded an odd assortment of incidents from an unusual cast of characters. There was, for example, the attempt by the Black Panthers to write a new constitution for the United States based upon communist principles. The meetings and convention for that purpose drew large crowds of members and sympathizers, but the Black Panther organization fell quickly into disarray immediately thereafter, as its leaders, Huey Newton and Eldridge Cleaver, argued over direction. To a great extent, it was not the FBI that destroyed the Black Panthers but the Panthers themselves.

A related oddity was the case of Angela Davis, a black communist Black Panther member and Ph.D. student in California. She was implicated in one of the most notorious murders in California history as an accomplice. It involved Jonathan Jackson, a black teen companion of Davis's, who tried to arrange a jail break for some criminals by taking over a court in San Rafael and seizing hostages. Jackson used weapons registered in Davis's name, thus implicating her. Her arrest, arraignment, and trial evoked the sympathy of a large contingent of Americans and resulted in a "Free Angela!" campaign. She was ultimately acquitted. A third oddity was the case of Joan Little, a black female petty thief serving a short sentence in a North Carolina jail, who in October 1977 killed a white guard with an ice pick and escaped to New York. Upon capture and trial, she claimed self-defense, saying the guard had tried to rape her using the ice pick as his weapon but that she had wrested it from his hand. The news coverage made the trial a minisensation similar to that of Angela Davis six years earlier, complete with a public campaign to free Little. In the end, she did go free of murder charges, but she served the remainder of her time for the original charges of petty thievery.

Several interesting racial developments that came out of the nation's capital in 1970s are worth mentioning. One involved New York's black Democratic congresswoman, Shirley Chisholm, who ran for president of the United States in 1972. The first African American of either sex to be taken seriously as a candidate for that high office, Chisholm made a courageous but not impressive showing. Another involved the Michigan congressman Charles Diggs (D), the first chair of the Congressional Black Caucus. In March 1978, he was indicted for taking kickbacks, and eight months later was sentenced to three years in jail. Despite pleading guilty to the scandal and being convicted on all 29 counts of misusing funds, Diggs was reelected by his Detroit constituents in a strong show of support. He subsequently resigned his seat in Congress and served seven months in jail. Meanwhile, the esteemed body of which he was a member, the House of Representatives, held hearings in August 1978 on the possibility of a conspiracy in the assassination of Martin Luther King, Jr., a decade earlier, in which convicted killer James Earl Ray testified. Nothing substantial came of the hearings. Within a year, the unrelated issue of forced busing, which had proved a sore spot for white Americans throughout the decade, finally came to a head in Congress. The House considered and defeated a constitutional amendment to ban it.

Two victories for racial justice that came out of the late 1970s involved Ku Klux Klansmen who were indicted or convicted of murder in cases stemming from events in the '60s. In November 1977, Robert E. Chambliss was convicted in the 1963 "bombingham" case, and in September 1978 Gary Thomas Rowe, Jr., who served as an FBI informer for the KKK in Alabama in 1965, was indicted for the murder of Viola Liuzzo. Even so, white supremacists in the form of the KKK, the American Nazi party, and the National Socialist Party of America, among other smaller groups, continued to attract a growing radical fringe of whites in both the South and the North.

AMERICAN INDIANS

To a large extent, American Indians did not follow the course set by African Americans in the 1970s. Whereas the Black Power movement had basically played itself out by about 1972, the Red Power movement was just getting started. The most visible Native American activist group at the beginning of the decade was the Indians of All Tribes, but it was quickly displaced by the American Indian Movement (AIM), which grew increasingly more radical as the decade wore on. By about 1979, however, AIM had accomplished about as much as it could to draw attention to the plight of the Indians, and its influence and headline-grabbing ability waned thereafter.

As the '60s gave way to the '70s, the major news item for the Indians was the occupation of Alcatraz Island in San Francisco Bay. Having begun the occupation on November 19, 1969, the Indians of All Tribes staged the event partly to raise awareness of Indian issues and partly to gain more leverage in negotiating with the federal government for better treatment of their people. The Nixon administration indeed went through the motions of negotiating with the Indians, but ultimately the government yielded nothing of substance to them because of the occupation. Nixon must be credited, however, with not ordering or allowing a strong-arm approach in driving out the Indians in a bloody confrontation. Instead, he outlasted the Indians, whose numbers and public support dwindled as 1970 rolled over to 1971. By June 11, 1971, what had been more than 200

Indians had withered to fewer than 20. Nixon then sent in U.S. marshals to evict the tired and beleaguered little band, and the most dramatic event in American Indian history since the Wounded Knee massacre of 1890 was over.

Meanwhile, as the occupation dragged on for that year and a half, AIM got busy staging other similar protest occupations. In 1970, it took over an unused naval air station near its home base of Minneapolis, the Bureau of Indian Affairs' (BIA) office in Washington, D.C., and, most dramatic, the *Mayflower II* (a ship on the Massachusetts coast built for reenacting the landing at Plymouth Rock in 1620). In 1971, it took over a hydraulic power dam run by the Northern States Power Company, in Wisconsin, and Mount Rushmore, in South Dakota. These and similar actions all worked together to garner some concessions from the federal government that benefited Indians. In 1972, AIM once again marched on Washington and seized control of BIA headquarters. This time it issued a statement and list of demands called the "Trail of Broken Treaties," which contained 20 points that can be summarized as follows:

1. Restoration should be made of tribal treaty making rights which were ended by Congress in 1871;

2. A treaty commission should be established for making new treaties with sovereign individual tribal nations;

3. Indian leaders should be given the right to address Congress;

4. A congressional and presidential review of treaty commitments and violations should be conducted;

5. All treaties between the federal government and various tribes that were never ratified by the Senate should be brought up for a vote in the Senate;

6. All Indian tribes should be governed according to rules contained in treaties;

7. Restitution should be made to various tribes for violations of treaties over the years;

8. Indians should be given leeway to interpret treaties for themselves rather than have the BIA interpret for them;

9. A joint Congressional Committee should be formed on establishing better relations between the federal government and the Indians;

10. Restoration should be made to the various tribes of 110 million acres of land taken from them in violation of treaties by the United States;

11. Restoration of terminated tribal rights should be made;

12. All state jurisdiction over Indian tribes should be abolished;

13. Federal protection should be secured for offenses against Indians;

14. The Bureau of Indian Affairs should be abolished, and a new office of Federal Indian Relations should be created to replace it;

15. The new office should remedy the breakdown in the constitutionally pre-scribed relationships between the United States and the various tribes;

16. Indian tribes should not be compelled to follow state laws restricting commerce and trade;

17. Indian religious freedom and cultural integrity should be protected by the federal government;

18. Indians should have separate and special voting rights;

19. Indian organizations should be free from governmental controls;

20. The federal government should take affirmative steps to improve health, housing, employment, economic development, and education for all Indian people.[3]

Less than three months after issuing the "Trail of Broken Treaties," in February and March 1973, AIM choreographed its most notable protest ever. It occupied the town of Wounded Knee on the Pine Ridge Reservation in South Dakota for 71 days. In the standoff between government forces and the militant Indians, two people were killed and hundreds arrested. Once again, the Nixon admin-istration avoided a bloodbath when it could have easily ordered one. Nixon's overall record on Indian affairs looked good, if only because earlier presidents had done so little to improve the situation of Native Americans. Nixon sup-ported restoration of tribal status to groups that had been previously detribalized. He also encouraged Indians to take pride in their heritage, increased funding for programs to help them, and promoted a generous policy regarding their land claims.

The main problem that plagued AIM throughout the '70s was the same one that had helped destroy the Black Panthers: government opposition. As a result of the Wounded Knee standoff, in and after 1973 the FBI targeted the group as subversive and tried to drive it out of existence. This led to constant surveil-lance of Indian leaders and occasional arrests and shootouts. The most infamous case involved the arrest and conviction of the AIM member Leonard Peltier for allegedly killing two U.S. marshals in a shootout on June 26, 1975, at the Pine Ridge Reservation. Peltier, who still sits in prison today, has consistently maintained his innocence and has developed a cult following that is convinced he was framed. Efforts reminiscent of the "Free Huey!" and "Free Angela Davis!" campaigns have been launched, but so far with no success. Other infamous cases involved Richard Mohawk and Paul Skyhorse, who were charged with murder in a 1974 case in Los Angeles, and Harry Hanson, Jr., who in 1979 led an Indian takeover of the Red Lake Reservation in Minnesota in which the BIA office was burned down, federal officials were assaulted, and Indians were killed. Whereas Mohawk and Skyhorse were acquitted, in 1978, Hanson was convicted, in July 1979.

Not all Indian protests involved violence, trials, or incarceration. In July 1976, while the vast majority of Americans celebrated the Bicentennial, Indian activists commemorated the Battle of Little Big Horn, instead. That battle, in which General Custer and his men were killed by Crazy Horse, the Sioux, and their allies in Montana, occurred barely a week before the nation's Centennial, in 1876. Just as the battle cast a pall upon the nation while it prepared to celebrate its one-hundredth birthday, so the 1976 re-enactment was designed to do the same. It failed, going largely unnoticed by the media and the American public. From February 11 through July 17, 1978, AIM engaged in its most ambitious undertaking ever when it staged "The Longest March," from San Francisco to Washington, D.C.[4] The 2,700-mile transcontinental journey, which ended on the steps of the U.S. Capitol, drew attention to the needs of Indians, but it did not have as much impact as AIM had hoped. On July 18, AIM leaders expected to get a conference with President Carter but had to settle for a meeting with Vice President Walter Mondale and Secretary of the Interior Cecil Adams. Carter rejected their request to meet with him.

HISPANICS

The Hispanic population grew dramatically in the 1970s. By the end of the decade, more than 12 million Latinos lived in the United States. The largest increase came in the number of Mexican Americans, which doubled to almost 7 million. The other 5 million-plus comprised more than 1.5 million Puerto Ricans, nearly 1 million Cubans, and about 3 million people from other Central and South American countries. About 600,000 Chicanos lived in the East Los Angeles metropolitan area alone. Likewise, about 600,000 Cubans lived in the Miami area alone, and most Puerto Ricans lived in New York City. Otherwise, the Hispanic population was largely scattered throughout the southwestern United States, from Texas to California.

The main reason for the influx of Mexicans seems to have been the abolition of the Bracero program in 1964. Over the next 15 years, more Mexicans began immigrating to the United States, both legally and illegally, than ever before. The U.S. Immigration and Naturalization Service reported that it arrested nearly a million illegal aliens during those years, which marked a significant increase. The problem of illegal immigration did not attract much national attention in the 1970s, however. Social scientists and government officials barely began even to study the problem during the decade. The lack of research into the extent and nature of illegal immigration at the time led to wild speculation about the number that might be crossing the border each year. Low estimates ranged from 80,000 to 100,000; high estimates ranged from 220,000 to 250,000.

The growth of the Hispanic population in the 1970s caused problems in relation to the nation's affirmative action laws. Determining someone's racial classification was difficult, since Hispanics came from so many different nationalities and since their skin color might range from dark brown to nearly lily white. The Carter administration grappled with the problem and came up with *conversion procedures* through the federal Office of Personnel Management. It attempted to clarify who was Hispanic, who was not, and how a federal employer could tell the difference. The result was tortured legal hair-splitting. Even so, by 1980 the U.S. Census Bureau had included for the first time the "Hispanic" classification on its form, which basically allowed people to call themselves by that term if they chose, rather than allow a government official to determine their race. The results of that census illustrate perfectly the complexity of the problem: 6.4 percent of Americans described themselves as Hispanic, yet more than half of them simultaneously listed their color as "white" rather than "brown" or something else.

The growth of the Latino population translated directly into more Hispanic elected officials in the 1970s. Both New Mexico and Arizona elected Hispanic governors in 1974. The former elected Jerry Apodaca and the latter Hector Castro. At the beginning of the decade, there were five Latino congressmen and one U.S. senator. The number increased over the next few years, such that by 1977 a Congressional Hispanic Caucus could be formed. Two years later, the National Association of Latino Elected and Appointed Officials was founded; the group included state and local officials, as well as those in the federal government. A major effort to create a viable third party especially for Hispanics in the Southwest surfaced in 1970 when Jose Angel Gutierrez formed the *La Raza Unida*. The party won a few races in Texas but otherwise flopped. It turned out that Hispanic voters and candidates could function well enough in the two major mainstream parties as to make a separatist third party ineffective and unnecessary.

Inasmuch as old-stock English-speaking white Americans were concerned about the growth of the Hispanic population at all in the 1970s, they focused on the social needs of the Spanish speakers. California passed the first state Bilingual-Bicultural Education Act in 1976. Congress followed suit two years later with the federal Bilingual Education Act. America's Anglo-centric mind set and the comparatively small number of Spanish speakers in the United States had mostly prevented such reforms prior to the 1970s. Although Hispanic civil rights activists did their part to raise awareness among Anglo Americans on this issue, it was, ironically, a Chinese American who forced the issue of bilingual education to the fore through a case that went to the U.S. Supreme Court in 1974, *Lau v. Nichols*.

ASIAN AMERICANS

Asians from various countries accounted for 25 percent of the total immigrants in 1970. By 1980 that figure had increased to 44 percent. The total Asian American population in 1970 was about 1.5 million. By 1980 it had increased to around 5 million. After Mexico, the Philippines and South Korea were the two largest sources of immigrants in the 1970s. Five of the top 10 immigrant groups came from Asia.

One group of Asian Americans, the Vietnamese, became the highest-profile minority group in the United States in the late 1970s. The war in Vietnam ended in American and South Vietnamese defeat in 1975, the Ford and Carter administrations and Congress had to clean up the mess, and the American people had their commitment to humanitarianism sorely tested. Refugee camps were set up in America to take in families and individuals dislocated by the war and fortunate enough to get passage out of Vietnam before the communists assumed control. Ford asked Congress to appropriate $327 million to aid the refugees, but Congress refused. Public opinion polls showed that most Americans agreed with Congress and opposed Ford's plan. At a refugee camp in Arkansas, white Americans protested the arrival of the Vietnamese "gooks" ostensibly because their presence was a painful and constant reminder of the lost war and in many cases lost loved ones. Congress approved Ford's request, however, to create a $2 million fund to pay for the relocation of 2,000 South Vietnamese orphans in the United States. In April 1975, Ford flew to San Francisco to welcome the first plane loads of 325 children arriving from Vietnam. In a made-for-TV-news display of presidential leadership, Ford dramatically entered one plane and carried Vietnamese babies out in his arms. Ford's action changed public opinion, convincing a majority of Americans to accept Vietnamese refugees in their midst. Altogether, some 120,000 refugees found new homes in the United States thereafter.

An unrelated but symbolically important event occurred on January 19, 1977, when President Ford officially pardoned Iva Toguri D'Aquino, better known as "Tokyo Rose," for treason against the United States during World War II. Born in Los Angeles, Tokyo Rose was an American citizen who was visiting relatives in Japan when the war broke out. She got stuck there and subsequently went to work as a radio propagandist for the imperial government of Japan. After the war, she was convicted on the basis of false, or at least controversial, testimony and sentenced to 10 years in prison. By pardoning her, Ford not only tried to right a wrong done to an individual but, more important, tried to make a symbolic gesture of goodwill to both the Japanese and Japanese Americans. He likewise began the healing process with regard to the roughly 120,000 Japanese Americans who had been interned in war camps in the United States during World War II by saying that the internment was "wrong." It would remain for other government officials in a later decade to take the next step in making restitution.

Law and Government

Three characteristics stand out as differentiating the 1970s from the 1960s in terms of laws and legal affairs as related to racial issues. First, in the '60s the emphasis was almost exclusively on civil rights legislation and litigation aimed primarily at helping African Americans. The '70s saw a rise in interest in helping other minorities, including women and the disabled, as well as various racial and ethnic groups. Second, the volume of legislation and litigation in the '70s that ranks as important enough to discuss is a veritable drop in the bucket compared to that passed during the '60s. Third, whereas most of the civil rights bills and cases that surfaced in the '60s were passed into law or ruled upon favorably for minorities, the '70s brought a mixed bag of successes and failures.

The Nixon administration concocted the Family Assistance Plan in 1969 to reform the federal welfare system. Had it become law, it would have guaranteed every American family a minimum income of $1,600 per year. Although it was not designed specifically to aid minorities but just the poor in general, it would have helped a disproportionate percentage of minorities. It passed in the House of Representatives in two different forms in 1970 and 1971, only to be defeated in the Senate each time. A similar type of program, called the Humphrey-Hawkins bill, was introduced in 1974. Sponsored by the white Minnesota Democrat Hubert Humphrey and the black Democrat Gus Hawkins of California, it was supposed to guarantee full employment. Again, though not specifically aimed at helping minorities, it would have helped them the most. The Congressional Black Caucus strongly supported the bill and pushed it as the most important item on its agenda. The bill finally passed in 1978 as the Full Employment and Balanced Growth Act after President Carter and opponents in Congress had forced changes in it so substantial as to nullify its purpose.

The biggest racial challenge facing the various branches and agencies of the federal government in the 1970s was arriving at a consensus on affirmative action. The issue spawned several important court cases, and both the Nixon and Carter administrations wrestled with how to interpret the statutes already on the books. Carter introduced the Uniform Guidelines on Employee Selection Procedures, which attempted to clarify what the courts and the administration expected from employers regarding minority hiring. In summation, the guidelines held that any hiring practice that had a demonstrably negative impact on a minority group must be deemed illegal. Few civil rights issues raised the dander of conservatives on the bench or in the general public like affirmative action. Several notable cases that touched on some aspect of affirmative action wound their way through the American justice system in the 1970s and ended with Supreme Court rulings. In 1971, in *Griggs v. Duke Power Company*, the Burger Court said that neither a high school diploma nor an intelligence test could be used to determine employment eligibility if they adversely affected minorities primarily. A 1976 case, *Washington v. Davis*, added a limiting stipulation to that ruling, however, saying that if a certain kind of test could be shown to indicate a person's ability or lack thereof to perform a specific job, then it was legal, even if it had a disproportionately negative effect on the hiring of minorities.

More notable among affirmative action cases of the 1970s were those alleging reverse racism. The most famous was *Regents of the University of California v. Bakke*, which originated in 1974 and was ruled on in 1978. Allan Bakke, a white student, applied to a public medical school in California, only to be denied admission in order to make room for minority applicants with lower test scores.

His suit generated one of the hottest debates over affirmative action in American history, a debate that still goes on today. The Supreme Court's complex ruling favored Bakke, but in an indirect way. It invalidated the California medical college's admission process, which automatically reserved a certain number or percentage of slots for minority students regardless of test scores, but it upheld the right of public universities to use race and ethnic background as one criterion in the admissions process. At the same time the Bakke case began its torturous journey through the courts, in Louisiana another set of cases and countersuits that involved a white employee of the Kaiser Aluminum Company named Brian Weber started on the same path. Weber sued the company because he had been passed over for a promotion training program because of his race. Black workers received the training, instead. The Court ruled that the company's policy did not violate the intent of the affirmative action laws in place at the time, and thus no reverse racial discrimination could be proven.

Other than affirmative action cases, the most important Supreme Court ruling involved forced busing of black and white students across school district lines to achieve more racially balanced public school systems. The ruling in *Swann v. Charlotte-Mecklenburg Board of Education*, in 1971, started the process of forced busing, and the *Keyes v. Denver School District No. 1* ruling, in 1973, reinforced it. These rulings caused the worst white backlash of the decade, partly because they affected northern cities more than the rural South. The most intense opposition came from white parents, teachers, administrators, and city officials in Boston. In 1974–1975, frequent rioting broke out there as a result of cross-town busing of students. Various cities and school districts around the country sought redress against forced busing by going to court. In most cases, they lost. As late as 1979, the cities of Dayton and Columbus, Ohio, both were ordered to engage in cross-town busing. In that same year, the House of Representatives voted upon and defeated a constitutional amendment to ban forced busing. The one major victory for antibusing proponents came in 1974 in *Millikin v. Bradley*, a case arising in the Detroit area. The court ruled that forced busing between inner-city schools and suburban schools to achieve a racial balance in a general metropolitan area was not acceptable when some of the schools being forced to participate had violated no law and could be shown to have made all reasonable efforts to comply with the spirit of the law.

A few Supreme Court cases that involved racial issues but were not related to affirmative action or busing also had important ramifications for American society from the 1970s to the present. Perhaps the most important was *Lau v. Nichols*, in 1974. It involved Chinese American students in San Francisco who had an academic deficiency in English. Based on the Civil Rights Act of 1964, they claimed that the San Francisco educational establishment discriminated against them by not offering them alternatives to the sink-or-swim choice of mastering English or failing school. The Court agreed and forced the implementation of bilingual educational services or remedial courses in English with a different scale to measure success. This ruling has affected far more Spanish speakers than Chinese-speaking students over the years. Hispanic students lost a major court battle in 1973, however, in *San Antonio Independent School District v. Rodriguez*. Chicanos argued in the case against the formula for funding public schools in Texas, which depended mainly on local property taxes. Since Chicanos were poorer on average than Anglos, they owned less valuable property for tax purposes. Consequently, their school districts received less funding. The litigants argued for some type of judicial oversight to produce a more equitable funding formula, but the Court said no. On the positive side for Chicanos, cases involving unreasonable stops, searches, arrests, and detentions of people crossing the border by the U.S. Border Patrol were brought successfully to the Supreme Court.

MEDIA AND MASS COMMUNICATION

Prior to the 1970s, racial minorities in the United States were usually depicted in the mass media as subservient to whites, if not altogether inferior to them. The civil rights movement began the transition away from negative stereotypes and toward positive portrayals, but by 1970 little had changed noticeably. The new decade, however, saw a revolution in the way the media depicted minorities, not only giving them billing on an equal basis with whites but bringing positive representations of them into vogue. Indeed, what had been culturally taboo in the '60s with regard to how the media treated minorities became not only socially acceptable in the '70s but required by law. This trend seemed to fit perfectly with the growing emphasis on affirmative action in the new decade. While many of the early steps made in this direction resulted from the mandates of affirmative action laws and court rulings that basically required white employers and power brokers to spread the wealth to minorities, as the decade moved along much of the change became increasingly voluntary. It turned out there was quite a market in the capitalist economy for positive portrayals of minorities, and the American public was ready to gobble up whatever it could get in the way of nonwhite stars. That same public became equally hungry for new opportunities to view the world through the eyes of minorities, especially African Americans.

These changes showed up in obvious venues such as television, radio, and the movies, but they also showed up in more subtle forms, such as academic literature and minority-studies programs. Social scientists and literary critics, among others, began researching, writing about, and arguing the merits of black culture and language patterns. In 1970, Clarence Major published A *Dictionary of Afro-American Slang*, which treated black slang not only as worthy of serious study and scholarly acceptance but as a language form just as legitimate as standard English. In 1972, J. L. Dillard published *Black English: Its History and Usage in the United States*, which made the same argument from a literary critic's point of view. In 1973, R. L. Williams coined a now-familiar term for this black slang, some of which had been spoken for decades—"ebonics."[5] Because of the work of these and other scholars, a debate began about whether or not black students should be forced to learn standard English. The pro-ebonics argument said no, that American society should instead embrace the diversity in black language just as it had begun to accept racial differences in other walks of life; ebonics should not be considered inferior or substandard English. The debate did not catch on outside the ivory tower in the 1970s. Not until the 1990s would it become a mainstream public debate.

Prior to the '70s, educators commonly forced minority students to conform to rigid, preset standards used for whites. The idea that public education should be tailored to the needs of minorities received a boost from Pat Conroy's 1972 book *The Water Is Wide*, which became the basis for the critically successful (if not so commercially popular) 1974 film *Conrack*, starring Jon Voight. Voight played a white man who took a job that virtually no one else wanted teaching black elementary school children on one of the Sea Islands off the coast of Beaufort, South Carolina. Because the children and their families grew up and lived their whole lives on the island, they had not absorbed standard American or even South Carolinian culture. Nor did they have any reason to. They spoke their own language, which blended Gullah slave idioms and vocabulary with English. Normal educational concepts were alien to them because they had no basis for understanding what they had never seen, heard, or been exposed to. This forced Voight's character to be creative and innovative as he struggled to give the students a reason to embrace schooling. He learned to speak their language, in other words, before he tried to teach them his, and it worked.

For Hispanics, the 1970s were a break-out decade in academia and educational advancement. Chicano social scientists at UCLA in 1970 started *Aztlan*, a journal devoted to studying Latino issues. Two years later, the National Association of Chicano Studies was formed, and Chicano-studies programs sprang up throughout the Southwest. As bilingual education became a major political football, in 1974 the *Bilingual Review* was started. It was a scholarly journal that studied the issue and made recommendations about how to implement bilingual programs in schools. Thanks to the journal, energetic lobbyists, and a Supreme Court case, bilingual education became a staple of the American public school system after the 1970s.

African Americans made major inroads in the mass media in the 1970s. Ed Bradley, a black free-lance journalist, earned acclaim as a CBS news reporter in Vietnam and Cambodia from 1972 through 1975. CBS then elevated him to its White House correspondent position, which he held from 1976 to 1978. Although Bradley essentially made the big time by his own efforts, the next generation of black news people would benefit from the work of the National Association of Black Journalists, founded in 1975. Hispanics also made important advances, as the number of radio stations broadcasting in Spanish in the United States topped 500 by the end of the decade. Also by 1980, 23 Spanish language TV stations operated in the United States. *La Raza*, a politically oriented newspaper printed in Spanish and published in Chicago, became another important voice for Latinos in the 1970s.

CULTURAL SCENE

If the 1960s was a time for breaking down the dam of racial segregation and minority exclusion in American society, the 1970s was the time that minorities came flooding through, sweeping across the landscape. The success of blacks especially, and other minorities to a lesser degree, in sports, music, film, television, and literature was nothing less than astounding. In boxing, for instance,

Atlanta Braves' Hank Aaron eyes the flight of the ball after hitting his 715th career homer in a game against the Los Angeles Dodgers in Atlanta, Georgia, Monday night, April 8, 1974. Aaron broke Babe Ruth's record of 714 career home runs. Dodgers southpaw pitcher Al Downing, catcher Joe Ferguson, and umpire David Davidson look on. AP Photo/Harry Harris.

Muhammad Ali solidified his hold on the self-proclaimed title "the greatest of all time," although fellow black pugilists Joe Frazier, George Foreman, and Larry Holmes made impressive showings in the heavyweight division, as well. The white film maker Sylvester Stallone, playing on white America's desire to achieve even a little parity in professional boxing, scored an incredible hit with his unlikely fictional white boxing champion, Rocky Balboa, in the movie *Rocky* (1976), which won the Oscar for Best Picture in 1977. Real life would not be so kind to white boxers, however.

Football and especially basketball followed basically the same track as boxing. Blacks became so dominant in these sports that their participation alongside whites was no longer a novelty after the early 1970s. Even so, in professional football, two prizes eluded African Americans—head-coaching jobs and quarterback positions on championship teams. In professional baseball, black dominance as a whole was never achieved, although parity certainly was, and certain individuals dominated their respective positions. The black Oakland Athletics pitcher Vida Blue won both the Cy Young Award and the American League MVP Award in 1971, becoming the youngest MVP winner ever. The pinnacle of black baseball success, however, came when Henry "Hank" Aaron of the Atlanta Braves broke Babe Ruth's all-time home run total, hitting number 715 on April 8, 1974. He ultimately hit 755 home runs before retiring after the 1976 season. In 1975, Frank Robinson became the first black manager in professional baseball history, managing the Cleveland Indians for three seasons.

Hispanics began to make inroads into professional sports as well in the 1970s. Jim Plunkett of Stanford University became the first Mexican American to win the Heisman Trophy as college football's best player, in 1970. In professional golf, Lee Trevino continued the success he had begun in the late 1960s, becoming the first Mexican American to win the PGA Player of the Year Award, in 1971. He followed that success by winning the PGA championship and World Series of Golf titles in 1974. In 1978, Nancy Lopez became the first Mexican American woman to win the LPGA championship.

In music, the 1970s witnessed an outpouring of all types of new sounds, styles, and racially mixed bands. "Soul" music became a catch-all name for the various black musical styles that arose during and after the civil rights movement. Building upon the groundbreaking successes of the previous decade, African American artists not only achieved parity with whites on the mainstream pop charts in the '70s but dominated during some years. Roberta Flack won the Record of the Year Grammy twice, for instance, while Stevie Wonder won the Album of the Year twice, all within the first six years of the decade. The Jackson Five, starring the 12-year-old prodigy Michael Jackson as the lead vocalist, became cultural icons not only for their hit songs but also for having their own television cartoon in 1971–1972. This black family from Gary, Indiana, had four number one hits for Motown Records on the mainstream American pop charts in 1970 alone.

The '70s brought the new musical form called "reggae" to the fore. A black Jamaican style developed in the previous decade, reggae was practically synony-

Funkadelic. Courtesy of Photofest.

mous with Bob Marley and the Wailers, the main proponents of the style in the U.S. market. Reggae's greatest success came in 1974, however, when the British rock guitar legend Eric Clapton turned Marley's "I Shot the Sheriff" into a number one single. The mid-70s saw the rise of the soul group Earth, Wind, & Fire, which managed to draw in both black and white audiences while celebrating its African heritage and promoting integration at the same time. Another important development in the mid-'70s was the black musical genre called "funk." Groups such as George Clinton's Parliament-Funkadelic, which put on glamorous, high-tech stage productions, turned funk into gold.

In the late 1970s, disco music became all the rage. It was a style that black and white artists alike embraced and made successful. K. C. and the Sunshine Band, an integrated group out of Miami, was as responsible as any individual musical act for starting the disco craze. The group had a white lead vocalist/keyboardist/front man, but almost all the backup musicians and singers were black. Mainly a dance-oriented genre of music, disco would have been a commercial success without any outside help, but the phenomenal box-office hit movie *Saturday Night Fever* (1977) made it all the more so. The movie's soundtrack, written mainly by the white Australian brothers who performed as the Bee Gees, and sung by them and several others of various racial and ethnic groups, became the best-selling soundtrack of all time. The Village People, a theatrical integrated group, became a disco icon of the decade with their exotic role-playing and characters dressed as a policeman, an Indian chief, a cowboy, a construction worker, a sailor, and a leather-clad biker. Their hits included "Macho Man" and "YMCA," both of which came out in 1978. A final notable musical development in the late '70s was the beginning of "rap" music. The first rap song was "Rapper's Delight," by the Sugarhill Gang. Although very popular, it did not start an immediate rap craze but merely laid the foundation for others to build upon in later decades.

In the motion picture industry, a major development in the early 1970s in Hollywood was the rise of the "blaxploitation" genre of film making. The black producer Mario Van Peebles started it with *Sweet Sweetback's Baadasssss Song* (1971), but the black director Gordon Parks followed it with more commercial success in *Shaft* a year later. The latter was such a hit that it spawned many imitators, including Parks's successful follow-up *Superfly* (1973). Although these inner-city racial sex-drugs-and-crime dramas were made by and starred African Americans, white audiences devoured them. These movies also received sharp criticism from the Coalition against Blaxploitation and others who considered them harmful to blacks because of the negative, although self-induced, stereotyping involved.

Flip Wilson on his NBC show. Courtesy of NBC/ Photofest. © NBC.

Critics said the same about television situation comedies made about blacks, such as *Sanford and Son*, *Good Times*, and *The Jeffersons*, each of which was hugely successful with audiences of all races in the 1970s. Yet such programs were at least a long-overdue starting point toward racial equality in television.

Not all racial movies and TV programming were so easily criticized. The film *Sounder*, starring Cicily Tyson, in 1972, was both a commercial and a critical success for its excellent production, thought-provoking screenplay, and award-winning casting. Made from the book of the same name by William H. Armstrong, who won the Newberry Award for children's literature for it in 1970, the movie is about the trials of a black family and its dog in 1930s Louisiana. Debuting in 1970, the TV variety series *The Flip Wilson Show* likewise received rave reviews from audiences and critics of all races. Wilson, a lovable and talented comedian-actor, had an impressive four-year run on NBC. His character "Geraldine," which he played in drag, became as famous as Wilson himself. Geraldine's oft-repeated line "The devil made me do it" became a cultural catchphrase. The black comedian-actor Bill Cosby scored an impressive hit with his "Fat Albert" children's cartoon, which debuted in 1972 and lasted an incredible 12 seasons on NBC TV. Another successful racial program was *Soul Train*, which was basically a black version of the long-running pop music and dance show *American Bandstand*. Produced and

Louis Gossett, Jr. (as Fiddler) and LeVar Burton (as Kunta Kinte), in the miniseries *Roots*, which aired in January 1977. Courtesy of ABC/Photofest. © ABC.

hosted by Don Cornelius, the show began in Chicago in 1970 and has aired in syndication across the country from 1971 to the present.

By far the most important cinematic event of the 1970s was the airing of the first made-for-TV "miniseries," *Roots*. Adapted from the best-selling book of the same name, which won a Pulitzer prize in 1977 for the black author Alex Haley, *Roots* took the nation by storm for eight nights in a row, beginning January 23, 1977. A partly factual but mostly fictional account of Haley's search for his ancestors, the story followed Kunta Kinte and his family through captivity on the west coast of Africa through the early generations of slavery in the American South. The book and miniseries spawned a genealogical research craze, as people of all races began to try to discover their own family tree's "roots." Although lauded by popular audiences, Haley's story quickly came under fire for egregious plagiarism. Haley settled out of court, paying a large amount of money. The furor over the plagiarism never equaled the celebration of *Roots* as a great work of entertainment, if not history. Mainly it got people talking about slavery and started a constructive dialogue about race relations in America, as few events have ever done.

Native Americans likewise saw white perception of their ancestry and history reformed in the 1970s. Having always been portrayed in books and movies by white authors and film makers as villains or inferior savages, Indians began to be treated as complex people worthy of serious study. This resulted largely from the Indian civil rights movement of the late '60s and early '70s, which brought pressure on whites to end racial stereotyping. The book *Bury My Heart at Wounded Knee* (1970) by Dee Brown captivated readers as no other account of Indian history had done. A true story of the various tribes on the Great Plains, the desert Southwest, and the Pacific Northwest in the late 1800s, it cemented the popular Red Power slogan "Custer Died for Your Sins" in the minds of many observers. It played a role in bringing AIM's attention to the Pine Ridge Reservation and to the town of Wounded Knee, South Dakota, which became the centerpiece of the Indian civil rights struggle in and after 1973. A movie that came out in 1970 that fitted in perfectly with the popular genre of realism in film making at the time was *Little Big Man*, starring Dustin Hoffman. Hoffman's character, Jack Crabb, claims to be the only white survivor of Custer's Last Stand in 1876. After that fateful day, Crabb is adopted by the Cheyenne tribe. He spends the rest of his life in and out of Indian tribal life and white America, viewing each through a lens that few have ever had the privilege to see.

In contrast to blacks and Indians, Hispanics did not gain a great deal of exposure in the 1970s in movies or on TV. There were notable exceptions, however. The Los Angeles-based comedy duo Cheech and Chong (Richard "Cheech" Marin and Thomas B. "Tommy" Kin Chong) became cultural icons with stand-up routines, songs, and the 1978 film *Up in Smoke*. Their shtick was playing two urban hippies whose main goal in life was to smoke marijuana at every chance. The situation comedy "Chico and the Man" aired from 1974 to 1978 and starred

Bruce Lee in *Enter the Dragon* (1973). Courtesy of Warner Bros./Photofest. © Warner Bros.

Freddie Prinze as a half–Puerto Rican, half-Mexican man living in Los Angeles. Prinze became a huge star, one of the biggest of the decade. Unable to cope with fame and fortune, after battling drugs and depression, sadly he took his own life, on January 28, 1977. Tony Orlando, a half-Puerto Rican, half-Greek entertainer, along with his backup singers "Dawn" (two African American females), had a string of number one hits from 1970 to 1974, including "Tie a Yellow Ribbon 'Round the Old Oak Tree" and "Knock Three Times." In 1974–1975, he had his own variety show on TV, which was hailed as the first for a Hispanic.

Finally, one interesting development in the early 1970s combined several different cultural elements and racial groups: the martial arts. Originally a collection of related Asian fighting styles, the martial arts included karate, kung fu, and judo, among others. The fad of studying and practicing the martial arts caught on in mainstream America, especially among young men and boys, thanks largely to the success of movies such as Tom Laughlin's *Billy Jack* (1971) and Bruce Lee's *Enter the Dragon* (1973). The fad spawned the hit TV show *Kung Fu,* starring David Carradine, and the hit song "Kung Fu Fighting," by Carl Douglas. The most amazing thing about this fad can be found among the four examples just given: Laughlin was white but played an American Indian martial arts expert who fought injustice on a reservation; Lee was Chinese, and his movie was set in Hong Kong but was shot in Hollywood; Carradine was white but played a Chinese kung fu fighter living in the old American West; and Carl Douglas was a black Jamaican who scored big in the United States using an Asian theme. Martial arts, therefore, did about as much to bring various cultures and racial groups together as any single fad could do.

INFLUENTIAL THEORIES AND VIEWS OF RACE RELATIONS

Few history books, and even fewer economic-history books, have ever caused such alarm and debate as *Time on the Cross: The Economics of American Negro Slavery* (1974), by Robert Fogel and Stanley Engerman. A major revisionist work that explored the socioeconomic nature of southern slavery rather than its political nature, this book stood the academic world on edge while standing the historical issue of slavery on its head. It then filtered down from the ivory tower and out into the general public where it stirred much interest—a rare thing for a scholarly academic book. The authors, Fogel and Engerman, were professors of history and economics at the University of Rochester, and Fogel was a former communist. They used a historical approach called cliometrics that was still relatively novel in the early 1970s. This approach used extensive numbers crunching to formulate a statistical model of the supposed normal characteristics of slavery in the South on the eve of the Civil War. The conclusions were startling because they challenged some very basic assumptions about how bad slavery was for the African Americans who were held captive, not only from an economic point of view but, more important, from a moral perspective.

Prior to the publication of *Time on the Cross*, five assumptions about slavery were generally regarded as common knowledge in the historical profession. In summation, they were:

1. Slavery was generally an unprofitable institution.
2. Slavery was a dying institution at the time of the Civil War because it was unprofitable.
3. Slave labor was less efficient than free labor.
4. Slavery retarded the South's economy.
5. Slaves were worse off physically and materially than free workers in the North.

Fogel and Engerman's evidence refuted all five beliefs and added more controversial findings on top of them. Their conclusions can be summarized in 10 points:

1. Slaves were a highly profitable investment for slave holders and traders —as profitable as any northern industrial capitalist's investments.

2. Not only was slavery not dying out on the eve of the Civil War, it was actually thriving better than ever.

3. Southern political leaders anticipated even more growth in their "peculiar institution" in the 1860s, which is why secession looked like such an attractive option at the time.

4. Not only was slavery an efficient labor system, it was actually 35 percent more efficient than free northern labor during that era.

5. Slaves were typically not lazy and uncooperative but actually worked harder and were more determined to do a good job than free white workers.

6. Demand for slaves as a labor force was growing faster in towns and cities than on plantations and farms in 1860.

7. Slaveholders had a financial interest in keeping slave families together, so selling individual family members down the river was rare.

8. Slaves were just as well off materially as free factory workers in the North.

9. Slaveholders did not confiscate all the wealth generated by their slaves but actually gave back about 90 percent of it, either directly or indirectly.

10. Not only was the South's economy not held back by slavery, but it actually grew at a faster rate than the North's economy between 1840 and 1860.

Such revelations of supposed empirical research caused a flurry of fellow cliometricians to begin crunching the numbers, scrutinizing the sources, and either reinforcing these conclusions or debunking them. Scholars churned out a plethora of economic history studies in response to *Time on the Cross*. Perhaps the most important refutation came from Herbert Gutman's 1975 book *Slavery and the Numbers Game*, which, along with similar studies, showed how statistics can be manipulated to reach a desired conclusion. Both sides quickly created a cadre of disciples that defended their chosen point of view, and various members of each side tended to focus on one or more of the arguments rather than all of them. Fogel and Engerman's points 7, 8, and 9, often caused the most acrimony, because they dealt more with the moral aspect of slavery than with abstract economic theory. If black families were not routinely destroyed by white slave-holders but were instead encouraged to stay together, then slavery could no longer be used as an excuse for the problems facing black families in the 1970s. Likewise, the idea that slaves were remunerated for their labor, even if only indirectly, chipped away at the foundation of the growing notion that modern African Americans deserved reparations for their ancestors' "time on the cross."

RESOURCE GUIDE

SUGGESTED READING

Black Panthers

Cleaver, Kathleen, and George Katsiaficas, eds., *Liberation, Imagination, and the Black Panther Party: A New Look at the Panthers and Their Legacy*. New York: Routledge, 2001.
Foner, Philip S., ed. *The Black Panthers Speak*. Philadelphia: J. B. Lippincott, 1970.
Marine, Gene. *The Black Panthers*. New York: New American Library, 1969.
Seale, Bobby. *Seize the Time: The Story of the Black Panther Party and Huey P. Newton*. New York: Random House, 1970.

Angela Davis

Davis, Angela Y. *Angela Davis: An Autobiography*. New York: Random House, 1974.
Jackson, George. *Soledad Brother: The Prison Letters of George Jackson*. New York: Putnam, 1970.
Parker, J. A. *Angela Davis: The Making of a Revolutionary*. New Rochelle, N.Y.: Arlington House, 1973.

Wounded Knee and Native American Issues

Means, Russell. *Where White Men Fear to Tread: The Autobiography of Russell Means*. New York: St. Martin's Press, 1995.

Boston Busing Controversy

Hampton, Henry, and Steve Fayer, eds. *Voices of Freedom: An Oral History of the Civil Rights Movement from the 1950s through the 1980s*. New York: Bantam Books, 1990.
Theoharis, Jeane F. "'We Saved the City': Black Struggles for Educational Equality in Boston, 1960–1976," *Radical History Review* 81 (Fall 2001): 61–93.

Richard M. Nixon and Civil Rights

Mason, Robert. *Richard Nixon and the Quest for a New Majority*. Chapel Hill: University of North Carolina Press, 2004.
Nixon, Richard. The Memoirs of Richard Nixon. New York: Grosset and Dunlap, 1978.

Gerald R. Ford and Racial Issues

Mieczkowski, Yanek. *Gerald Ford and the Challenges of the 1970s*. Lexington: University Press of Kentucky, 2005.

Jimmy Carter and Civil Rights

Amaker, Norman C. "The Faithfulness of the Carter Administration in Enforcing Civil Rights," in Herbert D. Rosenbaum and Alexej Ugrinsky, eds., *The Presidency and Domestic Policies of Jimmy Carter*. Westport, Conn.: Greenwood Press, 1994, pp. 737–46.

Hispanics and Asians

Duignan, Peter J., and L. H. Gann. *The Spanish Speakers in the United States: A History*. Lanham, Md.: University Press of America, 1998.

Gutierrez, David G., ed. *The Columbia History of Latinos in the United States since 1960*. New York: Columbia University Press, 2004.

Min, Pyong Gap, ed. *Asian Americans: Contemporary Trends and Issues*. Thousand Oaks, Calif.: Sage, 1995.

Pinchot, Jane. *The Mexicans in America*. Minneapolis: Lerner Publications, 1989.

General Culture and Society

Bailey, Beth, and David Farber, eds. *America in the 1970s*. Lawrence: University Press of Kansas, 2004.

Berkowitz, Edward D. *Something Happened: A Political and Cultural Overview of the Seventies*. New York: Columbia University Press, 2006.

Sagert, Kelly Boyer. *The 1970s*. Westport, CT: Greenwood Press, 2007.

Media and Mass Communications

Barnouw, Erik. *Tube of Plenty: The Evolution of American Television*, rev. ed. New York: Oxford University Press, 1982.

Brasch, Walter M. *Black English and the Mass Media*. Amherst: University of Massachusetts Press, 1981.

Rome, Dennis. *Black Demons: The Media's Depiction of the African American Male Criminal Stereotype*. Westport, Conn.: Praeger, 2004.

Affirmative Action

Mills, Nicholaus, ed. *Debating Affirmative Action: Race, Gender, Ethnicity, and the Politics of Inclusion*. New York: Delta Books, 1994.

Time on the Cross Controversy

Fogel, Robert W., and Stanley L. Engerman. *Time on the Cross: The Economics of American Negro Slavery*. Boston: Little, Brown, 1974.

Black Leaders

Abernathy, Ralph David. *And the Walls Came Tumbling Down: An Autobiography*. New York: Harper and Row, 1989.

Reynolds, Barbara A. *Jesse Jackson: The Man, the Movement, the Myth*. Chicago: Nelson-Hall, 1975.

Blacks in Sports

Ashe, Arthur, Jr. *A Hard Road to Glory: A History of the African American Athlete since 1946.* New York: Warner Books, 1988.

Hauser, Thomas. *Muhammad Ali: His Life and Times.* New York: Simon and Schuster, 1991.

Torres, Jose, and Bert Randolph Sugar. *Sting Like a Bee: The Muhammad Ali Story.* New York: Contemporary Books, 2002.

FILMS/VIDEOS

Conrack (prod. and dir. Martin Ritt, 20th Century Fox, 1974).

Roots (dir. Marvin Chomsky, ABC Television, 1976).

Rocky (dir. John G. Avildsen, United Artists Films, 1976).

Saturday Night Fever (dir. John Badham, Paramount Pictures, 1977).

Shirley Chisholm '72: Unbought and Unbossed (dir. Shola Lynch, Lantern Lane Entertainment, 2004), a made-for-TV documentary about Chisholm's run for the presidency in 1972.

Sounder (dir., Martin Ritt, for 20th Century Fox, 1972).

WEB SITES

Affirmative Action

American Association for Affirmative Action, "About Us." July 2005, http://www.affirmativeaction.org/about.html (accessed August 27, 2007).

Angela Davis

Claris, "History of Consciousness Faculty: Angela Y. Davis." humwww.ucsc.edu/HistCon/faculty_davis.htm (accessed August 27, 2007).

Roots

Bird, J. B., The Museum of Broadcast Communications. "Roots: U.S. Serial Drama." http://www.museum.tv/archives/etv/R/htmlR/roots/roots.htm (accessed August 27, 2007).

Time on the Cross

Weiss, Thomas. "'Review of Robert William Fogel and Stanley L. Engerman, Time on the Cross: The Economics of American Negro Slavery.' EH.Net Economic History Services." November 16, 2001, http://eh.net/bookreviews/library/weiss.shtml (accessed August 27, 2007).

Wounded Knee II

FreePeltier.org, "The Case of Leonard Peltier." April 5, 2004, http://www.freepeltier.org/wounded_knee.htm (accessed August 27, 2007).

NOTES

1. Quoted in Jeane F. Theoharis, "'We Saved the City': Black Struggles for Educational Equality in Boston, 1960–1976," *Radical History Review* 81 (Fall 2001): 76.

2. DeWitt, Larry. "Moynihan, Welfare Reform, and the Myth of "Benign Neglect." October 2005, http://www.larrydewitt.net/Essays/Moynihan.htm (accessed August 27, 2007).

3. American Indian Movement Grand Governing Council, "Trail of Broken Treaties 20-Point Position Paper." http://www.aimovement.org/archives/index.html (accessed August 27, 2007).

4. Freeman, Jo. "Indians End Longest Walk in Washington DC on July 15, 1978." http://www.jofreeman.com/photos/Longest_Walk.htm (accessed August 27, 2007).

5. Williams, Robert L. "The Ebonics Controversy," *Sage Journals* Online (1997). http://jbp.sagepub.com/cgi/content/abstract/23/3/208 (accessed August 27, 2007).

Selected Bibliography

BOOKS

Abernathy, Ralph David. *And the Walls Came Tumbling Down: An Autobiography*. New York: Harper and Row, 1989.

Arsenault, Raymond. *Freedom Riders: 1961 and the Struggle for Racial Justice*. New York: Oxford University Press, 2006.

Ashe, Arthur, Jr. *A Hard Road to Glory: A History of the African American Athlete since 1946*. New York: Warner Books, 1988.

Bailey, Beth, and David Farber, eds. *America in the 1970s*. Lawrence: University Press of Kansas, 2004.

Barbour, Floyd B., ed. *The Black Seventies*. Boston: Porter Sargent, 1970.

Barnouw, Erik. *Tube of Plenty: The Evolution of American Television*, rev. ed. New York: Oxford University Press, 1982.

Bass, Amy. *Not the Triumph but the Struggle: 1968 Olympics and the Making of the Black Athlete*. Minneapolis: University of Minnesota Press, 2004.

Bass, Patrick Henry. *Like a Mighty Stream: The March on Washington, August 28, 1963*. Philadelphia: Running Press, 2002.

Berkowitz, Eric D. *Something Happened: A Political and Cultural Overview of the Seventies*. New York: Columbia University Press, 2006.

Branch, Taylor. *Parting the Waters: America in the King Years, 1954–1963*. New York: Simon and Schuster, 1988.

Brasch, Walter M. *Black English and the Mass Media*. Amherst: University of Massachusetts Press, 1981.

Brown, H. Rap. *Die! Nigger, Die!* New York: Dial Press, 1969.

Bruns, Roger. *Cesar Chavez: A Biography*. Westport, Conn.: Greenwood Press, 2005.

Carmichael, Stokely, and Charles V. Hamilton. *Black Power*. New York: Vintage Books, reissued 1992.

Carson, Clayborne. *In Struggle: SNCC and the Black Awakening of the 1960s*. Cambridge, Mass.: Harvard University Press, 1981.

Carter, Rubin. *The Sixteenth Round: From Number 1 Contender to #45472*. New York: Penguin Reprint, 2005.

Cleaver, Eldridge. *Soul on Ice*. New York: Dell, 1968.

Cleaver, Kathleen, and George Katsiaficas, eds. *Liberation, Imagination, and the Black Panther Party: A New Look at the Panthers and Their Legacy*. New York: Routledge, 2001.

Davis, Angela Y. *Angela Davis: An Autobiography*. New York: Random House, 1974.

Deloria, Vine. *Custer Died for Your Sins: An Indian Manifesto*. New York: Macmillan, 1969.

Dinnerstein, Leonard, et al., eds. *Natives and Strangers: A Multicultural History of Americans*. New York: Oxford University Press, 1996.

Duignan, Peter J., and L. H. Gann. *The Spanish Speakers in the United States: A History*. Lanham, Md.: University Press of America, 1998.

Escott, Paul D. et al., eds., *Major Problems in the History of the American South*, Vol. II: *The New South*. Boston: Houghton Mifflin, sec. ed., 1999.

Farmer, James. *Lay Bare the Heart: An Autobiography of the Civil Rights Movement*. New York: Arbor House, 1985.

Fogel, Robert W., and Stanley L. Engerman. *Time on the Cross: The Economics of American Negro Slavery*. Boston: Little, Brown, 1974.

Foner, Philip S., ed. *The Black Panthers Speak*. Philadelphia: J. B. Lippincott, 1970.

Franklin, John Hope, and Alfred A. Moss, Jr. *From Slavery to Freedom: A History of African Americans*, 7th and 8th eds. New York: McGraw-Hill, 1994, 2000.

Garrow, David J. *Bearing the Cross: Martin Luther King Jr., and the Southern Christian Leadership Conference*. New York: William Morrow, 1986.

Gentile, Thomas. *March on Washington: August 28, 1963*. Washington, D.C.: Self-published, 1983.

Gillon, Stephen M. *The American Paradox: A History of the United States since 1945*. Boston: Houghton Mifflin, 2003.

Greenberg, Milton. "The Negro in America," *Collier's 1964 Year Book: Covering the Year 1963*. New York: Crowell-Collier.

Grier, William M., and Price M. Cobb. *Black Rage*. New York: Basic Books, 1968.

Gutierrez, David G., ed. *The Columbia History of Latinos in the United States since 1960*. New York: Columbia University Press, 2004.

Haley, Alex, ed. *The Autobiography of Malcolm X*. New York: Grove Press, 1965.

Hampton, Henry, and Steve Fayer, eds. *Voices of Freedom: An Oral History of the Civil Rights Movement from the 1950s through the 1980s*. New York: Bantam Books, 1990.

Hartmann, Douglas. *Race, Culture, and the Revolt of the Black Athlete: The 1968 Olympic Protests and Their Aftermath*. Chicago: University of Chicago Press, 2004.

Hauser, Thomas. *Muhammad Ali: His Life and Times*. New York: Simon and Schuster, 1991.

Hirsch, James S. *Hurricane: The Miraculous Journey of Rubin Carter*. Boston: Mariner Books, 2000.

Jackson, George. *Soledad Brother: The Prison Letters of George Jackson*. New York: Putnam, 1970.

Johnson, Troy. *The Occupation of Alcatraz Island: Indian Self-Determination and the Rise of Indian Activism*. Urbana: University of Illinois Press, 1996.

Johnson, Troy, et al., eds. *American Indian Activism: Alcatraz to the Longest Walk*. Urbana: University of Illinois Press, 1997.

Jones, Le Roi, and Larry Neal. *Black Fire*. New York: William Morrow, 1968.

Kerner, Otto, et al. *Report of the National Advisory Commission on Civil Disorders*. New York: Bantam Books, 1968.

King, Martin Luther, Jr. *Why We Can't Wait*. New York: New American Library, 1964.

———. *Where Do We Go from Here?* Boston: Beacon Press, 1968.

Lester, Julius. *Look Out Whitey! Black Power's Gon' Get Your Mama!* New York: Grove Press, 1969.

Levine, Daniel. *Bayard Rustin and the Civil Rights Movement.* New Brunswick, N.J.: Rutgers University Press, 2000.

Levy, Jacques. *Cesar Chavez: Autobiography of La Causa.* New York: W. W. Norton, 1975.

Lowery, Charles D. and John F. Marszalek, eds., *The Greenwood Encyclopedia of African American Civil Rights: From Emancipation to the Twenty-first Century,* 2nd ed. Westport, Conn.: Greenwood Press, 2003.

Marine, Gene. *The Black Panthers.* New York: New American Library, 1969.

Mars, Florence. *Witness in Philadelphia.* Baton Rouge: Louisiana State University Press, 1977.

Mason, Robert. *Richard Nixon and the Quest for a New Majority.* Chapel Hill: University of North Carolina Press, 2004.

Means, Russell. *Where White Men Fear to Tread: The Autobiography of Russell Means.* New York: St. Martin's Press, 1995.

Meier, August, and Elliott Rudwick. *CORE: A Study in the Civil Rights Movement, 1942–1968.* New York: Oxford University Press, 1973.

Meredith, James. *Three Years in Mississippi.* Bloomington: Indiana University Press, 1966.

Mieczkowski, Yanek. *Gerald Ford and the Challenges of the 1970s.* Lexington: University Press of Kentucky, 2005.

Mills, Nicholaus, ed. *Debating Affirmative Action: Race, Gender, Ethnicity, and the Politics of Inclusion.* New York: Delta Books, 1994.

Min, Pyong Gap, ed. *Asian Americans: Contemporary Trends and Issues.* Thousand Oaks, Calif.: Sage, 1995.

Moody, Anne. *Coming of Age in Mississippi.* New York: Dell, 1968.

Moquin, Wayne, ed. *A Documentary History of the Mexican Americans.* New York: Praeger, 1971.

Nixon, Richard. *The Memoirs of Richard Nixon.* New York: Grosset and Dunlap, 1978.

Parker, J. A. *Angela Davis: The Making of a Revolutionary.* New Rochelle, N.Y.: Arlington House, 1973.

Pfeffer, Paula. *A. Philip Randolph: Pioneer of the Civil Rights Movement.* Baton Rouge: Louisiana State University Press, 1990.

Pinchot, Jane. *The Mexicans in America.* Minneapolis: Lerner Publications, 1989.

Rainwater, Lee, and William L. Yancey. *The Moynihan Report and the Politics of Controversy.* Cambridge, Mass.: M.I.T. Press, 1967.

Reilly, Edward J. *The 1960s.* Westport, Conn.: Greenwood Press, 2003.

Reynolds, Barbara A. *Jesse Jackson: The Man, the Movement, the Myth.* Chicago: Nelson-Hall, 1975.

Rome, Dennis. *Black Demons: The Media's Depiction of the African American Male Criminal Stereotype.* Westport, Conn.: Praeger, 2004.

Rosenbaum, Herbert D., and Alexej Ugrinsky, eds. *The Presidency and Domestic Policies of Jimmy Carter.* Westport, Conn.: Greenwood Press, 1994.

Rosenberg, Jonathan, and Zachary Karabell. *Kennedy, Johnson, and the Quest for Justice: The Civil Rights Tapes.* New York: W. W. Norton, 2003.

Sagert, Kelly Boyer. *The 1970s.* Westport, Conn.: Greenwood Press, 2007.

Schlesinger, Arthur M., Jr. *A Thousand Days: John F. Kennedy in the White House.* Boston: Houghton Mifflin, 1965.

Seale, Bobby. *Seize the Time: The Story of the Black Panther Party and Huey P. Newton.* New York: Random House, 1970.

Sears, David O., and John B. McConahay. *The Politics of Violence: The New Urban Blacks and the Watts Riot.* Boston: Houghton Mifflin, 1973.

Silver, James W. *Mississippi: The Closed Society.* New York: Harcourt, Brace and World, 1964.

Sobel, Lester A., ed. *Civil Rights, 1960–1966.* New York: Facts on File, 1967.

Stang, Alan. *It's Very Simple: The True Story of Civil Rights.* Boston: Western Island, 1965.

Taylor, Ronald B. *Chavez and the Farm Workers.* Boston: Beacon Press, 1975.

Theoharis, Jeane F. "'We Saved the City': Black Struggles for Educational Equality in Boston, 1960–1976." *Radical History Review* 81 (Fall 2001): 76.

Torres, Jose, and Bert Randolph Sugar. *Sting Like a Bee: The Muhammad Ali Story.* New York: Contemporary Books, 2002.

Upchurch, Thomas Adams. *A White Minority in Post–Civil Rights Mississippi.* Lanham, Md.: Hamilton Books, 2005.

Washington, James M., ed. *A Testament of Hope: The Essential Writings and Speeches of Martin Luther King, Jr.* San Francisco: Harper San Francisco, 1990.

Wheelen, Francis. *Television.* London: Century, 1985.

Williams, Juan. *Eyes on the Prize: American Civil Rights Years, 1954–1965.* New York: Viking Press, 1987.

Williams, Juan, ed. *My Soul Looks Back in Wonder: Voices of the Civil Rights Experience.* New York: AARP Sterling, 2004.

Woll, Allen L., and Randall M. Miller, eds. *Ethnic and Racial Images in American Film and Television: Historical Essays and Bibliography.* New York: Garland, 1987.

WEB SITES

Affirmative Action

American Association for Affirmative Action, "About Us." July 2005, http://www.affirmativeaction.org/about.html (accessed August 27, 2007).

American Indian grievances

American Indian Movement Grand Governing Council, "Trail of Broken Treaties 20-Point Position Paper." http://www.aimovement.org/archives/index.html. (accessed August 27, 2007).

FreePeltier.org, "The Case of Leonard Peltier." April 4, 2004, http://www.freepeltier.org/wounded_knee.htm (accessed August 27, 2007).

United Native America, "Bureau of White Affairs." 2004, http://www.unitednativeamerica.com/bureau/index.html (accessed August 25, 2007).

American Indian Movement occupation of Alcatraz

Berger, Alan L. "American Fuehrer: George Lincoln Rockwell and the American Nazi Party," *Holocaust and Genocide Studies* 2003 17(1): 180–85. http://hgs.oxfordjournals.org/cgi/content/citation/17/1/180 (accessed August 25, 2007).

Amiri Baraka

Hiltz, Virginia, and Mike Sell. "Black Arts Movement." 1998, http://www.umich.edu/~eng499/ (accessed August 25, 2007).

Sherman, Scott. "A Turbulent Life." http://www.dissentmagazine.org/article/?article (accessed August 25, 2007). Black Power movement

Bloody Sunday 1965

U.S. National Park Service, "We Shall Overcome." August 2001, http://www.cr.nps.gov/nr/travel/civilrights/al4.htm (accessed August 25, 2007).

Ruben "Hurricane Carter"

Deal, Cal. "Hurricane Carter: The Other Side of the Story." http://www.graphicwitness.com/carter (accessed August 25, 2007).

Chicago Freedom movement

Center for Urban Research and Learning, Loyola University Chicago, "40 Anniversary." May 8, 2004, http://www.luc.edu/curl/cfm40/ (accessed August 25, 2007).

Lowenstein, Jeff Kelly. "Resisting the Dream." http://www.chicagoreporter.com/ (accessed August 25, 2007).

Angela Davis

Claris, "History of Consciousness Faculty: Angela Y. Davis." http://www.ucsc.edu/HistCon/faculty_davis.htm (accessed August 27, 2007).

Ebonics

Williams, Robert L. "The Ebonics Controversy, Sage Journals Online." (1997). http://jbp.sagepub.com/cgi/content/abstract/23/3/208 (accessed August 27, 2007).

Greensboro Sit-ins

International Civil Rights Center & Museum, "They Opened One Door for All." http://www.sitinmovement.org (accessed August 25, 2007).

NRinteractive, "Greensboro Sit-Ins: Launch of a Civil Rights Movement." 1998, http://www.sitins.com (accessed August 25, 2007).

Life of Martin Luther King, Jr.

The Martin Luther King, Jr., Research and Education Institute, http://www.stanford.edu/group/King/ (accessed August 25, 2007).

Latino issues

Pearson, Kim. "Wetback." 2004, http://kpearson.faculty.tcnj.edu/Dictionary/wetback.htm (accessed August 25, 2007).

"The Making of MEChA:." http://studentorgs.utexas.edu/mecha/archive/research.html (accessed August 25, 2007).

Long, Hot Summer of 1967

Haymes, Don. "The Long Hot Summer." http://www.mun.ca/rels/restmov/texts/race/haymes43.html (accessed August 25, 2007).

1963 March on Washington

Abbeville Press, *The Civil Rights Movement, The March on Washington, 1963:* "We Stood on a Height." http://www.abbeville.com/civilrights/washington.asp.

International Information Programs, "John Lewis Leads Commemoration of March on Washington." July 25, 2003, http://usinfo.state.gov/scv/Archive/2005/Aug/15-620146.html (accessed August 25, 2007).

Nammour, Chris. "The March on Washington for Jobs and Freedom." http://www.pbs.org/newshour/extra/features/july-dec03/march_8-27.html (accessed August 25, 2007).

"Speech prepared for the March on Washington, August 1963." February 10, 2006, http://www.hartford-hwp.com/archives/45a/641.html (accessed August 25, 2007).

White, Jack E. "Aug. 28, 1963." March 31, 2003, http://www.time.com/time/magazine/article/0,9171,1004520,00.html (accessed August 25, 2007).

Younge, Gary. "I Have a Dream." *The Guardian.* August 21, 2003, http://www.guardian.co.uk/Columnists/Column/0,5673,1026385,00.html

Daniel Patrick Moynihan and "benign neglect"

DeWitt, Larry. "Moynihan, Welfare Reform, and the Myth of 'Benign Neglect'." October 2005, http://www.larrydewitt.net/Essays/Moynihan.htm (accessed August 27, 2007).

New Urban Black hypothesis

Mason, T. David and Jerry A, Murtagh. "Who riots? An empirical examination of the "new urban black" versus the social marginality hypotheses." January 10, 2005, http://www.springerlink.com/content/w6252x3441564x62/ (accessed August 25, 2007).

Roots miniseries

Bird, J. B., The Museum of Broadcast Communications. "Roots: U.S. Serial Drama." http://www.museum.tv/archives/etv/R/htmlR/roots/roots.htm (accessed August 27, 2007).

Time on the Cross

Weiss, Thomas. "'Review of Robert William Fogel and Stanley L. Engerman, Time on the Cross: The Economics of American Negro Slavery.' EH.Net Economic History Services." Novmber 16, 2001, http://eh.net/bookreviews/library/weiss.shtml (accessed August 27, 2007).

Watts Riot

Government Documents Department and the Doheny Electronic Resources Center at the University of Southern California, "Violence in the City: An End or a Beginning?" http://www.usc.edu/libraries/archives/cityinstress/mccone/contents.html (accessed August 25, 2007).

Reitman, Valerie and Mitchell Landsberg. "Watts Riot, 40 Years Later." August 11, 2005, http://www.latimes.com/news/local/la-me-watts11aug11,0,7619426.story?coll= la-home-headlines (accessed August 25, 2007).

Index

About the Author

THOMAS UPCHURCH is Assistant Professor of History at East Georgia College.